PAX ROMANA
and the Peace of Jesus Christ

PAX ROMANA
and the Peace of Jesus Christ

Klaus Wengst

Fortress Press Philadelphia

Translated by John Bowden from the German
Pax Romana. Anspruch und Wirklichkeit. Erfahrungen und Wahrnehmungen
des Friedens bei Jesus und im Urchristentum,
published 1986 by Christian Kaiser Verlag, Munich.

First Fortress Press edition 1987

Library of Congress Cataloging-in-Publication Data
Wengst, Klaus.
Pax Romana.

Translation of: Pax Romana.
Bibliography: p.
Includes index.
1. Peace—Religious aspects—Christianity—History of doctrines—Early church, ca. 30–600. 2. Rome—Civilization. 3. Jesus Christ—Teachings. 4. Peace—Biblical teaching. I. Title.
BT736.4.W4413 1987 261.8'73 87–45320
ISBN 0–8006–2067–4

3052D87 Printed in the United Kingdom 1–2067

Contents

For Helga

Preface

In present-day discussions among Christians about peace, certain passages and sections of the New Testament are constantly cited and 'applied', or there are sweeping references to 'the New Testament'. Because of this, it is important to put questions in a more specifically historical way and with more historical reflection. In the time of Jesus and the New Testament writers there was political peace: there was the Pax Romana. How did Jesus and the early Christians experience, perceive and evaluate this peace? How did they live in and with it or even against it? If we attempt to answer these questions, differences and indeed contradictions emerge. How are we to deal with them? Are some evaluations less appropriate than others? Are there theological criteria for answering these questions? Can we discover anything from them about present-day discussions about peace? This book is meant to be a contribution to the discussion by attempting to go into questions of this kind.

But is it not too late for that? At the beginning of this year a friend expressed the hope that there would still be readers for my book. The peace movement is no longer making headlines; it is impossible to miss the resignation here and there. But it could be that now is not the time for great demonstrations and actions but a time for reflection, a time not so much of action and reaction related to the politics of the day as of fundamental reflection. At all events, I hope that this book will prove helpful to the peace movement beyond the narrow circle of those with theological training.

It began in discussions and lectures in church communities in the winter of 1981/1982. I gave a very provisional report on my work on this topic in my contribution to the Festschrift for Walter Kreck's seventy-fifth birthday (ed. Hannelotte Reiffen, Cologne 1983, 252-68). I made progress in the summer semester of 1983 through a series of joint lectures with my colleagues and friends Hans-Eckehard Bahr and Jürgen Ebach on the theme 'The Interruption of Violence'. This book owes a great deal to what I heard from them and have learnt from them in conversations. The joint work made me feel that I must work on my own contribution for publication. A free semester in winter 1984/85 gave me the opportunity for this. I finished a draft manuscript in March 1985 and then worked over it once more in August of that year.

Present and former colleagues have given me substantial support in producing this book. Frau Edith Lutz not only typed the manuscript and, together with my wife, undertook the laborious task of reading the proofs, but also helped in my survey of ancient literature. I also received further help in this and in work on the secondary literature from a number of my students – Karoline Hafer, Uta Küppers, Dirk Bockermann and Stefan Hucke – and also from my assistant Heike Nadolph, who in addition checked the translation of all the Latin quotations, and Susanne Tatusch. The four last-mentioned and Frau Lutz, together with my assistant Martin Leutzsch, also read the manuscript and made numerous critical and constructive suggestions for its improvement. I have taken over personal contributions from Martin Leutzsch at several points; these are marked by his initials. I would like to express my thanks here to everyone who has been of help.

Bochum, February 1986 Klaus Wengst

Note to the English translation

For the English translation I have agreed to the omission of material from the notes where this refers to discussion which is being carried on specifically within the German-speaking world.

I INTRODUCTION

Interruption of Violence

Themes have their day. Even investigations into so important a theme as peace are not always carried on with the same urgency. If peace is relatively taken for granted, there is hardly any discussion of it. Things are different in our present-day situation, since on the one hand the safeguarding of peace by deterrrence leads to an arms race with costs which become more and more unimaginable, and on the other hand this arms race begins to demonstrate a progression which suggests the possibility of winning a war even under the conditions of nuclear warfare, thus bringing it back into the sphere of the probable.

So if the theme of peace is at all topical, it certainly is also topical for churches and Christians, in so far as they coexist in time with other individuals and institutions and are affected to the same degree by the problems which oppress all of us. However, there is another way in which churches and Christians have this theme thrust upon them as a task more than any other, assuming that they feel themselves bound to the New Testament as the primal document of their faith and to the history of Jesus Christ to which it bears witness. The basis of this preeminence is not that the word 'peace' occurs particularly often in the New Testament, though it is by no means rare;[1] of much greater significance is the fact that the central content of the proclamation of the primitive church, the evidence of the death and resurrection of Jesus,[2] is characteristically bound up with conceptions of peace.

In one respect that is quite obvious: Jesus was killed by being executed on the cross, in other words by the Roman forces of occupation.[3] He did not die by chance or by accident but was executed by Roman soldiers after a trial which resulted in his condemnation by the Roman procurator of Judaea, Pontius Pilate. Whatever may have been the details of the contribution by leading circles among Jesus' fellow-countrymen to this condemnation – Jesus had certainly not won their friendship and in Jerusalem his symbolic action in the temple and the prophecy announcing its end had been a particular provocation to the Sadduceean priestly aristocracy[4] – the decisive authority was Rome in the person of the procurator. The fact that he had Jesus executed on the cross shows that the death of Jesus is indissolubly bound up with the political peace that there was at that time, the Pax Romana, produced and guaranteed by Roman power. In the view of the procurator this execution, like many others, was virtually an act to secure the peace. Extant reports of the implementation of the Roman punishment of crucifixion in Palestine at the time of Jesus mention only rebels as criminals.[5] Further evidence of a political connection is the fact that Jesus was crucified with two 'robbers' (Mark 15.27), a designation for rebels which was current at the time.[6] Finally the notice about Jesus' guilt, 'The king of the Jews' (Mark 15.26), needs to be mentioned.[7] It follows conclusively from all this that in the eyes of the Roman provincial administration Jesus was a rebel who endangered the existing peace. A disturber of the peace was done away with, by legal means, by the power responsible for peace. It follows from this that not only was Jesus' understanding of peace different, but above that all his activity cannot have conformed to the Pax Romana but must have been contrary to it. The accounts of his activity give plenty of indications that his execution was not unconnected with what he said and did. The statements in the New Testament which relate to the death and resurrection of Jesus, which form its focal point, are thus indissolubly connected with a historical event, the crucifixion of Jesus, that belongs in the context of the political peace activity of the time. However, it is an extremely strange focal point, a focal point on the periphery – an execution in a relatively insignificant part of a province in the east of the Roman empire.

Among the evangelists it is Matthew in particular who shows dimensions in the account of the crucifixion of Jesus which otherwise were not at all part of a routine execution. Whereas the occupying forces thought that they could do away with the disturbance of their peace brought about by Jesus by executing him and thus go back to the order of the day, with impressive imagery Matthew shows that this order has been fundamentally interrupted. In 27.45,51 he not only takes over from the Gospel of Mark the miraculous sign of three hours of darkness before the death of Jesus[8] and the rending of the curtain of the temple when he died,[9] but in vv.52f. also tells how the earth quaked, graves opened, 'and many bodies of the saints who were asleep were raised', came out of the graves and appeared to many. Thus the death of Jesus was accompanied by signs of the messianic time which with him breaks into the old age. Along with the graves, world history, which has gone its way over corpses, 'is opened', and thus the actual course of history is deprived of the triumph of being final and gives space and time to oppressed hopes.

Matthew did not read that off the mere event of the crucifixion of Jesus: he could not have made the readers and hearers of his Gospel perceive this crucifixion in such dimensions were he of the view that the execution was the last word about Jesus. Rather, with the whole of earliest Christianity he shared the belief that God had raised Jesus from the dead. Only to a superficial inspection are the documents in this case evidently closed once and for all; nor have they merely been reopened for an appeal, with a view to a posthumous rehabilitation. If God is proclaimed as the one who has raised Jesus for the dead, we are given a glimpse of a reality which simply transcends such human possibilities.

At some points in the New Testament this reality is described in terms of peace. It is the victim of the violence perpetrated in the name of Roman peace who brings reconciliation and peace. So the author of Colossians, a pupil of Paul, takes up and interprets in 1.15-20 an earlier hymn and states that it pleased God, through 'the firstborn from the dead' (v.18), the risen Christ, 'to reconcile in himself all things, whether on earth or in heaven, making peace by the blood of his cross' (v.20).[10] The crucifixion and resurrection of Jesus understood as a single event accordingly form the basis of universal reconciliation and all-embracing peace. But that implies that the state of the world as it appears without Christ cannot be described as cosmic and social harmony. And that also raises the question whether the Pax Romana really deserves the name of peace. The author protects the proclamation of peace and reconciliation through Christ from being a merely enthusiastic disregard of an unpeaceful reality by defining the community as the sphere in which peace and reconciliation may be experienced under the Lordship of Christ.[11] Another pupil of Paul, the author of Ephesians, takes the same course when in 2.14-18 he describes Christ as 'our peace'.[12] He proclaims the cross of Christ as the abolition of enmity between Gentiles and Jews, as the reconciliation of these separated groups in a new unity of peace which is a reality to be preserved in the church made up of Jews and Gentiles, as an anticipation of reconciled humanity.[13] The reality of the crucified and risen Jesus thus manifests itself as new creation in the community, and this is explicitly mentioned in v.15 as the creation of a new humanity made up of Jews and Gentiles. Here the author takes up Pauline statements about the 'new creation'[14] in which not only is the opposition between Jews and Gentiles done away with but also that between slaves and free, men and women, barbarians and Greeks.[15] But specifically that can only mean that privileges are done away with, the exalted brought low and the lowly exalted so that they can meet on the same level, as sisters and brothers – all aspects which run strictly counter to the subjugation model of the Pax Romana.

The testimony to the resurrection of the crucified Jesus challenges the 'inexorable continuity'[16] of the history of violence and proclaims its end. God does not leave history to itself, i.e. to the victors, but in the resurrection of this one crucified man with a promise and with the prospect of a future takes the side of the humiliated and the victims, the tortured and the hanged. In some stories of resurrection appearances in the Gospel the risen Christ proves his identity with the wounds of the crucifixion;[17] through them he remains bound up with the suffering and the sufferers of the world. According to Walter Benjamin, for the Jews the future was 'not a homogenous and empty time. For in it every second was the narrow gate through which the Messiah could appear.'[18] Would not the resurrection of Jesus open up that gate once and for all, and so offer a basis for unquenchable hope against the deadly continuity of ongoing history?

Thus at the focal point of the New Testament, the testimony to the death and resurrection of Jesus, two completely opposed modes of peace clash. On the one hand there is violence which interrupts and indeed breaks off – the 'interruption of violence' as interruption and breaking off by force – there is the Pax Romana in the name of which Jesus was executed, a peace produced and secured from the then centre of power, above all by military means, an order going out from the metropolis and orientated on it. On the other hand there is the interruption of violence as violence itself being interrupted, indeed broken off: there is peace and reconciliation as the abolition of oppositions and enmity, as new creation which takes shape on the periphery of society.

In the world defined by the Pax Romana, the history of which continues as though nothing has happened, there is therefore a witness which runs contrary to it. How did those who bore this testimony attempt to express their belief that peace was made in the death and resurrection of Jesus in specific actions for peace? Was the interruption of violence which was thought to have happened expressed in their own achievement of interruptions of violence, in a praxis contrary to the Pax Romana? How was its reality perceived and evaluated? How was what is 'realistic' defined in the field of tension between ongoing history and faith and a praxis which seeks to be in accordance with it? Such questions will be investigated in the second part of this book by means of the earliest Christian writings. Here it will emerge that in this respect, too, already in primitive Christianity reality was by no means always experienced in the same way. There is no clear 'evidence of the facts';

that is to a large degree dependent on how one is affected at any point. The writings of primitive Christianity are by very different authors who lived in very different places, came from very different social strata and thus had different experiences of the Pax Romana.

I shall not be investigating all the evidence that could provide an answer to the questions I have raised. First of all we shall discover the attitude of Jesus himself to the Pax Romana. Then I shall be concerned to work out from the letters of Paul, the Gospel of Luke and Acts, the Letter of Clement of Rome and the Revelation of John four characteristic positions in earliest Christianity. This is certainly only a selection, but it contains by far the most contrasting statements of the writings of earliest Christianity on the Pax Romana and thus demonstrates their whole breadth. The statements do not just represent different gradations; in part they are virtually opposed to each other. From that it will emerge that at the least one cannot speak over-hastily of *the* evidence of the New Testament or even of the Bible on peace. The differences which even amount to contradictions must first of all be taken seriously in all their sharpness. Here it will also be important to investigate the conditioning of the various positions. However, if we are not just to register a loose juxtaposition, ultimately we cannot rule out the question whether criteria can be discovered which show particular statements to be more appropriate than others. The final part will discuss how we should deal with the different attitudes in earliest Christianity to peace, and what emerges from them today for action for peace by the church and Christians.

Before describing the perception of the Pax Romana by Jesus and by the earliest Christian authors I have mentioned, in the first part I shall attempt to describe the various aspects of the peace which emanated from Rome. Here for the most part we shall be listening to witnesses from antiquity. They will not necessarily be read as their authors intended, since I shall be bringing out information the giving of which was at any rate not their primary intention. It is often also important to recognize as it were the 'underside' of statements that have been transmitted – in contrast to the glorification of the first two centuries of the Roman empire which can often be noted in history writing. There need be no dispute that there was great splendour during these centuries, but the important thing is not to be silent about the cost of the splendour and not to forget the suffering of those who contributed to it. Here, though, I am not concerned to maintain a 'balanced' view but to have a view from below which investigates what effect the Pax Romana had on the many nameless people whose immeasurable tears and sufferings, whose hopes, are hardly attested, or if they are, are attested only indirectly. Thus while it is important to produce many specific details which illuminate the circumstances in which these people lived and which are to be understood as an expression of the Roman system of rule, there is no need here for me to give a picture which is differentiated according to the various emperors. Certainly these were very different individuals, each of whom had his own emphasis during his reign, but for the daily life of the majority of the population of the empire the change at the top will have been relatively insignificant. The view from below is not least a guard against the kind of historiography which subsequently legitimates what happened on the grounds of its necessity. Against this truly fatal glorification of the power which in fact came to establish itself and which excludes alternatives, it is important to keep alive the hopes of the powerless.

II PART ONE

Pax Romana

or: 'The best and happiest period in world history'

or: 'We should be grateful that we have already had forty years of peace'

1. 'A Golden Age'?

In spring 143 the Greek orator Aelius Aristides, who came from Asia Minor, gave a speech in Rome in the presence of the emperor Antoninus Pius and his court. Towards the end of this speech 'to Rome' he criticized Hesiod for beginning his description of the ages with the age of gold and then going on to describe a decline thereafter; he said that if he had chosen this approach, he would have had to announce the rule of Rome as the end of the age of iron. Had he been 'a perfect poet and seer, he would have lamented those who had been born before your time'.[1] Referring to Augustus, Virgil had already said that the age of gold had returned: 'This, this is he whom so often you hear promised to you, Augustus Caesar, son of a god, who shall again set up the golden age in Latium amid the fields where Saturn once reigned, and shall spread his empire past Garamant and Indian, to a land that lies beyond the stars.'[2]

Virgil and Aristides, Augustus and the Antonine emperors, mark out the period which even in antiquity and thereafter all down history produced comments of the utmost admiration. This is at the same time the period of the ministry of Jesus, the rise and growth of the church. Later Christian authors saw an intrinsic connection between the birth of Jesus Christ and the time of peace under Augustus, between the growth of the church and the growth of the Roman empire.[3]

Peace – that was the decisive and most important sign of this time. A modern historian sees the 'Pax Romana, peace in the empire and security on the frontiers', as 'perhaps the most amazing achievement of the Romans. Compared with all that the then world knew of its past, this state of affairs must have seemed to all those alive at the time to be the golden age.'[4]

In this verdict he agrees with Aelius Aristides, who said that before the rule of the Romans 'the dregs came to the surface and everything happened through blind chance; but since your appearance confusion and revolt have come to an end. Order has returned everywhere and in everyday life and in the state there is clear light of day. Laws have come into being, and faith has been found at the altars of the gods.'[5] Who could not be impressed at the splendour which was now apparent? Roman peace prevailed in an enormous area, 'from the mouth of the Rhine to Dobruja, from Brittany to the edge of the Sahara, from the Straits of Gibraltar to Constantinople and the Euphrates'.[6] No war devastated the land and destroyed the cities: arts and crafts could unfold and agriculture develop; vines were grown even by the Rhine; trade and commerce flourished; new cities came into being, and old ones were redeveloped in splendour; the same law applied everywhere. We can understand why Aelius Aristides resorted to superlatives: 'Cities now gleam in splendour and beauty, and the whole earth is arrayed like a paradise.'[7]

The author of this 'paradise' was Rome. Of course it had presented itself as the bringer of peace even before the time of Augustus, so that there are already characteristics of the Pax Romana in the period before him; however, his time was felt to be the great turning point. With his principate the turmoil of the civil war came to an end, and for the moment he stopped the policy of expansion. In the account of his actions which he wrote shortly before his death, he himself stressed two symbolic actions which clearly express his feeling that he was the one who brought peace to the Roman empire. First he points out that three times he had had the doors of the temple of Janus Quirinus shut, something which was only permissible when peace prevailed throughout the empire; it had happened only twice in history before him.[8] Secondly, he writes, 'When I returned from Spain and Gaul... after successful operations in those provinces, the senate voted in honour of my return the consecration of an altar to "Pax Augusta".'[9]

The awareness of the dawn of a new time of peace was not limited to Augustus and the Roman senate; this feeling was also shared in the provinces. Two well known inscriptions are indications of this. In the calendrical inscription of Priene, near to the provincial capital, Ephesus, dated 9 BC, Augustus is celebrated as the ruler given by providence, 'who has brought war to an end and has ordained peace': thus 'for the world, the birthday of the god (viz. the emperor Augustus)' means 'the beginning of his tidings of peace.'[10] In an inscription from Halicarnassus, also in Asia Minor, which among other things celebrates Augustus as 'saviour of the whole human race', the reason for this is said to be that: 'Land and sea have peace, the cities flourish under a good legal system, in harmony and with an abundance of food, there is an abundance of all good things, people are filled with happy hopes for the future and with delight at the present...'[11] So was this a golden age for which Rome deserved the praise?

According to Aelius Aristides, 'no words are good enough for this city, indeed it is impossible to see it as one should'.[12] For that one would need the eyes of Argus: Rome is so great that it is impossible to see it all. That makes him ask the rhetorical question, 'What standpoint do you take?'[13] But that is in fact the decisive question, namely the standpoint which the observer adopts, the perspective that he gains as a result. Aelius Aristides goes for the highest possible standpoint; he chooses the perspective 'from above' in order to be able to perceive the splendour which emanates from Rome and thus gain an overall perspective. Here he is in line with the way in which Rome itself saw things, as is clear from the name which it gave to the peace which was a characteristic of the time. The Senate had had an 'altar of the peace of Augustus' built, so to begin with this peace was named after the supreme authority of the Roman empire: Pax Augusta.[14] This connection continued to hold for the concept of 'Roman peace', Pax Romana, which then became current. That is particularly clear from a passage in Seneca, who is the first to use the term. In it he speaks of the emperor as a general:

> For he is the bond by which the commonwealth is united, the breath of life which these many thousands draw, who in their own strength would only be a burden to themselves and the prey of others if the great mind of the empire should be withdrawn.
>
> If safe their king, one mind to all,
> bereft of him, their trust must fall.
>
> Such a calamity would be the destruction of the Roman peace, such a calamity would force the fortune of a mighty people to its downfall. Just so long will this people be free from that danger as it shall know how to submit to the rein; but if ever it shall tear away the

> rein, or shall not suffer it to be replaced if shaken loose by some mishap, then this unity and this fabric of mightiest empire will fly into many parts, and the seed of this city's rule will be one with the end of her obedience.[15]

According to this the Pax Romana is indissolubly connected with the *imperium Romanum*, with the authority which goes forth from Rome. Thus the concepts themselves already make it clear that this is a peace determined from above, appointed by the centre of power. Aelius Aristides seeks to match this supreme standpoint by his perspective, and this perspective is in turn matched by his status. Certainly he is a man from the provinces, but he has Roman citizenship, and above all substantial means which relieve him of all concerns about the material needs of life. The authors of the inscriptions quoted above, which celebrate the time of peace under Augustus, are also members of the upper classes. The first inscription was commissioned by the council of the province of Asia and the second by the council of the city of Halicarnassus. The question whether the period of Pax Romana between Augustus and the Antonines was a golden age must therefore be supplemented by another simple question, for whom?[16]

The perspective 'from above' on the splendour of Rome does not show us the whole reality; it blinds us. It reflects a complex of meaning which would be challenged by its victims. That makes it important to exchange the perspective for one 'from below', so as not to consign real sufferings to oblivion through a triumphalist interpretation and and so that the victors of history do not once again triumph over their victims in the way in which history is written.[17] Among the ancient historians it is Tacitus above all who guards against such glorification. After the death of Augustus, he tells us, there were positive assessments of his work: 'The empire had been fenced by the ocean or distant rivers. The legions, the provinces, the fleets, the whole administration, had been centralized. There had been law for the Roman citizen, respect for the allied communities; and the capital itself had been embellished with remarkable splendour. Very few situations had been treated by force, and then only in the interests of general tranquillity.'[18] But other assessments had taken the opposite line: 'After that there had been undoubtedly peace, but peace with bloodshed.'[19]

Pax Romana – a golden age or a peace with bloodshed? At all events it is certain that the reality of this peace was experienced in different ways by different people. I shall now go on to depict the different aspects of the Pax Romana, and in so doing will above all give an opportunity for experiences that were different from those of Aelius Aristides to find expression.

2. 'A peace established through victories' – the military aspect of the Pax Romana

It is no coincidence that the Emperor is spoken of as general in connection with one of the earliest mentions of the concept of the Pax Romana.[20] The military aspect of this peace takes pride of place. The building of the 'altar of the peace of Augustus' was understood above as a symbolic act; no less symbolic was the place where this altar was built, 'on the Campus Martius'.[21] A modern admirer of Rome sees 'a deep and significant meaning' in this location: 'The field of Mars, too, is now to bear witness that the times of war are ended, that the rule of the goddess Pax, the golden age of peace, in which wars and distresses alone find their meaning, has dawned.'[22] The significance of the history of violence here lies in the success of the victor: on this altar the sacrifices burn away to nothing.[23] The altar of the peace of Augustus was an altar of burnt offering; the fact that it was built on the field of Mars shows that this peace had been won on the battlefield. The other passage mentioned above, from the Acts of Augustus, confirms this with all the clarity that could be desired: the temple of Janus was to be closed 'whenever there was peace, secured by victory, throughout the whole domain of the Roman people on land and sea'.[24] So the first thing that we must note is that the Pax Romana is a peace which is the political goal of the Roman emperor and his most senior officals and is brought about and secured by military action through the success of his legions.

(a) 'Mars, Victoria, Pax'

Here the evidence of coinage is very eloquent: Mars the god of war is in full armour, on his left shoulder a standard and on his outstretched right arm the goddess of victory, along with the inscription *Mars Victor*.[25] Another coin portrays Victoria on the hand of the goddess Roma, who is herself sitting on the weapons of conquered opponents.[26] Portrayals of Victoria are particularly frequent: she has her right foot on the globe and is inscribing a shield with the victory which has just been won;[27] standing behind the head of Augustus she is putting a laurel wreath on his brow.[28] Pax, the goddess of peace, usually portrayed in the Greek sphere with a cornucopia, also appears in this form on Roman coins, e.g. on the obverse of a denarius from the early period of Augustus' sole rule; the head of the goddess has an olive branch in front and a cornucopia behind; but on the reverse side Octavian is portrayed in military clothing with a spear.[29] On a tetradrachm from the same period Pax is standing on a sword with the staff of peace in her hand.[30] This peace is an 'armed peace', and the legions which have achieved it are evidently 'peace troops'.[31]

The portrayal of the goddess of peace is most vivid on coins of Trajan: she has her right foot on the neck of a vanquished foe.[32] 'War, victory and peace'[33] – these three associated aspects are represented in an impressive way on a sestertius of Nero: the emperor is depicted on a triumphal arch in a quadriga facing forward; Victory is standing on the right beside him with a garland and a palm branch, and on the left is Pax with cornucopia and staff of peace, somewhat lower down on the ambulatory of the arch on both sides is a legionary soldier, and Mars is in the left niche that can be seen.[34] War leading to victory is the presupposition of the happy time of peace in which the emperor triumphs, and this is in turn guaranteed by the legions. The peace which Rome brings is a victory-peace for the Romans, while for the vanquished it is a peace of subjection. This aspect, too, is vividly reflected in the imagery of coins: the emperor Commodus on a horse with Victoria behind him, crowning him with a garland, a sign of victory in front of him, and below him sitting on the ground a fettered prisoner on whose head the emperor's horse is putting its left fore hoof;[35] the emperor galloping away over an adversary lying weaponless on the ground, protecting himself with one arm and imploring vainly with the other.[36] The vanquished, too, are impressively portrayed. In the centre of a sestertius of Titus is a palm; with her back to it on the left a mourning Jewish woman is sitting, her head propped up with her right hand; on the other side a Jew is moving to the right to meet an unknown fate as a prisoner of war, his hands fettered behind his back, his head turned towards the woman.[37] On various coins of Domitian a German woman is sitting on a shield, mourning, with a broken spear beneath her.[38] One wonders with what feelings members of subject peoples will have looked at such coins.[39]

In the introduction which the Ancyra copy of the acts of Augustus provides, it is aptly said that those acts of Augustus are reported through which 'he subjected the earth to the rule of the Roman people'. First, success in waging war demonstrates who has the power, and then peace is ordered. Thus at one point Plutarch already writes about Caesar in respect of his enterprises in Spain: 'After bringing the war to a successful close, he was equally happy in adjusting the problems of peace.'[40]

The details of this practice of peace through war and victory can briefly be demonstrated from the conquest of northern Britain by Agricola. Tacitus portrays his father-in-law Agricola as a most honourable man who in his career was always a strict observer of the law and did not enrich himself in a self-seeking way. But the 'right of war' is something special. So Tacitus writes at one point: 'Accordingly he sent forward the fleet to make descents on various places, and to spread a general and vague panic.'[41] At another point Tacitus tells of devastating forays which were suddenly undertaken: 'After he had terrorized them sufficiently, he paraded before them the enticements of peace. By these means many states which up to that time had dealt with Rome on equal terms were induced to give hostages and abandon their hostility.'[42] Here the Roman power produced terror and uncertainty and then offered itself as an active guardian of peace.[43] However, Tacitus indicates briefly that this peace did not just contain 'enticements', when in respect of the conquest of Britain he speaks of tribes 'which feared our peace'.[44]

Peace produced and maintained by military force is accompanied with streams of blood and tears of unimaginable proportions. Looking back to Numa, a king of peace of a different kind, from the earliest days of Rome, Plutarch says, 'But that which was the end and aim of Numa's government, namely, the continuance of peace and friendship between Rome and other nations, straightway vanished from the earth with him. After his death the double doors of the temple which he had kept continually closed, as if he really had war caged and confined there, were thrown wide open and Italy was filled with the blood of the slain.'[45] An example of the way in which with the further extension of the Roman empire areas increasingly remote from Rome came to be filled 'with the blood of the slain' may be taken from an episode from Germanicus' first campaign in Germany in AD 14: 'For fifty miles around he wasted the country with sword and flame. Neither age nor sex inspired pity: places sacred and profane were razed indifferently to the ground.'[46] Plutarch immediately continues in the passage quoted above: ' "What, then!" some one will say. "was not Rome advanced and bettered by her wars?" That is a question which would need a long answer, if I am to satisfy men who hold that betterment consists in wealth, luxury and empire, rather than in safety, gentleness and that independence which is attended by righteousness.'[47]

However, Plutarch does not give this detailed answer. Did he regard it as hopeless? Those whom he has in view here combined peace and security with rule on a military basis which brought them riches and luxury. By associating peace and security with justice and contentment – in contrast to domination – Plutarch himself is here indicating – timidly enough – a different understanding of peace from the Pax Romana based on 'the blood of the slain'.

(b) 'Born to rule...'

How did Rome come to introduce peace, as it understood it, everywhere? Plutarch attributes to Caesar 'an insatiable love of power and a mad desire to be first and greatest'.[48] Is Caesar thus the embodiment of typical Romanhood? At all events he is the embodiment of Romanhood as it set out on the road to victory and then found itself virtually compelled to continue along it. Thus when Aeneas has been taken by the Sibyl of Cumae to the underworld after landing in Italy, Virgil makes Anchises, there among the pious, tell him: 'Remember, O Roman, to rule the nations with your power – there shall be your arts – to crown peace with law, to spare the humbled and to tame in war the proud.'[49] The establishment of an order of peace through Roman rule here seems to be virtually the will of divine fate. How could such a will not be obeyed?[50] At another point Virgil says that Augustus 'gave a victor's laws to willing nations'.[51]

This notion is also echoed by Aelius Aristides: 'Since from the very beginning you (viz. the Romans) were born free and in a sense directly to rule, you admirably provided for all that serves this end, founded a form of state such as no one had yet had, and established firm laws and rules for all.'[52] The prophecy of Roman rule over the world which Virgil puts in the mouth of Anchises is of course a *vaticinium ex eventu*, a statement made in the form of a prophecy after the event has already taken place; it is thus none other than an ideology born of success, but one which in fact calls for new successes.[53] Successes in war, which are always also lucrative for the victors, strengthen self-awareness. Thus Plutarch writes that the announcement in Rome of the victory over King Antiochus 'filled the people with the proud feeling that it was able to master every land and sea'.[54] That too appears as a prophecy, indeed from Jupiter himself: 'I set neither bounds nor periods of empire; dominion without end have I bestowed.'[55]

This awareness of being 'lords of the world'[56] calls for deeds to match. Thus the Emperor Claudius was not content with the triumph accorded him by the Senate, but 'desiring the glory of a legitimate triumph, he chose Britain as the best place for gaining it, a land that had been attempted by no one since the deified Julius'.[57] What were the Romans after in Britain? Their self-awareness and the ambition of the imperial ruler of the world called for its conquest.

According to the account of Josephus in his *Jewish War*, Titus also appealed to the Roman self-awareness when before the attack on the city of Tarichaea he addressed his cavalry: 'Romans! For it is right for me to put you in mind of what nation you are, in the beginning of my speech, that so you may not be ignorant who you are, and who they are against whom we are going to fight. For as to us, Romans, no part of the habitable earth has been able to escape our hands hitherto... and a sad thing it would be for us to grow weary under good success.'[58]

According to a speech by Vespasian which was also written by Josephus, Roman honour called for victory 'since they are not forced to fight, but only to enlarge their own dominions'.[59] This sense of Roman superiority is so great that the motives of their opponents for fighting, however noble, pale into insigificance, as is again made clear by the speech of Titus to his soldiers: 'Your fighting is to be on greater motives than those of the Jews; for although they run the hazard of war for liberty, and for their country, yet what can be a greater motive to us than glory? and that it may never be said that after we have got dominion of the habitable earth, the Jews are able to confront us as equals.'[60] Here we are looking as it were deep into the soul of a world power. It must not be provoked by a third- or even fourth-class military power. Woe to those who dare as much!

(c) '...to yield to those that are too strong...'

The sense of superiority on the part of the Romans is matched on the side of those whom they conquer by the recognition of this power, which is compelling in the truest sense of the word. As an example of this I would like once again to cite the Jewish historian Flavius Josephus, who to begin with was in command of the Jewish rebels in Galilee and then when beaten became an admirer of Rome. He called the Roman military power 'irrestistible'.[61] At the siege of Jerusalem he made himself the spokesman of Rome and called out to the defenders:

> Men may well enough grudge at the dishonour of owning ignoble masters over them, but ought not to do so to those who have all things under their command: for what part of the world is there that has escaped the Romans, unless it be such as are of no use because of their heat or cold? And it is evident that fortune has gone over to them on all sides, and that God, when he had gone round the nations with this dominion, is now settled in Italy. That moreover, it is a strong and fixed law, even among brute beasts, as well as among men, to yield to those who are too strong for them; and to suffer those to have the dominion, who are too hard for the rest in war.[62]

So impressed was Josephus by the power of Rome that he virtually claimed that God supported the right of the stronger which he had just proclaimed. Therefore the Jewish rebels were 'waging war not only against the Romans but also against God'.[63]

Secondly, I would cite the Greek philosophizing writer Plutarch who, commenting on what politicians can do in subjected Greece, says with resignation:

> But the best thing is to see to it in advance that factional discord shall never arise among them and to regard this as the greatest and noblest function of what may be called the art of statesmanship. For observe that the greatest blessings which states can enjoy – peace, liberty, plenty, abundance of men and concord – so far as peace is concerned the peoples have no need of statesmanship at present; for all war, both Greek and foreign, has been banished from among us and has disappeared; and of liberty the peoples have as great a share as our rulers grant them, and perhaps more would not be better for them; but bounteous productiveness of the soil, kindly temperance of the seasons, that wives may bear 'children like their sires', and that the offspring may live in safety – these things the wise man will ask the gods in his prayers to send his fellow-citizens. There remains, then, for the statesman, of those activities which fall within his province, only this – and it is the equal of any of the other blessings: – always to instil concord and friendship in those who dwell together with him and to remove strifes, discords and all enmity, as in the case of quarrels among friends... Then he will instruct his people both individually and collectively and will call attention to the weak condition of Greek affairs, in which it is best for wise men to accept one advantage – a life of harmony and quiet, since fortune has left us no prize open for competition. For what dominion, what glory is there for those who are victorious? What sort of power is it which a small edict of a proconsul may annul or transfer to another man and which even if it last, as nothing in it seriously worth while?'[64]

There is nothing to quibble at in the balance of power; that is clear. Pliny expresses that from the Roman side, on the occasion of his consulate in AD 100, in the following way in his speech of thanks to Trajan: 'Now once more terror is in their midst (he is referring to external enemies who had become arrogant before the accession of Trajan); our enemies are afraid, and crave permission to obey commands. They see that Rome has a leader who ranks with her heroes of old, whose title of Imperator was on seas stained with the bloodshed of victory and on battlefields piled high with the bodies of the dead. They pray, they implore, we grant, we refuse – both in accordance with the majesty of sovereign power.'[65] Only those with illusions about this balance of power could dare to spark off a rebellion against Rome. Josephus spends many pages giving an extended account of the superior

Roman military might.[66] He ends with the words: 'This account I have given the reader, not so much with the intention of commending the Romans, as of comforting those who have been conquered by them, and for the deterring others from attempting innovations under their government.'[67]

Anyone who nevertheless ventured to wage war came to feel what, according to the passage from Virgil about the task of Rome which I quoted above, it meant to 'tame in war the proud'. This happened with cruel harshness. Towards the end of an account of the way in which Roman soldiers captured a Galilean city in the Jewish War, Josephus tells us: 'The Jews went on fighting for six hours; but when the fighting men were spent, the rest of the multitude had their throats cut, partly in the open air and partly in their own houses, both young and old together. So there were no males now remaining apart from infants, which, with the women, were carried as slaves into captivity.'[68]

(d) 'Who cares about war in wild Spain?'

Because 'the whole earth' is ruled by Rome,[69] the world has peace. This claim to comprehensive peace is even maintained when wars are being discussed. Thus Aelius Aristides writes:

> People no longer believe in wars, indeed doubt whether they ever happened; stories about them are usually regarded as myths. But if wars should flare up somewhere on the frontiers, as is natural given such an immeasurably great empire, given the folly of the Dacrians, the difficult situation of the Libyans or the miseries of the people by the Red Sea, who are incapable of enjoying the blessings of the present, these wars quickly disappear again, just like myths, as do the stories about them. So great is the peace that you now have, though waging war is a tradition among you.[70]

It is no coincidence that those words are spoken in Rome. At the centre, wars on the periphery were played down; they were hardly noticed. So Horace can ask the rhetorical question: 'Who cares about war in wild Spain?'[71] But this question can be answered quite simply and in all seriousness: those who are involved in the war there, and especially the Spaniards. Despite all the assertions to the contrary, the Pax Romana was not really a world peace. This peace, gained and secured by military force, had its limits at the limits of the Roman empire. In the *Annals* of Tacitus the description of this war occupies page after page.[72] Here the laws of power and glory govern the action. In the Armenian campaign at the time of Nero Domitius Corbulo compares the city of Artaxata to an earthquake, 'For in view of the extent of the walls it was impossible to hold it without a powerful garrison, and our numbers were not such that they could be divided between keeping a strong retaining force and conducting a campaign; while, if the place was to remain unscathed and unguarded, there was neither utility nor glory in the bare fact of its capture.'[73] The glory of war is documented in ruins. In this action the inhabitants escaped with their lives because they had surrendered to the Romans with 'what they had'. In the continuation of the description of this campaign, however, Tacitus reports of the Roman general, 'he devastated with fire and sword the districts he found hostile to us'.[74]

In a very similar way Germanicus had called on his soldiers in a battle with the Germani 'to go on with the carnage. Prisoners were needless; nothing but the extermination of the race would end the war.'[75] Seneca may have such events in mind when he speaks of giving vent to one's fury in state life: 'We check manslaughter and isolated murders; but what of war and the much-vaunted crime of slaughtering whole peoples?'[76] Of course that did not always have to be practised. So Augustus writes in his *Res Gestae*: 'The foreign nations which could with safety be pardoned I preferred to save rather than to destroy.'[77] Here we have a clear picture of the sovereign brutality of great military power which gives itself the semblance of humanity.

War on the periphery is almost unavoidable for peace gained and secured by military means. Horace expressly wishes that Rome may take its weapons to 'whatever limit bounds the world'.[78] According to Aelius Aristides the Romans did not build walls round their city, but round their empire: 'You have built them as far outside as was possible... worth seeing for those who dwell within the ring'[79] – evidently not for those outside, since war can be taken to them at any time. This principle of the Pax Romana, transferring war and its evil consequences to the periphery, is expressed with astonishing openness by Horace when he says of the god Apollo: 'Moved by your prayer he shall ward off tearful war, wretched plague and famine from the folk and from our sovereign Caesar, and send these woes against the Parthian and the Briton.'[80]

The character of this peace, which is imperial in the truest sense of the word, is very evident: it extends so far because the *imperium* which goes out from the centre can be imposed by weapons. The connection between peace and military power, between *pax* and *imperium*, is explicitly shown in two sentences in Augustus's *Res Gestae*: 'I extended the boundaries of all the provinces which were bordered by races not subject to our empire. The provinces of the Gauls, the Spains and Germany I reduced to a state of peace.'[81] And in this peace of course

Roman orders held. The arrogance of power as over against those on the periphery is very evident in an episode recounted by Tacitus:

> A leader of the Germani faithful to the Romans over fifty years led his tribe to unoccupied land on the frontier, which however the Roman soldiers kept as occasional pasturage for their cattle. The German thought, 'By all means let them keep reservations for cattle in the midst of starving men, but not to the extent of choosing a desert and a solitude for neighbours in preference to friendly nations.' However, the answer of the Roman governor was, 'All men have to bow to the command of their betters; it had been decreed by those gods... that with the Roman people should rest the decision what to give and what to take away, and that they should brook no other judges than themselves.'[82]

Can what took place on the periphery of the Roman empire be dismissed as a 'marginal occurrence' of no further importance? Or do we not see here on the periphery the tremendous price which was paid for this peace?[83]

3. 'Being able to enjoy one's possessions in peace' – the political aspect of the Pax Romana

First of all it must be remembered that the Pax Romana rested on compelling military power; the military aspect is the dominant one. But it also contained other elements to which the victors were glad to refer as justification for what they did, and which were also echoed by some of those whom they conquered. Closely connected with the military aspect is the political one, which we must now go on to consider.

(a) 'Peace and security'

Roman power offered security. 'Peace and security' belong closely together. A Syrian inscription reads: 'The Lord Marcus Flavius Bonus, the most illustrious Comes and Dux of the first legion, has ruled over us in peace and given constant peace and security to travellers and to the people.'[84] According to Aelius Aristides what is said here of a small area applied all over the world: 'Now the earth itself and its inhabitants have been granted universal security which is evident to all.'[85]

What is primarily envisaged here is protection against any threat from outside the boundaries of the empire. Seneca speaks of a time 'in the midst of peace': 'When weapons are everywhere at rest and when peace prevails throughout the world.'[86] Those who disturb the peace and are or seek to be in military conflict with Rome are offered security. Thus according to Josephus' report, in the Jewish War Titus invited the defenders of the city of Gischala to surrender, 'especially when they have seen cities much better fortified than theirs, overthrown by a single attack upon them; while as many as have entrusted themselves to the security of the Romans' right hands enjoy their possessions in safety.'[87] Josephus makes Antipater say very much the same things in Judaea after Caesar had reordered affairs in the province of Syria and unrest broke out after his departure. If they complied, 'he argued to his fellow countrymen, they would be able to live in happiness and enjoy their possessions'.[88]

The passage I have just quoted also shows that the security ordained by Rome involved the exclusion of internal disputes and controversies between different areas of the realm. Caesar appeared in Palestine as the one who settled quarrels within Judaism over the leadership;[89] he deprived the Jews of conquests which had been made formerly and 'restored their legitimate citizens' to the cities, of course by subjecting them to the superior rule of the governor of the province of Syria.[90] Aelius Aristides praises the end of the controversies between the cities as an escape from certain death, as the realization of a dream, for in his view 'as a consequence of their mutual discord and unrest the cities were already as it were on the refuse heap; but then they received a common leadership and suddenly came alive again'.[91]

Thus security includes not least 'internal security'. Horace is delighted to be able to say in respect of Augustus: 'Neither civil strife nor death by violence will I fear, while Caesar holds the earth.'[92] Tacitus calls the time after the Civil War between Otho and Vitellius the time 'of security restored':[93] according to him 'the security of peace' includes work without anxiety in the fields and houses open.[94] Not to be plundered by robbers either at home or on journeys is 'peace and security'.[95] So Aelius Aristides ends the section on the possibility of unhindered travel with the statement: 'It is security enough to be a Roman or rather one of those who live under your (viz., the Romans') rule.'[96] According to Seneca, 'the benefits of this peace which extends to all are more deeply appreciated by those who make good use of it.'[97] With reference to Domitian Pliny speaks of 'those comfortless times' and is glad now to be able to live more safely and more happily under Trajan.[98] However, Martial could already write in 94, under Domitian: 'No savagery of captains is here, no frenzy of the sword; we may enjoy unbroken peace and pleasure.'[99] Here it becomes clear that the one who praises this security bases that praise on limited perception.

Both aspects, internal and external security, guarded by the power of Rome, are given impressive expression in the speech which Tacitus makes the Roman general Cerialis give in Trier to the Treviri and the Lingones after their revolt has been put down:

> Roman commanders and generals entered your land and the lands of the other Gauls from no desire for gain but because they were invited by your forefathers, who were wearied to death by internal quarrels, while the Germans whom they had invited to help them had enslaved them all, allies and enemies alike... We have occupied the banks of the Rhine not to protect Italy but to prevent a second Ariovistus from gaining the throne of Gaul... There were always kings and wars throughout Gaul until you submitted to our laws. Although often provoked by you, the only use we have made of our rights as victors has been to impose on you the necessary costs of maintaining peace; for you cannot secure tranquillity without armies, nor maintain armies without pay, nor provide pay without taxes; everything else we have in common... For, if the Romans are driven out – which heaven forbid – what will follow except universal war among all peoples? Therefore love and cherish peace and the city... be warned by the lessons of fortune both good and bad not to prefer defiance and ruin to peace and security.[100]

(b) 'Peace and concord'

Internal conditions ordered by Rome, security from external enemies guaranteed by Rome, paid for by tribute, maintained by obedience – the advice to 'love and cherish peace and the city' aptly sums it all up. From a Roman perspective the provision of peace by Rome is matched by concord on the side of those who have been pacified. Peace rests on concord between Rome and the other peoples and cities, and on concord among these others. The connection between peace and concord and the stress on concord with Rome already appears in an inscription from the year 139 BC which in connection with Rome and the cities of Asia Minor talks of 'preserving mutual goodwill with peace and all concord and friendship'.[101] Goodwill towards Rome is stressed by an inscription from Ephesus dating from 85 BC in connection with the war against Mithridates. Here it becomes clear that goodwill means specific obedience, the recognition of Roman rule: '...the people preserves its old goodwill towards the Romans, the saviours of all, and readily agrees to their ordinances in all things. And because from the beginning our people has maintained goodwill towards the Romans... it has resolved to undertake the war against Mithridates for the Roman empire and for common freedom.'[102]

The quotation from Plutarch[103] given at length above already showed that, given the circumstances, the politicians of Greek cities had no alternative but to seek concord. Peace is the framework appointed by the Romans which has to be filled out with mutual concord.[104] This is matched on the other side by the desire expressed by Tacitus that to the peoples outside the frontiers of the empire, 'if not love for us, at least hatred for each other may last for a long time. Since now that the destinies of the empire have passed their zenith, fortune can guarantee us nothing better than discord among our foes.'[105]

Concord is also a particularly important concept within Rome.[106] This becomes clear when, according to Plutarch's account, Otho makes it known in his last speech before he commits suicide in order to end the civil war, that he wants to sacrifice himself for 'peace and concord'.[107] As a rule, however, discord tended to come from elsewhere. When there was social unrest in Puteoli in 58, a cohort of Praetorians was sent in, 'the terrors of which, together with a few executions, restored the town to concord'.[108]

Significantly this last term also occurs in a context which demonstrates quite clearly to what concord the Roman peace is ultimately due: a coin of Nero depicts two hands linked in a handshake and behind them is a standard, on which the inscription runs: 'Concord of the army/the armies', namely with one another or with the emperor.[109]

(c) 'Freedom and other specious names...'

Aelius Aristides praises as the greatest quality of the Romans: 'Of all those who ever possessed an empire, you alone rule over people who are free.'[110] However, the very way in which this is put already shows that this freedom is related to domination. Thus in the inscription quoted above the council of Ephesus had decided 'for Roman rule and common freedom';[111] and Plutarch had indicated clearly enough that the Greek cities had as much freedom as the Romans allowed them.[112] For non-Roman citizens, freedom under the conditions of the Pax Romana is freedom that has been granted, and scant enough at that. They are to maintain it by 'fidelity to the law and concord'.[113] From the Roman side care can be exercised. Thus Pliny advises a friend who is going as governor to Achaea: 'To snatch from such a people the shadow that remains would be a harsh, cruel, indeed barbarous act. Physicians, you see, though in sickness there is no difference between slaves and freemen, yet give the latter milder and more gentle treatment.'[114]

Such considerations play no part at all when it comes to barbarians. Thus according to Tacitus, Agricola sees as one of the benefits of a possible conquest of Ireland that for Britain 'Roman troops would be everywhere and liberty would sink, so to speak, below the horizon.'[115]

Here again we can see as it were the principle of the Pax Romana: the use of weapons, which is indispensable for it, is shifted as far as possible to increasingly distant 'frontiers' so that in this way it is possible to have peace from revolts in an increasingly large centre and to be able to exercise rule undisturbed. When Tacitus makes barbarians speak in his works, he occasionally expresses that quite clearly. He tells of Civilis, the rebel prince of the Batavians, who in secret conversations 'reminded them of the miseries that they had endured so many years while they falsely called their wretched servitude a peace'.[116] He also makes the Britannic prince Calgacus compare subjection to Rome with slavery.[117] In the speech of Cerialis to the Treviri and Lingones in Trier, from which I have already quoted, the final reference to the plundering and oppressive Germani is made amazingly general, so that his contemporary readers would perforce have been reminded more of the Romans than of the Germani: 'Freedom, however, and other specious names are their pretexts: but no man has ever been ambitious to enslave another or to win dominion for himself without using those very same words.'[118]

According to Josephus, the last king of Judaea, Agrippa II, tells those resolved on revolt that given his estimation of the balance of power their hope for peace is simply 'nonsensical'.[119] He can certainly understand why they break out into lamentation because of unjust attacks by the governor, but he firmly rebukes them for at the same time bursting into songs in praise of freedom: it is impossible to have both together.[120] Now is evidently not the time for freedom.[121] In Italy one can see among hostages sent by the Parthians 'the nobility of the east (the Parthians) enslaved under the pretext of peace'.[122] So Josephus, the friend of Rome, makes Agrippa give those intent on rebellion this advice: 'Nothing so much damps the force of blows as bearing them with patience; and the quietness of those who are injured diverts the injurious persons from afflicting... such crimes as we complain of may soon be corrected, for the same procurator will not continue for ever; and it is probable that the successors will come with more moderate inclinations.'[123] Tacitus makes the Roman general Cerialis give very much the same advice to the conquered rebels: 'You endure barren years, excessive rains, and all other natural evils: in like manner endure the extravagance or greed of your rulers. There will be vices as long as there are men, but these vices are not perpetual and they are compensated for by the coming of better times.'[124]

The system as slavery and slavery as a system, heightened slavery but as a natural event – this cynicism on the part of the rulers makes it clear that the freedom of Roman peace is in the first place *Roman* freedom.

The coin mentioned above, on the reverse of which the goddess Pax is depicted standing on a sword,[125] has on the obverse the head of Augustus with the inscription 'Protector of the freedom of the Roman people'.[126] Roman freedom and peace based on force of arms are indeed two sides of the same coin. From Rome, from the centre, it was possible to speak of 'peace and freedom' otherwise than in the provinces. In connection with comments about the 'universal peace' which is produced by the emperor and from which the philosophers in particular profit, Seneca says: 'The great and true goods are not divided in such a manner that each has but a slight interest. They belong in their entirety to each individual... At a distribution of grain men receive only the amount that has been promised to each person... The goods, however, are indivisible – I mean peace and liberty – and they belong in their entirety to all men just as much as they belong to each individual... rich leisure, control of his own time and a tranquillity uninterrupted by public employments.'[127] At the latest these specific instances show that the great benefits of peace and freedom really were 'indivisible' in so far as they were not in fact shared but formed the privilege of a few: they belonged to all only as a slogan.

However, it is clear again and again from, say, the works of Tacitus that even in Rome itself freedom was limited. Thus he says of remarks by Tiberius on the election of consuls: 'In words the policy was specious; in reality it was nugatory or perfidious and destined to issue in a servitude all the more detestable the more it was disguised under a semblance of liberty.'[128] That rule abroad was based on domestic militarization even in the early period of Roman expansion is made clear by Plutarch in his description of Aemilius Paulus as a general. He is said to have told the citizens of Rome: 'If they had confidence in him they must not make themselves his colleagues in command, nor indulge in rhetoric about the war, but quietly furnish the necessary supplies for it.' Plutarch ends the section with the sentence: 'Thus was the Roman people, to the end that it might prevail and be greatest in the world, a servant of virtue and honour.'[129]

(d) 'To distinguish merit in every degree'

The Romans Tacitus and Pliny the Younger had already seen that the Pax Romana was not a sphere of freedom. For non-Romans, in fact, it amounted to servitude, though with the spheres of freedom which were allowed them. Most politically responsible Romans were aware that excessively harsh servitude could produce a potential for rebellions and unrest, and so their statesmanship consisted essentially in giving the upper classes of subject peoples a share in exercising rule.

Again it is Tacitus who openly speaks of the 'old and long-received principle of Roman policy, which employs kings among the instruments of servitude', who then prove themselves to be faithful friends of the Romans.[130]

King Agrippa II, who has already been mentioned, was one of them, as already were his ancestors down to Herod and Antipas. However, the initiative for such collaboration did not just come from Rome. The favour of Roman power was also wooed by indigenous potentates in order to free themselves of unwanted competitors and to gain or establish positions of power. Thus Herod had first of all appealed to Mark Antony, who made him king and thus ended disputes among the Jews.[131] After Antony's defeat and death, however, 'Herod was under immediate concern on account of his friendship with Antony, who was already defeated at Actium by Caesar.'[132] He resolutely went to the victor and had his kingdom confirmed by him. Herod showed his gratitude with gifts.[133] One need only ask where he got the wherewithal for presents which could pacify an Octavian, to see who was collaborating with whom, at whose expense. The great-grandson of Herod the Great, Agrippa II, acted in precisely the same way towards Vespasian. He welcomed the general and future emperor 'and his army in his richly adorned house with the added purpose of securing his endangered throne with Roman help'.[134]

Whatever the immediate occasion may have been, the collaboration of Rome with the indigenous upper classes was at all events an explicit piece of political calculation. It could relate both to the existence, extension and security of the empire and to the internal situation of the province in question or the friendly monarchy. As an example of the one case I might cite the appointment of Herod as king by the Roman senate on the orders of Mark Anthony because that could 'only be an advantage in the Parthian wars'.[135] In connection with the other instance Pliny writes to a friend who is governor in Baetica that he would like to commend his concern for justice (*iustitia*) to the people of the province through great humanity (*humanitas*). We shall be investigating both terms, *iustitia* and *humanitas*, later. Pliny goes on to describe the most important part of this *iustitia* as being 'to distinguish merit in every degree and so to gain the love of the lower rank, as to preserve at the same time the regard of their superiors'. Then as his final advice he says: 'Keep up the distinctions of rank and dignity. For to level and confound the different orders of mankind is far from producing an equality among them; it is, in truth, the most unequal thing imaginable.'[136]

Rome was able to produce a sharing of interests between itself and the native upper classes – and again this involved above all those at the top of society. This community of interests was above all of an economic kind. Roman peace guaranteed the preservation of the existing order and therefore the continuation of the status of the indigenous upper classes. On the other hand Rome guaranteed a peace in the province or in the allied kingdom which was the presupposition for the money and offerings in kind which had to flow to Rome as duties and taxes. Thus the sparing of the subjected mentioned in the famous Virgil passage[137] was motivated not least by economic considerations. According to Josephus it was in the 'nature' of the Romans to be 'naturally mild in their conquests, and they preferred what was profitable before what their passions dictated to them; which profit of theirs did not lie in leaving the city empty of inhabitants, nor the country desert'.[138] That the interest of the native upper classes in the preservation of the *status quo* and also their love of peace – i.e. of Roman peace – was motivated by economic reasons is also clearly stated by Josephus. He describes how shortly before the outbreak of the Jewish War, when storm signals were already out because of the forays of the governor Florus, the chief priests and all the other influential people and the council went to King Agrippa II to discuss the difficult situation. He describes these people as those who were 'desirous of peace because of the possessions they had'.[139] At another point he reports how the influential people of Gadara, during the war in Galilee, when Vespasian was already approaching the city, made him an offering 'out of the desire they had of peace, and for saving their effects, for many of the citizens of Gadara were rich men'.[140] He says that as a matter of course, without offence; he himself was not poor.

4. 'The Common Market for the Produce of the Earth' – the economic aspect of the Pax Romana

At the end of the preceding section we had already seen how the economy played a decisive role in Roman peace. Economic considerations were not decisive for the indigenous upper class only: the economic contribution of the province was in fact important for the survival of Rome.

(a) 'Building roads through forests and swamps'

The lands round the Mediterranean conquered by Rome also differed very widely in economic terms. Using present-day terminology one could say that in addition to developed countries – from the perspective of Rome – there were also 'developing countries' which still had to be exploited economically. This exploitation took place along with conquest. The Roman legionary soldier was at the same time an economic pioneer.[141] That is already clear from his equipment. According to Josephus he 'carries almost as much as a mule'; Josephus goes on to describe the equipment of the ordinary foot soldier like this: 'spear and long shield, then a saw and a basket, a spade and an axe, a thong of leather and a hook and handcuffs'.[142] The sequence of this list is extremely illuminating. First come the weapons which are used for the conquest of foreign territory. The implements listed after this certainly also had a military purpose, in that they were used for digging trenches and building camps, but they also served for the economic exploitation of conquered territory. The handcuffs at the end stand for the maintenance of the new situation brought about by force of arms.[143] This context of peaceful implements, weapons and handcuffs is clear. It gives the economy an atmosphere of military force and at the same time shows whom above all it had to and indeed did serve.

Pliny shows in one of his letters how the conquest of a land was already accompanied with measures for its economic exploitation. He is enthusiastic about the intentions of a poet to describe Trajan's Dacian war. Pliny points out that in it he must not only describe warlike events and the two triumphs celebrated in Rome: rather, he puts in first place: 'You will sing of rivers turned into new channels, and rivers bridged for the first time, of camps built on craggy mountains.'[144] Aelius Aristides is full of admiration at such achievements by the Romans: 'You have measured out the whole earth, spanned rivers with bridges of different kinds, pierced through mountains to lay roads, established post stations in uninhabited areas and everywhere introduced a cultivated and ordered way of life.'[145]

Both Pliny and Aristides can be enthusiastic at the Roman measures for the economic exploitation of the provinces, because they do not ask who has to do the work of changing the courses of rivers and building bridges and roads and forts, and because that was not of course a problem for the Roman citizen for whose benefit the arrangements for irrigation, sea travel and commerce – the forts are again on the level of the handcuffs[146] – were being made. Things look different to those who have been conquered. Thus according to Tacitus, Calgacus prince of the Britanni tells his fellow countrymen: 'Our life and limbs will be used up in building roads through forests and swamps to the accompaniment of gibes and blows.'[147] Constructing roads and other building measures were thus carried out not only by the Roman legionary soldiers but where possible also by forced labour.[148] Whom they benefit is illustrated by a piece of rabbinic tradition which tells of a conversation between

Rabbi Jehuda and Rabbi Simon. Rabbi Jehuda is amazed at the Roman achievements: 'How fine are the works of this people. They have made streets, they have built bridges, they have erected baths.'[149] Simon answers him: 'All what they made they made to themselves, they built market places, to set harlots in them; baths, to rejuvenate themselves, bridges, to levy tolls for them.' This statement often appears in variant forms; thus it is attributed to Rabbi Gamliel II: 'This empire consumes us with four things: with its tolls, with its baths, its theatres and natural produce.'[150] So what Rome needed in order to exploit a province economically was above all the provision of an infrastructure, though this was tailored to its own needs. If the term 'development aid' had already been in existence it would have been just as much a euphemism for exploitation as it is today.

This imperial structure is also reflected very clearly at another level when in the letter mentioned above, in which Pliny welcomes the planned undertaking of his correspondents in describing the Dacian war, he says in connection with difficulties: 'It will also be quite difficult to reconcile these barbarous and uncouth names, especially that of the king himself, with the harmony of Greek verse.'[151] Foreign land cannot remain what it is; it must match the norms of the victor. Just as the names of the conquered are distorted to fit the metre current among the victors, so the economic riches of a conquered land and its economic capacity are directed towards the needs of Rome.

(b) 'Putting up with being a source of income for the Romans'

The profit which Rome got from the provinces came by right, namely by the right of the victor. The Romans 'always exacted from their conquered opponents the recognition that the war was entirely their fault',[152] so the first right of the victor is that to the spoil. In his description of Britain Tacitus states that it 'also contains gold, silver and other metals', and immediately adds, 'as the prize of victory'.[153] The mineral treasures are not for those who live there and work on them – the barbarians would not in any case know what to do with them – but for those who are superior, the victors. The gold in particular exerted a great power of attraction. After Josephus has reported the storming of the Jerusalem temple by the troops of Titus he continues: 'And now all the soldiers had such vast quantities of the spoils which they had got by plunder, that in Syria a pound weight of gold was sold for half its former value.'[154] But what the soldiers could take immediately was only a small part of the total booty of war. The depictions on victory pillars and triumphal arches are even now impressive testimony to what was taken off to Rome after a victory. The literary evidence confirms that. Josephus describes in detail the triumphal procession of Vespasian after the Jewish War and in so doing stresses the splendour that was set on show, which was to bear witness to 'the magnitude of the Roman empire'.[155] The connection between the booty of war and Roman peace is given a marked symbolic expression in the temple of peace which Vespasian had erected; according to Josephus 'it was beyond all human expectation and opinion; for having now by providence a vast quantity of wealth, besides what he had formerly gained in his other exploits, he had this temple adorned with pictures, and statues; for in this temple were collected and deposited all such rarities as men aforetime used to wander all over the habitable world to see, when they were situated in various places.'[156]

Plutarch cites the abundant spoil as a motive for military enterprises and demonstrates how this motive was disguised by being overlaid with another one, in remarks which he attributes to some of the noblest Romans and a few Greeks directly before the battle of Pharsalus, between Caesar and Pompey. Both generals would 'have now been willing quietly to govern and enjoy what they had conquered, the greatest and best part of earth and sea was subject to them, and if they still desired to gratify their thirst for trophies and triumphs, they might have had their full of wars with Parthians and Germans. Besides, a great task still remained in the subjugation of Scythia and India, and here their greed would have had no inglorious excuse in the civilization of barbarous people.'[157]

As for the damage which the population of conquered areas had to suffer, it should not be forgotten that those who waged war included soldiers who at least wanted to be fed and paid and sometimes also had to be given quarters.[158] Of course the pay was usually provided by the state treasury – except that this in turn had to be filled, above all from the provinces. It is ideal – from the Roman point of view – when the plunder is so great that a general can 'make the war pay for itself'.[159] After the conquest of a city, people like to plunder it; so wrote Tacitus of the troops in Gaul during the disputes of 68 and 69: 'They preferred to secure rewards rather than mere pay.'[160]

If peace was restored after the war, often enough a garrison was left behind which had the right to make requisitions. In an episode told by Apuleius a soldier robs a gardener of his ass because he has work for it: 'Along with other beasts of burden he has to get our governor's baggage from the place nearby.'[161]

Above all, however, peace had to be paid for by taxes, tolls, offerings, tribute and levies. I have already cited the passage from the speech by Cerialis in which he explains to the Treviri and the Lingones why all this is necessary, namely to ensure peace at home and abroad.[162] Tiberius Julius Alexander speaks about 'the security of the world' in exactly the same way as the prefect of Egypt in his edict on the occasion of the accession of Galba, and then goes on to talk about offerings and taxes.[163]

When Judaea was added to the province of Syria after the deposition of Archelaus son of Herod, its governor immediately arranged for an economic census: 'To begin with the Jews wanted to have nothing to do with this census, but they gradually abandoned their resistance on the persuasion of the high priest Joazar and on his advice quietly allowed an assessment of their resources.'[164] This assessment served as the basis for levying taxes, which were collected by the financial administration under the supervision of procurators. That could happen with great harshness. Plutarch gives a similar report of procurators in Spain at the time of Nero; anyone who was in debt over his tax was prosecuted and sold as a slave.[165]

A letter from the first century AD written by a smallholder in Egypt to his son shows what the levying of taxation looked like from his perspective and how it could ruin him. It goes:

> If you do not come I run the risk of having to give up the possessions that I have. My partner has not worked with me, indeed the sludge has not even been cleaned out of the cistern and moreover the irrigation is clogged with desert sand and the estate is untilled. None of the leaseholders wanted to do anything about it, and I alone am paying the public taxes without any income. The water is hardly enough to irrigate one field, so come immediately, as the plants are in danger of dying.[166]

The tax required of the owners 'was levied not on the basis of income but depending on the area irrigated, and this was calculated in an abstract way, depending on the height of the flooding of the Nile, without taking into account any deficiency in the irrigation'.[167] If the irrigation system was not in the best possible condition, for whatever reason, the burden of taxation was oppressive.[168] Many people in Egypt avoided the exaction of the debts for taxation by flight. Egypt was particularly important for Rome because it provided grain. Suetonius reports that for this reason Augustus had made it a Roman province: 'He reduced Egypt to the form of a province, and then to make it more fruitful and better adapted to supply the city with grain, he set his soldiers at work clearing out all the canals into which the Nile overflows, which in the course of many years had become choked with mud.'[169]

When the emperor Nero heard about difficulties experienced by the tax farmers who had to raise the public taxes, 'he hesitated whether he ought not to decree the abolition of all indirect taxation and present the reform as the noblest of gifts to the human race. His impulse, however, after much preliminary praise of his magnanimity, was checked by his older advisers, who pointed out that the dissolution of the empire was certain if the revenues on which the state subsisted were to be curtailed.'[170] According to Tacitus the result was an edict with various 'other extremely fair rulings, which were observed for a time and then eluded'.[171]

The burden on the provinces generally must have been oppressive. This is evident from the opposite picture, when Tacitus says of the Batavians as part of the Roman empire: 'They are not insulted, that is, with the exaction of tribute, and there is no tax-farmer to oppress them: immune from burdens and contributions, and set apart for fighting purposes only, they are reserved for war, to be, as it were, our arms and weapons.'[172] All the things which are mentioned here in the negative were therefore the rule elsewhere; that the special treatment described was again determined above all by military policy emerges very clearly. For the regular practice Josephus makes king Agrippa refer to the example of the Gauls, in the speech which he is supposed to have made to the rebels, and say quite openly that they 'put up with being a source of income for the Romans and allow the Romans to administer their riches'.[173]

A story told by Pliny shows one aspect of the burden which the provinces exploited by the Romans had to bear:

> On the shore of the North African city of Hippo a boy had tamed a dolphin, so that it could perform all kinds of tricks when swimming with him. Talk of this attraction got around and Roman officials came from all sides to enjoy the play. The city fathers of Hippo were not at all happy at this invasion: 'It was thought proper to remove the occasion of this concourse by privately killing the poor dolphin.' For 'the coming and staying was an additional expense which the slender finances of this little community could ill afford'.[174]

(c) 'Produce is brought from every land and every sea'

It stands to reason that the exploitation of the provinces and the booty of war above all benefited the city of Rome, and there in turn primarily the upper classes. Aelius Aristides says that the lands around the Mediterranean provide the Romans 'abundantly with whatever is in them. Produce is brought from every land and every sea, depending on what the seasons bring forth, and what is produced by all lands, rivers and lakes and the arts of Greeks and barbarians. If anyone wants to see it all he must either travel over the whole earth to see it in such a way or come to this city. For what grows and is produced among individual peoples is necessarily always here, and here in abundance.'[175] Anything that Rome did not seem able to use and that therefore did not come to the city was virtually denied existence: 'Anything that you do not see here does not count among what exists or has existed.'[176] Pliny talks in the same way as Aristides. First of all he puts special stress on Rome's grain supply: 'Now for the corn supply, equivalent in its generosity, I believe, to a perpetual subsidy', after which he adds the rhetorical question: 'Is it not plain to see that every year can abundantly supply our needs – and without harm to anyone?'[177] It is only logical that both Pliny and Aristides should praise the 'free market.' Rome's port Ostia, writes Aristides, is 'the common trading place for all people and the common market for the produce of the earth'.[178] That 'common' in reality means first and foremost 'for Rome' emerges as clearly as could be desired from the extended quotation given above. Pliny stresses that the Roman treasury really buys: 'The imperial exchequer pays openly for its purchases. Hence these provisions and the corn supply, with prices agreed between buyer and seller; hence, without causing starvation elsewhere, we have plenty here.'[179] The market flourishes, so it is not surprising that – as again Aristides says – there is also the ideology of achievement which generously overlooks the lower classes in the provinces: 'All ways stand open to all. No one is a stranger who shows himself worthy of an office or a position of the trust; on the contrary, in the world a universal democracy has developed under one man, the best ruler and guide. All stream as to one common market, each to obtain that which is his due.'[180]

The enthusiasm of Pliny and Aristides is qualified by Tacitus. He reports the shortage of grain in AD 51 and the famine that arises out of it and then notes with resignation: 'And yet, heaven knows, in the past Italy exported supplies for the legions into remote provinces; nor is sterility the trouble now, but we cultivate Africa and Egypt by preference, and the life of the Roman nation has been staked upon cargo boats and accidents.'[181]

He sarcastically lets Rome's parasitic attitude show through a speech of Tiberius: 'And if the harvests of the provinces ever fail to come to the rescue of master and slave and farm, our parks and villas will presumably have to support us.'[182]

But the provinces are virtually universally exploited, at least 'for the needs of the masters' and their exalted claims. The numerous lists of luxury goods shipped to Rome are an impressive indication of this. That is precisely summed up in one sentence: 'Triumphant luxury has long with greedy hands been clutching the world's unbounded stores – that she may squander them.'[183]

When after his victory over Otho Vitellius took his soldiers to Rome and quartered them in the city, 'they saw the riches of Rome with those eyes which had never seen such riches before, and found themselves shone round about on all sides with silver and gold'.[184] So it is not surprising that Rome was also a particularly expensive place to live in.[185]

There were constant attempts to limit the luxury which was always gaining the upper hand, but these continually proved unsuccessful. According to the account by Tacitus, in the time of Tiberius the senator Gallus Asinius countered these attempts by pointing to the corresponding growth of the empire. This once again clearly shows whom the Pax Romana primarily benefited: 'With the expansion of the empire, private fortunes had also grown: nor was this new, but consonant with extremely ancient custom. Wealth was one thing with the Fabricii, another with the Scipios, and all this was relative to the state. When the state was poor, you had frugality and cottages: when it attained a pitch of splendour such as the present, the individual also throve.' He then justifies the privileges of the senators and the *equites* by the special burdens borne by the members of these ranks – 'otherwise your distinguished men, while saddled with more responsibilities and greater dangers, were to be deprived of the relaxations compensating these responsibilities and these dangers'.[186]

The use which Rome made of the economic aspect of the Pax Romana is further shown in the splendour of the construction of the city. Augustus already points this out in his *Res Gestae* when, among other things, he stresses the building of many temples and the forum of Augustus, the preparation of the forum of Julia, the restoration of Pompey's theatre, and the repair and enlarging of the aqueducts and the renewal of streets and bridges.[187] According to Suetonius, Augustus 'so beautified it that he could justly boast that he had found it built of brick and left it in marble'.[188] In connection with his report on the expensive restoration of Rome under Nero after the fire of 64, Tacitus comments: 'Meanwhile Italy had been laid waste for contributions of money: the provinces, the federate communities, and the so-called free states, were ruined.'[189]

If the Roman plebs to some degree also profited from the building activity, that was even more true of the gifts of money and grain. Augustus refers to this at length in his *Res Gestae*.[190] After Pliny has described the distribution of imperial gifts under Trajan[191] he clearly brings out their connection with the nature of the emperor's rule and the privileges given to the rich: 'If he neglects his poorer subjects he protects in vain his leading citizens; who will become a head cut from a body, top heavy, soon to fall.'[192] The rulers need the loyalty of the masses; it is purchased by gifts. However, even a Pliny could be deceived over the sources of the imperial giving when he thinks that 'what is most welcome to the recipient is his knowledge that no one else has been robbed to provide for him, that there is one alone who is the power for so many thus enriched – his prince. And perhaps not even he – for anyone with a share in the commonwealth is as rich or as poor as the whole.'[193]

In addition to the emperor's distribution of gifts there was the organization of games. Suetonius stresses that here too Augustus clearly made a difference from the previous period: 'He surpassed all his predecessors in the number, variety and splendour of the shows.'[194] In his *Res Gestae* Augustus himself enumerates them all and devotes a whole section to the demonstration of a sea battle for which an artificial sea had to be made.[195] Tacitus counts it one of the 'peculiar and characteristic vices, taken on as it seems to me almost in the mother's womb – the passion for play actors and the mania for gladiatorial shows and horse racing'.[196] A saying handed down by Seneca is evidence of the widespread public satisfaction in Rome; he says that 'December (in which the feast of Saturnalia was held) used to be a month, but now it is a year'.[197] Giving an entertainment as a substitute for the desire for political activity is already clearly expressed by Juvenal: 'The people that once bestowed commands, consulships, legions and all else, now meddles no more and longs vaguely for just two things – bread and games.'[198]

The use which Rome made of its peace can be summed up from parts of the introduction to the poem about the Civil War which Petronius attributes to his Eumolpus:

> The conquering Roman now held the whole world, sea and land and the course of sun and moon. But he was not satisfied. Now the waters were stirred and troubled by his loaded ships; if there were any hidden bay beyond, or any land that promised a yield of yellow gold, that place was Rome's enemy, fate stood ready for the sorrows of war, and the quest for wealth went on. There was no happiness in familiar joys, or in pleasures dulled by the common man's use. The soldier out at sea would praise the bronze of Corinth; bright colours dug from earth rivalled the purple; here the African curses Rome, here the Chinaman plunders his marvellous silks, and the Arabian hordes

have stripped their own fields bare. Yet again more destruction, and peace hurt and bleeding. The wild beast is searched out in the woods at great price, and men trouble Hammon deep in Africa to supply the beast whose teeth make him precious for slaying men; strange ravening creatures freight the fleets, and the padding tiger is wheeled in a gilded palace to drink the blood of men while the crowd applauds... Tables of citron-wood are dug out of the soil of Africa and set up, the spots on them resembling gold which is cheaper than they, their polish reflecting hordes of slaves and purple clothes, to lure the senses. Round this barren and low-born wood there gathers a crowd drowned in drink, and the soldier of fortune gorges the whole spoils of the world while his weapons rust. Gluttony is a fine art. The wrasse is brought alive to table in sea-water from Sicily, and the oysters torn from the banks of the Lucrine lake make a dinner famous, in order to renew men's hunger by their extravagance.[199]

(d) 'All kinds of legal titles to robbery...'

I must now qualify substantially the statement above that the exploitation of the provinces and allied kingdoms, in the form of dues, taxes, tolls and tributes, was done in accordance with the law. Even by the standard of the law of the victors there were considerable grey areas extending even as far as crass acts of injustice. The post of governor was not only well paid but also carried with it the possibility of still further personal enrichment. Thus Juvenal writes: 'When you enter your long-expected province as a governor, set a curb and limit to your passion, as also to your greed: have compassion on the impoverished provincials, whose very bones have been sucked dry of marrow.'[200] He then says at length that once it was different, that one could bring home 'secret booty on heavily laden ships'. 'Nowadays on capturing a farm, you may rob our allies of a few yoke of oxen, or a few mares, with the sire of the herd, or of the household gods themselves, if there is a good statue left, or a single deity in his little shrine: such are the best and choicest things to be got now.'[201] Pliny reports on the trial of a governor of the province of Baetica, no longer alive, who was easily led astray: 'A boastful, exultant letter was also produced which he sent to one of his mistresses at Rome, wherein he expresses himself in these words: "Huzza! Huzza! I am coming back to you solvent, having raised four millions of sesterces upon the Baetici."'[202] The profits made by the dead man during his time as governor were confiscated, and his two minions were exiled for five years. Pliny ends this account with the statement: 'So very atrocious did that conduct now appear, which seemed at first to be doubted whether it was criminal at all.'[203]

This sentence makes it clear that it is legitimate here to speak of a grey area. There is evidence of more of them. Thus Juvenal writes: 'No man will get my help in robbery, and therefore no governor would take me on his staff.'[204] According to the account by Tacitus, when Agricola was quaestor in Asia Minor, he had refused when his governor had invited him to engage in this sort of thing, which almost went beyond the bounds of legality.[205] When later he himself became governor in Britain, 'he made demands for grain and tribute less burdensome by equalizing his imposts: he cut off every charge invented only as a means of plunder'.[206] Tacitus goes on: 'By repressing these evils at once in his first year he cast a halo over such days of peace as the carelessness or harshness of previous governors had made not less dreadful than war.'[207] That shows that the room for manoeuvre for the governor and his officials was considerable, and the many complaints about the avarice and cruelty of governors make it clear that it was often enough shamelessly exploited. One might recall the advice of Cerialis and the similar counsel of Agrippa to put up with rulers and governors like bad weather.[208] Josephus makes Agrippa offer the consolation that after a bad governor a gentler one would probably come along. He himself gives the lie to such consolation in his account of the series of governors in Judaea before the outbreak of the Jewish war.

To give one specific example of such criminal exploitation which was virtually unsuspected everywhere, one might mention the levy which was made among the Batavians under Vitellius. This levy – like taxes and tolls a heavy burden on the province – was for the recruitment of auxiliary troops, for whom 'it was a signal distinction if they fought without expending Roman blood'.[209] Tacitus writes of this levy among the Batavians: 'The burden, which is naturally grievous, was made the heavier by the greed and licence of those in charge of the levy: they hunted out the old and the weak that they might get a price for letting them off: again they dragged away the children to satisfy their lust.'[210] Wise Romans like Agricola and Pliny rejected such open acts of injustice.[211] They went against the Roman interest because they put at risk the consensus between the indigenous upper classes and Rome and thus created the conditions for possible rebellions. The levy among the Batavians described above was the immediate occasion for the revolt by Civilis.[212] He could refer to it and single it out in the preparations for revolt; Tacitus went on to report that 'he passed on to count over their wrongs, the extortion practised on them, and all the rest of the misfortunes of slavery... We are handed over to prefects and centurions; after one band is satisfied with murder and spoils, the troops are shifted, and new purses are looked for to be filled and varied pretexts for plundering are sought.'[213] So Rome had an interest in not extending the encroachments too far, and allowing at least the semblance of law. This was all the more the case since the claim to the validity of law was part of the Pax Romana, and this claim also served to legitimate it.

5. 'Imposing Roman law on the vanquished' – the legal aspect of the Pax Romana

When Marius invaded Spain, Plutarch tells us, 'it was a wild, uncivilized land where robbery was still regarded as a noble work'.[214] According to the speech by Cerialis, which I have already mentioned several times. in former times only despotism and war prevailed in Gaul, but now it had gone over 'to our law'.[215] In a speech by Jupiter to Mercury Virgil defines as one of the tasks of the Roman 'to bring all the world beneath his law'.[216] So Rome is under divine command, when it seeks to make its law prevail everywhere. Similarly, the Roman leader during the Parthian campaign of 62 announces that 'he will impose upon the conquered tributes, laws and... Roman jurisdiction'.[217]

(a) 'A legal security which stands high above all injustice....'

In fact there was a certain legal security in the Roman empire. When there were lynchings of Jews in Alexandria in 115 or 135, the prefect issued an edict, which stated: 'If anyone intends to accuse another, he has a judge appointed by the emperor for the purpose. For not even the prefect is allowed to execute without a judicial opinion; rather, there is a particular time and a particular place for a legal judgment, as also for the punishment of a particular action.'[218] Here the Roman power calls for and guarantees a process of state law. The emperor is named as the supreme authority, and in the province his representative is the governor, who has to administer the law. Thus in a passage in which at the same time law also emerges as an element of the Pax Romana, Epictetus makes his fictitious conversation-partner say: 'If some one beats you, go into the centre and call out, "Caesar, do I have to suffer this in your peace? Take me to the proconsul!"'[219] Before the proconsul, as judge, he will get his rights, since the security of the law is part of the imperial peace. Apuleius attests the same trust in the legal order in a passage in his *Metamorphoses*: after Lucius has been transformed into an ass, he is carried off by robbers; he has not yet noticed that as an ass he can only bray like an ass and not speak as a human being. The thought occurs to him: 'I determined with myself, though late, yet in good earnest, to seek some remedy of the civil power, and by invocation of the aweful name of the emperor to be delivered from so many miseries.' So when they go through a place where a great fair is being held, he tries to call on the 'great fair renowned name of the emperor'.[220] According to Seneca all subjects of Nero, who has just become emperor, confess that 'they are fortunate'; among the 'many compelling reasons for this confession' he mentions 'a security deep and abounding, and justice enthroned above all injustice'.[221] For himself he describes this security like this – in contrast to the emperor, who must be armed in the midst of his peace, 'It is possible for me to walk alone without fear in any part of the city I please, though no companion attends me, though I have no sword at my house, none at my side.'[222]

Pliny is similarly delighted to be able to live 'safely and happily under Trajan'; however, he says that looking back on the time of Domitian, in which that was not the case and which he calls 'that comfortless age'.[223] His contemporary Tacitus writes in similar vein: 'The rare good fortune of an age in which we may feel what we wish and may say what we feel.'[224] There are indications here that the law was patchy. That was not only the case for the inhabitants of the provinces, as the behaviour of the governor and his officials described above indicates, but also for Rome itself, even for its upper classes. Seneca, who so extravagantly praised his security under the young Nero, had to commit suicide about ten years later on the orders of the same Nero.[225]

(b) 'The law was certainly defeated...'

One need only read Suetonius, Tacitus or Plutarch to note the tremendous trail of blood which the principate, the imperial monopoly of rule, left behind it, specifically in the Roman upper classes.[226] That in such conditions the validity of the law was also continually limited elsewhere, goes without saying. So in the choice of a praetor the sons of Tiberius wanted the senate to set itself above a legal decree. In his account of this event, Tacitus describes this event as follows: 'Tiberius was overjoyed to see the senate divided between his sons and the laws. The law was certainly defeated, but not immediately and by a few voters only – the mode in which laws were defeated even in days when laws had force.'[227]

If law already proved patchy for the Roman nobility, that was of course also true for the upper classes in the provinces. Here the law was breached actually in the process of its administration. When Mucian was governor in Syria, he needed money for the civil war (fighting on the side of Vespasian): 'And in deciding cases which came before him as judge he had an eye not for justice or truth but only for the size of the defendant's fortunes. Delation was rife, and all wealthy men were seized as prey. Such proceedings are an intolerable burden;

nevertheless, though at the time excused by the necessities of war, they continued later in time of peace.'[228] Where the limits of law lie is clearly illustrated by an episode reported by Plutarch even before the time of the principate. When Pompey wanted to see Roman jurisdiction in the Sicilian city of Messina, but the inhabitants pointed out to him that there was a state treaty with Rome to the opposite effect, he replied to them: 'Cease quoting laws to us that have swords girt about us.'[229]

The right of the stronger which is evident here also applied, of course, within society in the Roman empire. Apuleius tells of the attempt of a rich landlord to take the small piece of land belonging to a neighbour by force and boundary litigation. It is argued against him: 'It is but a folly to have such trust in your riches, and to use your tyrannous pride to threaten, when the law is common for the poor alike, and a redress may be had by it to suppress the insolence of the rich.' The subsequent story shows that that is only a pious wish.[230]

Just as the freedom granted from above is only the cloak under which slavery and exploitation are concealed, so the law granted from above proves to be not only patchy but also class justice.

(c) *'Where money rules alone...'*

The class justice shows itself first in the mild treatment of members of the upper classes when found guilty at law. If a governor underwent trial because he had oppressed the leading members of provincial society too openly and too extortionately, he could count on senatorial solidarity, on compassion and mildness, on the intercession of influential friends.[231] Pliny allows himself to be persuaded by delegates of the province of Baetica to be advocate in the trial against the governor Classicus. On this he writes: 'I considered likewise, that Classicus being dead, the great objection of imperilling a senator was removed.'[232] At another point he speaks generally about his difficulties as an advocate: '... this annoyance of withstanding the private solicitations and public opposition of the defendant's friends'.[233] He is proud 'that in my practice as adovcate I have always refrained from making any bargain or accepting any fee, reward or so much as a friendly present'.[234] Under Trajan that has become the law; Pliny had already acted in that way voluntarily – but others had not.

Class justice is also showed secondly, of course, in discrimination against little people. Apuleius tells of a trial in which a well-to-do woman is convicted of an attempted murder and is condemned to lifelong exile; but a slave whom she used as the instrument for her action is condemned to crucifixion.[235] Petronius sums up the discrimination against the lower classes in a poem which at the same time stresses the corruptibility of the judge:

> Of what avail are laws
> where money rules alone
> and the poor suitor
> can never succeed?
> So a lawsuit
> is nothing but a public auction,
> and the knightly juror who listens to the case
> gives his vote as he is paid.[236]

Apuleius also stresses the corruptibility of the judge when immediately after the description of a scene in the theatre which depicts the judgment of Paris, he asks: 'Why then do you marvel, if the lowest of the people, the lawyers, beasts of the courts, and advocates that are but vultures in gowns, nay if all our judges nowadays sell their judgments for money?'[237] As might be expected, soldiers play a special role in the law. Juvenal discusses the advantages which all soldiers have:

> Let us first consider the benefits common to all soldiers, of which not the least is this, that no civilian will dare to thrash you: if thrashed himself, he must hold his tongue, and not venture to exhibit to the praetor the teeth that have been knocked out, or the black and blue lumps upon his face, or the one eye left which the doctor holds out no hope of saving. If he seeks redress, he has appointed for him as judge a hob-nailed centurion with a row of jurors with brawny calves sitting before a big bench...[238]

Against this background it rings hollow when Aelius Aristides praises the imperial proclamation of law: 'Here there is a comprehensive and laudable equality of the lowly with the mighty, the unknown with the known, the needy with the rich, the simple with the noble.'[239]

6. 'When were there so many cities...?' – culture and civilization under the Pax Romana

The Roman way of life spread with the Roman empire. City life was a basic feature of Roman civilization and culture. Rome colonized – in the truest sense of the word, as the establishment of colonies throughout the empire by the settling of military veterans was an element of Roman policy.

(a) 'Pillared halls, baths and choice banquets'

The urbanization of the population in barbarian provinces was a deliberate way of pacifying them to the advantage of Rome. The clearest evidence of this, expressed in almost disconcerting openness, is again provided by Tacitus. He writes of the activity of Agricola in Britain in winter 78/79:

> In order that a population scattered and uncivilized, and proportionately ready for war, might be habituated by comfort to peace and quiet, he would exhort indiviudals, assist communities, to erect temple, market-places, houses: he praised the energetic, rebuked the indolent, and the rivalry for his compliments took the place of coercion. Morever he began to train the sons of the chieftains in a liberal education, and to give a preference to the native talents of the Briton... As a result, the nation which used to reject the Latin language began to aspire to rhetoric; further, the meaning of our dress became a distinction, and the toga came into fashion: and little by little the Britons were seduced into alluring vices: pillared halls, baths and choice banquets. The simple natives gave the name of 'culture' to this factor of their slavery.[240]

The urbanization of the empire is highly praised by Aelius Aristides: he puts the rhetorical question: 'When were there so many cities, in the hinterland and by the sea?' He therefore stresses it as a particular advantage of the Romans over previous rulers 'that they were so to speak kings over empty land and strong fortresses, whereas you alone are rulers over cities'.[241] Roman rule was concerned with the construction of cities with public institutions. The correspondence between the emperor Trajan and Pliny during the latter's governorship in Bithynia and Pontus often refers to that. Here it is a matter of building baths and aqueducts, theatres and gymnasiums, covering over a stinking sewer next to a fine promenade.[242] Aristides also stresses: 'Everywhere there are gymnasiums, fountains, colonnades, temples, workshops and schools.'[243] Nor does he fail to stress that the Romans are the authors of these flourishing cities: 'The stream of gifts which flows from you to them (the cities) never ceases.'[244] Aristides of course overlooks the fact that the presupposition for this 'stream' is an essentially greater stream flowing in the opposite direction.

Kings treated as allies by the favour of Rome also advanced the Romanization of their realms. Thus Josephus reports of Herod the Great that:

> as a consequence of his love of splendour and the zeal with which he

> sought to gain the favour of the emperor and the Roman authorities he was also compelled to depart from ancestral customs and to transgress the laws, since to fulfil his ambitions he built cities and erected temples, though not in Judaea, because the Jews, to whom it is forbidden to worship statues and pictures after the manner of the Greeks, would not have tolerated it, but in other areas and cities.[245]

The prosperity of the cities also included the achievements of civilization which, according to Seneca:

> have come to light only within our own memory – such as the use of windows which admit the clear light through transparent tiles, and such as the vaulted baths, with pipes let into their walls for the purpose of diffusing the heat which maintains an even temperature in their lowest as well as in their highest spaces. Why need I mention the marble with which our temples and our private houses are resplendent? Or the rounded and polished masses of stone by means of which we erect colonnades and buildings roomy enough for nations? Or our signs for whole words, which enable us to take down a speech, however rapidly uttered, matching speed of tongue by speed of hand?[246]

Games must also be mentioned as a main aspect of city life. They were not only significant for Rome but occupied a prominent place everywhere throughout the cities of the provinces. According to Plutarch Lucullus already used the institution of games as a political instrument to secure Roman peace in the third war against Mithridates. He writes: 'Lucullus, after filling Asia full of law and order, and full of peace, did not neglect the things which minister to pleasure and win favour, but during his stay at Ephesus gratified the cities with processions and triumphal festivals and contests of athletes and gladiators.'[247] The holding of games in provincial cities served not least to consolidate the rule of the indigenous upper classes. Thus Apuleius tells of a man in Corinth who 'had passed all offices of honour in due course according as his birth and dignity required'. That was the occasion for him to hold gladiatorial games lasting three days, for which he also got beasts and gladiators from Thessaly.[248] Before that Apuleius had already spoken of gladiatorial games planned in Plataea which a certain Demochares wanted to arrange:

> He was come of a good house, marvellous rich, liberal and well deserved that which he had, and had prepared many shows and pleasures for the common people... First he had provided gladiators of a famous band, then all manner of hunters most fleet of foot, then

guilty men without hope of reprieve who were judged for their punishment to be food for wild beasts... He had ready a great number of wild beasts and all sorts of them, especially he had brought from abroad those noble creatures that were soon to be the death of so many condemned persons.[249]

How the poverty of the ordinary population contrasts with this expense emerges from the way the description goes on:

The animals were so afflicted by various diseases that they died one after another, and there were virtually none left, so much so that you might see their wrecks lying piteously in the streets and all but dead; and then the common people, having no other meat to feed on, and forced by their rude poverty to find any new meat and cheap feasts, would come forth and fill their bellies with the flesh of the bears.[250]

The Roman way of life as an effective means of establishing Roman peace – rebellious spirits which were not yet Romanized had recognized this. So according to the account by Tacitus, during the revolt of the Batavians under Civilis a German from the right bank of the Rhine went to Cologne and there called on his fellow countrymen: 'Away with those pleasures which give the Romans more power over their subjects than their arms bestow!'[251] But the Germans of Cologne did not want to do without the advantages of the Roman life-style and moreover pointed to their friendly relations with the Roman colonists.[252]

(b) *'Once avarice has eaten into men's hearts like rust'*

Harald Fuchs repeatedly quotes a text in which Pliny the Elder is amazed that no progress in culture and science corresponds to the great political development towards a single empire, but that on the contrary one can note a regression.[253] Petronius makes a similar comment to that of Pliny the Elder. He makes his poet Eumolpus give avarice as the cause of the decay of art and science:

Where is dialectic now, or astronomy? Where is the exquisite way of wisdom? Who has ever been to a temple and made an offering in order to attain to eloquence, or to drink of the waters of philosophy? They do not even ask for good sense or good health, but before they even touch the threshold of the Capitol, one promises an offering if he may bury his rich neighbour, another if he may dig up a hidden treasure, another if he may make thirty million in safety...So there is nothing surprising in the decadence of painting, when all the gods and men think an ingot of gold more beautiful than anything those poor crazy Greeks, Apelles and Phidias, ever did.[254]

Horace complained in just the same way that the Greeks had received from the muse 'the creative gift, the magic flow of discourse', whereas Rome's youth was learning to divide the as, the tiny copper coin, into a hundred pieces. In view of such a penny-pinching spirit he asks: 'Once avarice, like rust, has eaten into men's hearts, can we hope for poems to be fashioned worthy to be smeared with cedar-oil and kept in polished cypress?'[255] Virgil, too, sees this state of affairs, that Rome does not stand for art and science; however, he does not complain about it. He makes Anchises in the underworld say:

> Others, I doubt not, shall beat out the breathing bronze with softer lines; shall from marble draw forth the features of life; shall plead their causes better; with the rod shall trace the paths of heaven and tell the rising of the stars.[256]

But then quite deliberately he goes on to a passage which speaks of world rule and a comprehensive order of peace as the gift and task of the Romans.[257]

Excursus

'But may my lot bring me a modest and tranquil life...'

Over against this belligerent policy leading to and maintaining the position of a world power and the urban luxury based on it, other notes are also struck in the metropolis itself and its closer surroundings, namely in the elegaic poets Propertius and Tibullus, above all in the latter. They are rather like drop-outs, and therefore *de facto* reject the prevailing system, though they cannot be understood to be in principle opposed to Roman power politics either. On the one hand Propertius in particular can quite openly express the general hope of the conquest of even the remotest lands;[258] and he makes the wife of the Roman legionary who longs for her distant husband finally express the wish: 'But when the sons of Parthia are tamed may the headless spearshaft follow your triumphant steeds.'[259] On the other hand he can critically contrast the far-reaching conquests with the 'right way': 'Now o'er such wide seas are we tempest tossed; we seek out a foe and pile fresh war on war.'[260] He sees the cause of this as being avarice, of which he knows himself to be free: 'My soul is not so racked with lust for hateful gold, nor do I get bronze from your ruin, hapless Corinth.'[261] And to the one who deliberately goes after rich plunder in war he presents the vanity of such an undertaking in the face of death: 'Yet no wealth shall you carry to the waves of Acheron: naked, you fool, you shall be borne to the ship of hell. There victor and vanquished shades are mingled in the equality of death.'[262] With that he contrasts spending happy nights with his mistress: 'One such night might make any man a god! Ah! If all men desired to pass their life as I, and lie with limbs weighed down by deep draughts of wine, nor cruel steel would there be nor ships of war.'[263] So he declares that the god of love is the god of peace: 'Love is a god of peace, we lovers worship peace: enough for me the hard warfare I wage with my mistress.'[264] When he has become too old for that, he will then devote himself to scholarship.[265] Yet at the end of this fifth elegy of the third book, explicitly critical of Rome which is greedily conquering the world, one can still hear the tone of the nationalistic, warlike hope, albeit in a significant way: 'Do you to whom arms are dearest bring home the standards of Crassus.'[266] Propertius shares the hope for regaining the standards, but leaves others the war for that. He has decided otherwise for himself, namely for Amor, and – later! – for science.

The alternative to the Pax Romana is expressed more strongly in Tibullus than in Propertius. True, he wants 'still to celebrate Messalinus when he carries before his chariot pictures of the cities which he has conquered, himself wearing the laurel wreath; crowned with the laurel, the warrior then sings "Hurrah", exults "Triumph", so that it echoes around.'[267] Similarly, he makes the Sibyl announce the future rule of Rome to Aeneas.[268] But he puts this tradition in a context which has other accents. Alongside Rome which has become warlike and therefore powerful he sets 'Rome the shepherd'. This is not a romantic recollection of the good old days. Rather, he has prescribed for himself the simplicity and the toil of peasant existence: 'But may my lot bring me a modest and tranquil life, provided that the fire blazes constantly on my own hearth. If there is time, as a farmer I would plant the sweet grapes with a careful hand, grow noble apples; provided that my hope were not disappointed for the fruit to pile high and the vats be ever full with oily must.'[269] He is prepared to live in modest circumstances[270] and therefore he does not want to go to war. For like Propertius he sees the desire for riches as the cause of war. 'The cause is precious gold. There would be no war if the cup that one used at a meal were made simply of wood.'[271] So he contrasts 'the madness of bringing gloomy death upon oneself' with what he regards as being praiseworthy, namely 'the man on whom old age gently comes in a modest home surrounded by children'.[272] And before old age comes, 'it is good to follow the charms of love, as long as one shamelessly batters down doors and with desire begins to dispute with rivals'.[273] So others may go to war; Tibullus does not want to join in but to have just enough to live on: 'Standards and trumpets, away with you! Let men receive wounds who long for them! Get your treasures! Quietly on my plot I prefer to mock the rich, but at the same time to mock hunger.'[274]

Tibullus and Propertius are more than just detached from the powerful Pax Romana. They disregard the all-embracing concept of the Pax Romana when they understand peace without any reference to it as the goddess of love and thus reject the official ideology. Granted, their ideal of peace[275] remains private, and their modest circumstances are not so modest that they can do without this culture. They are not interested in an active alteration to the existing order of peace. But as 'drop-outs' who at least partially avoid the *imperium*, they can be regarded as isolated forerunners of those in whom Werner Raith sees the essential cause for the decline of the Roman empire, namely that 'the peoples of this gigantic world empire including its central country, Italy, largely on purpose and deliberately looked for alternatives to the *imperium*, one of which was a return to the country and to agriculture'.[276]

7. 'Serving on earth as vicar of the gods' – the religious aspect of the Pax Romana

From the perspective 'from above', from which people saw or wanted to see only the brilliant side, one could be caught up in enthusiasm about the Roman peace provided by a powerful central power in an enormous area. Aristides was no hypocrite when he spoke of a golden age. Nor is it a coincidence that he speaks in this way to the emperor,[277] for the emperor at the head of political power was the guarantor and representative of this peace.

(a) 'The great ruler and guide of all...'

The hierarchical structure of the Roman use of power is described by Aristides in utter wonderment: 'If an individual rules over so many people and his officials and emissaries stand so far below him, yet far higher than those over whom they have control, and carry out everything in peace, without tumult and agitation, and if there is no envy, but everywhere complete justice and respect reign and no one is deprived of the rewards for his achievement', then – and for Aristides this is not a programme but reality – a verse of Homer's which he has slightly changed applies: 'All is well within the reign of Olympian Zeus.'[278] Immediately before this he had described the structure of military command as 'surpassing any human order'.[279] In this system, he had already shown, 'everything is carried out to order and at a mere nod'. Granted, the governors had the power to rule, but at the same time they too were ruled. 'Therefore one could also say that they are distinct from those who are ruled in that they first show how one should allow oneself to be ruled. So great a fear of the great ruler and guide of all has been inculcated in all men.'[280] As the emperor stands over the empire in this way, the empire is structured towards him as its head, and in turn all the power of command emanates from him, then he becomes so to speak the embodiment of the empire. Thus Pliny suggests in connection with wishes 'for ourselves and the city': 'Should we not rather reverse this order, and beg the gods to grant that all your actions prove successful for yourself, for the state and for us, or, to shorten our prayers, for yourself alone?'[281] In a similar way, at the end of his *Panegyricus*, in the concluding petition to Capitoline Jupiter, Pliny says: 'We are not burdening you with vows – we do not pray for peace, concord and serenity, nor for wealth and honours: our desire is simple, all embracing and unanimous – the safety of our prince. This is no new concern we ask of you.'[282] Indeed this is 'no new concern', but the empire as it is. Shortly beforehand Pliny had said: 'To end my speech I call on the gods, the guardians and defenders of our empire, speaking as consul on behalf of all humanity.'[283] By protecting and sustaining the Roman empire the gods secure the safety of the world. That stands in peace, concord, security, riches and honour, all aspects of the Pax Romana which this empire provides. The gods protect and sustain it in the person of the emperor, who stands surety for all these benefits.[284]

Seneca suggests to the young emperor Nero a soliloquy the first part of which begins by stressing the tremendous power of the emperor:

> Have I of all mortals found favour with heaven and been chosen to serve on earth as vicar of the gods? I am the arbiter of life and death for the nations; it rests in my power what each man's lot and state shall be: by my lips fortune proclaims what gift she would bestow on each human being: from my utterance peoples and cities gather reasons for rejoicing; without my favour and grace no part of the whole world can prosper; all those many thousands of swords which my peace restrains will be drawn at my nod, what nations shall be utterly destroyed, which banished, which shall receive the gift of liberty, which have it taken from them, what kings shall become slave and whose heads shall be crowned with royal honour, what cities shall fall and which shall rise – this is mine to decree.[285]

Seneca thinks: 'This pronouncement, Caesar, you may boldly make, that whatever has passed into your trust and guardianship is still kept safe.'[286] And according to Aristides what the emperor decides is always 'truth, justice and law'.[287]

Given that the emperor has such an extraordinarily elevated position, it must be that his person stands out in an almost religious sense and also can be worshipped in a cult. So the imperial cult proves to be an indissoluble element of the Pax Romana.

(b) 'As God on earth'

When Tacitus says 'a prince does not enjoy divine veneration until he has ceased to be active among men',[288] that does not apply to the provinces, though it does to Rome and Italy. Cultic actions in honour of the living emperor may thus be excluded, but the person of Augustus was already exalted to religious dimensions even during his lifetime by poets like Virgil and Horace. In his Eclogues Virgil makes a shepherd say in an allusion to Augustus: 'O Meliboeus, it is a god who wrought for us this peace – for a god he shall ever be to me; often shall a tender lamb from our folds stain his altar.'[289] Horace praises Augustus as 'father and guardian of the human race';[290] and as a parallel to Jupiter, who reigns in heaven, he speaks of Augustus as 'god on earth'.[291] Even Seneca, who later could mock the dead Claudius in the *Apocolocyntosis* in a way as skilful as it was venomous, could write in his 'On Consolation' to Polybius: 'May this sun which has shed its light upon a world that had plunged into the abyss and was sunk in darkness ever shine.'[292] We may note almost as a matter of course that Martial, preferred under Domitian, wrote similar poems to this emperor who had himself designated 'lord and god'.[293]

The exaltation of the person of the emperor to a superhuman dimension is, however, not only shown in the exuberance of the language of Roman poets but also comes out in the servility of this system directed towards the emperor at its head dignified with the features of religion. That becomes clear when Aristides says of the senior representatives of Rome next to the emperor, namely the governors, that none of them 'can remain immobile if he but hears the name of the ruler, but he rises, praises and reveres him and says two prayers, one for the ruler to the gods and one to the ruler himself for his own well being'.[294] A letter from Pliny to the emperor Trajan which he writes to him on his accession, shows what such a prayer for the ruler might sound like: 'Therefore I pray that you, and through you all mankind, may enjoy every prosperity, as befits your reign; and as an individual no less than an official, noble emperor, I wish you health and happiness.'[295]

As a public institution there were vows for the well-being of the emperor even before Augustus. He says in his *Res Gestae*: 'The senate decreed that every fifth year vows should be undertaken for my health by the consuls and the priests... In addition the entire body of citizens, with one accord both individually and by municipalities, performed continued sacrifices for my health at all the couches of the gods.'[296] When Pliny was governor of the province of Bithynia and Pontus he reported to Trajan at the beginning of the year on the making and renewal of 'annual vows to ensure your safety and therefore that of the state'.[297] The day of the accession of the emperor was a solemn beginning to each year; as Pliny described it, 'we have offered prayers to the gods to keep you in health and prosperity on behalf of the human race, whose security and happiness depends on your safety. We have also administered the oath of allegiance to your fellow soldiers in the usual form, and found the provincials eager to take it, too, as a proof of their loyalty.'[298] The oath was also a commitment to obey the emperor and his orders. How important the making of this vow and the taking of the oath were understood to be emerges from the fact that when mention is made of them by Pliny, each time a formal confirmation by the emperor follows.[299]

If general well-being depends on the health of the emperor, then the individual has no right to complain about his fate 'as long as the emperor is preserved'. Thus Seneca writes to Polybius: 'As long as he is alive your dear ones are alive – you have lost nothing. Your eyes ought to be not only dry, but even happy; in him you have all things, he takes the place if all.'[300]

How the vows for the emperor were made in a religious community emerges from the description of a procession of initiates into the mysteries of Isis by Apuleius. At the end of this procession, which takes place on the occasion of the resumption of navigation in the spring, at the sanctuary there is a reading of 'vows for good fortune to the great prince, the senate, to the noble order of chivalry and generally to all the Roman people, and to all the sailors and ships as be under the puissance and jurisdiction of Rome'.[301]

(c) 'Romae et Augusto'

If Augustus was praised as God in Rome only in poetic language, in the provinces this was also done in official documents. In the calendar inscription of Priene mentioned at the beginning of this section, which records the decision of the conference of the province of Asia to transfer the birthday of the emperor to the beginning of the year, this day is designated 'the birthday of the god'.[302] The matter-of-fact way in which religious titles were used for the emperor is shown by an Egyptian document about the repayment of a loan which in giving the year calls Augustus 'son of god'.[303]

In the provinces the emperor was also worshipped as a god. In Lyons there is an altar dedicated to the goddess Roma and Augustus, which formed the focal point of the imperial cult in Gaul. It is depicted on a sestertius from the late period of Augustus with the inscription '*Romae et Augusto*', flanked by two pillars with victory goddesses on them.[304] Tacitus reports from the time of Tiberius that the cities of Asia Minor resolved on 'a temple to Tiberius, his mother and the senate'.[305] But they could not agree in which city it should be erected: eleven cities disputed over it. Their delegates left it to the senate in Rome to decide.

Pergamon opted out, because it already had its own temple of Augustus. Finally Smyrna received the altar because of its many 'good offices towards the Roman people'.[306] The imperial cult becomes 'the uniting bond of the *imperium*, the symbol of the loyalty of all citizens to emperor and state'.[307]

Seen from one particular perspective all this fits into an almost idyllic picture – like the obverse of a coin from Pergamum from the time of Commodus:[308] in the centre is a youthful Jupiter with a sceptre in his left hand and a lightning flash in his right, the Roman eagle at his foot, on his right the head of the sun god, on his left that of the moon goddess – impressive symbolization of the religious glorification of the Roman rule which spanned the world. Furthermore, on the right and left of the eagle, below the sun and moon, the earth goddess is depicted recumbent with a cornucopia and the sea goddess with a rudder: under Roman rule the earth gives her fruits in abundance and trade over the seas is secured, so that nothing any longer stands in the way of the happiness of humanity. According to Aristides, 'Thus the existing conditions are naturally satisfying and useful for both the poor and the rich, and there is no other way of living. Thus a single harmony of state order has developed which embraces all.'[309]

(d) 'Sacrifice before your image...'

If the emperor represents the empire in that the common good depends on his wholeness, then not to take part in the ritual processes which were meant to celebrate and establish the well-being of the emperor inevitably aroused the suspicion of fundamental political disloyalty.[310] When as governor Pliny was involved in the trial of Christians, he was testing political loyalty towards the Roman empire. Here it was his sole concern to see that religious rituals were carried out towards the emperor and the Roman gods. In this connection he reports to Trajan: 'I considered that I should dismiss any who denied that they were or ever had been Christians when they had repeated after me a formula of invocation to the gods and had made offerings of wine and incense to your statue (which I had ordered to be brought into court for this purpose along with the images of the gods), and furthermore had reviled the name of Christ: none of which things, I understand, any genuine Christian can be induced to do.'[311]

In the same letter Pliny had earlier described the way in which he dealt with people who had been informed on to him as being Christians. He asked them 'if they are Christians, and if they admit it, I repeat the question a second and third time, with a warning of the punishment awaiting them'. The procedure towards those who denied being Christians demonstrates that anyone who confessed that he was a Christian was thus regarded as having been convicted of disloyalty, and that therefore the very accusation of being a Christian was related to this political crime. Pliny continues his report by saying that he had those who confessed to being Christians, even after being asked for a third time, led off to execution. 'For whatever the nature of their admission, I am convinced that their stubbornness and unshakeable obstinacy ought not to go unpunished.'[312] That too is a contribution to an understanding of Roman law and peace.

8. 'An age more evil than that of iron?'

It has become clear time and again in the preceding description that even in antiquity there were critical voices which did not follow Aelius Aristides in seeing the Pax Romana as a golden age. There must have been more of them than have come down to us, voices 'from below' which no one has recorded. A Roman senator, Tacitus, has given words to some such voices. Above all his broken relationship with the principate led this Roman aristocrat to make and maintain many observations which he attributed to others.[313] The stony Seneca expresses himself in an ambivalent way. Whereas after the accession of Nero he speaks of 'the beginning of an age rich in blessings' and of 'golden times',[314] later he does not seem to have gone on thinking of the present in this way.[315] For he commends withdrawal into oneself: 'If you retreat to privacy, everything will be on a smaller scale, but you will be satisfied abundantly.'[316] As an example he twice cites the philosopher Stilpo. Having lost his wife, children and possessions in the conquest of his home town Megara by Demeterius, Stilpo was asked whether he had lost anything. He replied: 'I have lost nothing. My goods are all with me.'[317] Seneca explains: 'Justice, virtue, prudence; in other words he deemed nothing that might be taken from him a good.'[318] At a time when 'taking away' was virtually a Roman programme, this retreat into the private sphere and one's own person was a course available to someone who was critically detached from this system or became so.[319] Juvenal may be mentioned last among Romans who gave an unfavourable verdict about his own time, dominated by Rome. He who would so much have liked to be rich, who complained about his modest circumstances and felt misunderstood, but could call a small estate and a few slaves his own, writes about his own day, 900 years after the founding of Rome: 'An age more evil than that of iron, one for whose wickedness nature herself can find no name, no metal from which to call it.'[320]

There were critics of the Pax Romana above all also among the intellectual élite of the provinces. They have been described by Harald Fuchs.[321] However, he writes about these critics that 'much though they lacked, they could never have done without the prosperity of Roman peace'.[322] Among the intellectual élite of the provinces was also Plutarch, who adopted an ambivalent attitude to the Pax Romana. In his account of the Attic general Phocion he made him say after the constant arrival of tidings of victory in Athens on the attempt at securing freedom from Macedonian rule after the time of Alexander the Great: 'When will our victories cease?'[323] In expressing this wish was Plutarch also secretly thinking of the Romans? In the case of Phocion the wish arose out of the feeling that the victories disguised insight into the actual power situation and that this was not very good for the victors. One result of this investigation could be to show that a peace through victory like the Pax Romana is not good for the victors in the long run either. 'When will our victories cease?' would be a good wish for it. The victor must go on winning or fear defeat. The wish for victories to cease could be related to a third dimension beyond victory and defeat, to a balance of peace.

Finally I would like mention two voices 'from below' which uncompromisingly resisted the Pax Romana. One of them is a speech which Tacitus has put on the lips of the Britain Calgacus; it is delivered to his countrymen before a decisive battle against Agricola's troops. According to Fuchs this speech is 'one of the most powerful that was ever written in the Latin language'.[324]

Calgacus describes how dangerous the Romans are,

> whose arrogance you shun in vain by obedience and self-restraint. Harriers of the world, now that earth fails their all devastating hands they probe even the sea:[325] if their enemy has wealth, they have greed; if he is poor, they are ambitious; East and West have glutted them; alone of mankind they behold with the same passion of concupiscence waste alike and want. To plunder, butcher, steal, these things they misname empire; they make a desolation and call it peace.[326] Children and kin are by the law of nature each man's dearest possessions: they are swept away from us by conscription to be slaves in other lands; our wives and sisters, even when they escape a soldier's lust, are debauched by self-styled friends and guests: our goods and chattels go for tribute; our lands and harvests in requisitions of grain; life and limb themselves are used up in levelling marsh and forest to the accompaniment of gibes and blows. Slaves born to slavery are sold once for all and are fed by their masters free of cost;

but Britain pays a daily price for her own enslavement, and feeds the slavers.[327]

The other voice which we must listen to is a Jewish one.[328] Jewish criticism of Rome was articulated above all in the form of Sibylline oracles and apocalypses, in prophecies alleged to have come down from ancient times and in images which simultaneously concealed and disclosed. The very bizarre world of the apocalypses might be dismissed as the delusions of sick natures, but even if that were the case, it must be noted that the apocalyptists had been made sick by the evil reality which they had to suffer. However, their imagery also expresses the hope that the reality governed by Rome is not a permanent one, but that it will be overcome. The lion symbolizing the Messiah is shown to be superior to the Roman eagle. The real future is not the extended today of an 'eternal Rome' but the messianic age of an earth freed from violence. In perceiving the reality of suffering and in the proclamation of a counter-reality which overcomes it the apocalypses are not a flight into unreal imagery but politically explosive positions which confirm the conflict with Rome. The seer of so-called IV Ezra writes:

> And I looked, and behold, a creature like a lion was aroused out of the forest, roaring; and I heard how he uttered a man's voice to the eagle, and spoke, saying, 'Listen and I will speak to you. The Most High says to you, "Are you not the one that remains of the four beasts which I had made to reign in my world, so that the end of my times might come through them? You, the fourth that has come, have conquered all the beasts that have gone before: and you have held sway over the world with much terror, and over all the earth with grievous oppression; and for so long you have dwelt on the earth with deceit. And you have judged the earth, but not with truth; for you have afflicted the meek and injured the peacable: you have hated those who tell the truth, and have loved liars; you have destroyed the dwellings of those who brought forth fruit, and have laid low the walls of those who did you no harm. And your insolence has come up before the Most High, and your pride to the Mighty One. And the Most High has looked upon his times, and behold, they are ended, and his ages are completed! Therefore you will surely disappear, you eagle... so that the whole earth, freed from your violence, may be refreshed and relieved, and may hope for the judgment and mercy of him who made it."'[329]

From which perspective reality is perceived is evidently important. Calgacus and the author of IV Ezra live on the peripheries of the Roman empire, experience its enormous violence and thus see it 'from below'. Aelius Aristides gives his speech to Rome at the centre of the empire and before its head and looks for a standpoint which is as lofty as possible. He does not see in Roman rule the domination of violence.[330] Nor is he its victim; he profits from it. Aelius Aristides today has many names.

III PART TWO

'God's Servant' or 'The Beast from the Abyss' – Between Resistance and Adaptation: Jesus and the early Christians

1. 'But it is not like that among you' – Jesus' other way

Given the political conditions of his environment, Jesus experienced the Pax Romana in a different way. His Galilean homeland was not under Roman rule; there and in Peraea the ruler was Herod Antipas, a son of Herod the Great, a vassal dependent on Rome. But Judaea, along with Samaria and Idumaea, was a Roman procuratorship. Here, in Jerusalem, the fate of Jesus was very closely bound up with the Pax Romana: through his violent death he became its victim. In the tradition about his activity preceding his execution there are relatively few direct references to aspects of the Pax Romana, but there are more and above all clearer ones than his much-discussed answer to the 'question of the taxation coin'. However, implicitly the central content of his proclamation, the imminence of the kingdom of God, amounts to a questioning of the Pax Romana: anyone who prays for the coming of the kingdom of God, expects it very soon, and sees the sign of its dawning in his own action, has no faith in the imperial good tidings of a pacified world and human happiness in it;[1] he does not regard this situation as the peace that God wants, but is certain that it will soon end. Such a basic attitude must not only be inferred from the confrontation between the kingdom of God proclaimed by Jesus and the reality of the Pax Romana; it is also attested by his explicit attitude to this peace.

(a) *'Those who are supposed to rule over the Gentiles lord it over them...'*

Both a sober and a critical view is taken of the central feature of the Pax Romana, the way in which rule is exercised, when according to

Mark 10.42 Jesus says to his disciples: 'You know that those who are supposed to rule over the Gentiles lord it over them, and their great men exercise authority over them.' Here we have someone speaking from the provinces, someone moreover who is far from privileged in the provinces. Here there is no mincing of words, but it is clearly stated that the existing 'order of peace' is based on the oppressive rule of force.[2] That is the way in which Jesus and – as is shown by the 'you know', which at the same time summarizes a long historical experience – his disciples experience the reality of the Pax Romana. This brief opinion, a perception from 'below', can well be put alongside the speech which Tacitus makes the Briton Calgacus give.[3] In contrast to him, Jesus does not spell out the oppression in detail; he merely notes it briefly and evocatively. By not describing anything at length he shows that a description of the situation is not the most important thing for him. As the continuation of the text shows, this comment, which is a precise characterization of the way in which he experiences the exercise of rule, is merely the dark background for the assertion that among his disciples things are different. We shall have to go into that later. This contrast alone makes it clear that he does not recognize and accept the situation which he so describes as a sober realist: that is the way things are in the world and there is no way of changing them. The alternative which Jesus puts forward shows that he is not resigned, and the contrast again leads to a negative description of the reality he depicts: peace based on oppressive force is not what Jesus wants.

This oppressive force is not just used by the emperor as the head of the system. The saying of Jesus mentions 'those who rule over the Gentiles' and 'their great men'. That, too, is a perception from below and from the periphery: the central power does not come into view of itself, and explicitly, but merely its minions. From that it also becomes clear that there is little apparent difference whether, as in Judaea, one lives under direct Roman rule or, as in Galilee, under indirect rule. The oppression is the same in either place.

But Jesus is not content with merely noting this oppression; in noting it, at the same time he dissociates himself from it in a remarkable way when he speaks of those who 'are supposed to rule over the Gentiles' or – as the phrase can also be translated – 'seem to rule'. The fact of rule exercised by force is noted, but at the same time it is limited by another reality which is evidently superior to it. Unlike Calgacus, whose inflammatory speech against oppressive Rome is set by Tacitus in the interval before a decisive battle, Jesus is not confronting Rome for a last battle, so that he would have to gain detachment from it on the same level of violence. He has this detachment on another level. We shall have to go on to ask what praxis this makes possible. In this saying, at any rate it allows the possibility of disputing the claim of oppressive violence that it is the all-determining and decisive, the ultimate reality, and thus also in the long run of even questioning its legitimacy.

In this sovereign detachment, which virtually amounts to a lack of respect, Jesus also contrasts with the guarantor of the Pax Romana in his country, his ruler Herod Antipas. Antipas had already had John the Baptist executed. According to Josephus' account, 'he was afraid that the reputation of the man, whose counsel seemed to be followed everywhere, might incite the people to uproar, and therefore thought it better to remove him opportunely from the scene than to be endangered by a turn in events and then to be compelled to feel regret when it was too late'.[4] Jesus seems to have aroused the same suspicions in him, and so his intentions were the same. According to Luke 13.31f. Jesus is warned by some Pharisees: 'Get away from here, for Herod wants to kill you.' And he said to them, 'Go and tell that fox, Behold I cast out demons and perform cures today and tomorrow, and the third day I finish my course.' Here Jesus speaks quite disrespectfully of his ruler: he calls him a fox. In this context such a description presents a picture not so much of cunning as of vileness.[5] The threatening intervention of Herod cannot cause him to change his plans: 'Today and tomorrow' – which means day by day[6] – he will go on doing what he regards as being his task. God is the logical subject in the passive formulation about his consummation: God will decide his destiny; God, not Herod, will bring his work to an end.[7] Here, too, Jesus gains detachment from his *de facto* ruler in the light of this superior reality.

That Jesus did not speak respectfully of rulers also emerges from another passage. According to Matt.11.8/Luke 7.25 he says to a crowd with reference to John the Baptist: 'What did you go out into the wilderness to behold? A man clothed in soft raiment? Behold, those who wear soft raiment are in kings' houses!' As in this context Jesus speaks with great respect for John the Baptist, the tone in his comment on the luxury of the powerful which is introduced here as a contrast is not one of wonderment or of envy, but of contempt.

The three passages quoted here suggest that Jesus had a critical detachment from the rule exercised in his time, which secured the Pax Romana. First of all this basic negative tone in the evaluation of the Pax Romana is to be noted. We must also keep it in mind if we are to understand the answer which Jesus gave about the payment of tax, a direct expression of Roman rule.

(b) 'Pay taxes to Caesar, or not?'

The narrative about the 'taxation coin' has become famous and has had widespread and in some respects even notorious influence.[8] Mark 12.13-17 runs:

> And they (viz. the high priest, scribes and elders = the Sanhedrin) sent some of the Pharisees and some of the Herodians, to entrap him in his talk. And they came and said to him, 'Teacher, we know that you are true, and care for no man; for you do not regard the position of men, but truly teach the way of God. Is it lawful to pay taxes to Caesar, or not? Should we pay them, or should we not?' But knowing their hypocrisy, he said to them, 'Why put me to the test? Bring me a coin, and let me look at it.' And they brought one. And he said to them, 'Whose likeness and inscription is this?' They said to him, 'Caesar's.' Jesus said to them, 'Render to Caesar the things that are Caesar's, but to God the things that are God's.' And they were amazed at him.

Jesus' final comment in the narrative is often regarded as his only statement on the Roman *imperium*, and thus also implicitly on the peace that it provides; at the same time this passage is taken as a fundamental discussion of the problem of the state. But is that not to read too much into it? It should not be isolated from its context, but should be understood from the situation which it depicts.[9]

Whatever may have been the attitude of the questioners mentioned at the beginning of the narrative and those who put them up to it,[10] it is clear that Pharisees and Herodians are not to be regarded as types of the attitude of Judaism either hostile or well disposed to Rome;[11] they did not have that role at the level of the Gospel of Mark,[12] at that of the narrative,[13] or in history.[14] It is also clear that the scene depicted must have taken place in Judaea. Only there in the time of Jesus could the question of the payment of tax to the emperor have been raised meaningfully; for it was there that the imperial tax was levied, and not in Galilee. After the deposition of Herod's son Archelaus as ethnarch of Judaea, Samaria and Idumaea, in AD 6 this area came under a Roman procurator of the equestrian order, who was subject to the supervision of the legate of the province of Syria. He ordered a census as a basis for the levying of Roman taxes. The direct taxes consisted mainly in a land tax, which was essentially to be paid as part of the crop, above all in grain, and a poll tax, which had to be paid by every adult with property and income. The rise of the Zealot movement is bound up with the introduction of Roman taxation; this led to the armed warfare against

Rome which finally ended in the Jewish War of AD 66-70. The Roman claim to rule over land and people was documented in the tax. But Israel, the land of Palestine and the people belonged to God; they might may not serve any other master. It was on the basis of this strict either - or that the Zealots also called on the people to refuse to pay tax.[15] That is the background against which Jesus asks whether it is permissible to pay tax to Caesar. Here it is clear that the person who questions Jesus expects him to say no. That is emphasized by the extended *captatio benevolentiae* which stresses Jesus' sole concern for the will of God without consideration for human regard. The beginning of the narrative explicitly stresses that they want to trap him with a word. That can only mean that the rejection of paying tax which they expected him to express would brand him as a rebel with the Roman occupying forces. The hypocrisy of which the narrative speaks consists in the fact that they themselves pay taxes, but by their question want to make Jesus say no. Jesus sees through his opponents' intentions. For that very reason he cannot say a clear no. Nevertheless he does not simply say yes, which would involve him in no danger. That should be a warning against seeing his answer as being essentially affirmative.

Jesus first reacts to the demand of his questioners by asking them to give him a denarius, which was the Roman coin in which the tax was paid, 'a visible symbol of Roman power and authority'.[16] Commentators sometimes hasten to stress that it should not be concluded from this 'that he did not have any coins on him'.[17] Far less, however, is there any reason to draw the opposite conclusion. This was certainly not the first denarius that Jesus had ever seen; he would already have known why he wanted to be given one and what he would do with it. But by not taking the denarius from his own pocket he showed that this was not his problem. It was not his problem, not just because as a Galilean he was not subject to Roman taxation, but in an even more fundamental way. Herod Antipas, Jesus' ruler, also levied taxes and tribute. But Jesus and his followers may not have been subject to taxes: a carpenter (Mark 6.3) who is not engaged in his craft, fishermen who have left their fishing gear by the lake (Mark 1.16-20), a publican who has left his post (Mark 2.14) have no income and therefore cannot be taxed by their ruler – nor could they be taxed by the Roman authorities.[18] In fact they had escaped taxation long since – at the price of a very uncertain existence.

By getting his questioners to take the denarius from their purse, Jesus shows that their question was not meant seriously, that they had long since answered it by using the emperor's money.[19] The rhetorical question which Jesus asks, namely whose image and superscription is on the coin, can also be seen as having the same intention, namely of catching out the questioners in their usual practice. Of course the image and inscription are Caesar's.[20] Then 'Give Caesar what is his.'[21] If we refer this answer not just to the coin that has been shown but also to the question about the tax that has been asked, then it means: you have taken the emperor's money, you deal in it, so you must also allow him to ask it back again in the form of taxation when he wants it: 'If you already give way at the level of money, economics and therefore, of course, politics, then you must also bear the consequences and give his due to the one who is responsible for this system, namely the emperor.'[22] That could have been the end of the answer. Jesus has not allowed himself to be forced into a dangerous 'no'; he has shown that the question is not his problem but that it is not a serious problem for those who ask the question either: they have long since answered the question in the affirmative. In this way, however, he has not answered the question which was asked with a simple 'yes' either. This 'yes' follows only on the tacit presupposition of the questioners, that they have wholly and utterly given way to the reality appointed and controlled by Rome, as is shown by the Roman denarii in their pockets. The fact that Jesus' answer does not, however, stop here, then makes this very presupposition a problem: 'But[23] to God the things that are God's.' As what was Caesar's was emphatically associated with his picture on the coin, what is God's must primarily be thought of in terms of man in the image of God.[24] So the questioners are told that they themselves belong to God and therefore have to give themselves wholly to him. That *a priori* rules out a *laissez-faire* separation of the spheres, as though the emperor were responsible for the external order while God belonged within the internal sphere of human beings. Jesus thus not only shows the question which the questioners meant quite lightly as far as they were concerned, which indeed they meant only as a catch question for Jesus, to be a frivolous question, but also throws it back at them as a serious problem. Understood in this way, the famous statement of Jesus about giving to Caesar what is Caesar's and to God what is God's is not the solution of a problem but the indication of a problem – for those who took the payment of tax for granted and who wanted to trap Jesus with their question. If they themselves belong to God and are indebted to him first and in all things, what about the fact that they use Caesar's money and also pay taxes? That is a question which they have to answer, which Jesus answered in his own way and which he now puts to them.

Here the fact of Roman power is perceived by Jesus in the form of Roman money. He turns the matter-of-fact way in which his conversation partners accept this taxation into a problem. Therefore there can be no question of his recognizing this sphere of power or presenting it as necessary, of his attributing to it something like autonomy or even legitimating it. Once one has recognized that Jesus is asking about the presupposition of the question that has been raised, it seems quite possible that the very first part of his closing sentence contains a dimension which goes substantially further than indicating to the questioners the obvious consequence of what they do. The demand 'Give to Caesar what is Caesar's' referred to the superscription and image of the emperor on the coin which was used to pay the tax. But all denarii bear the superscription and image of the emperor. The demand could therefore go beyond the question of taxation and mean the return of all denarii to the emperor, a rejection of coins and currency in principle. The question which quickly arises, as to whether this is a realistic praxis, has given way to the assertion that Jesus and his disciples manifestly acted in this way. Also in favour of the probability of this thesis is the fact that Jesus drew a sharp alternative between God and mammon: 'No servant can serve two masters; for either he will hate the one and love the other, or he will be devoted to the one and despise the other. You cannot serve God and mammon' (Luke16.13/Matt.6.24). That the dimension of a refusal to have anything to do with coinage and currency could be read out of this answer by Jesus' conversation partners is suggested by the fact that Jesus was ultimately executed as a political rebel. The accusation mentioned in Luke 23.2 that Jesus prevented the people from paying taxes to Caesar need not therefore necessarily be false, but can have some basis here. Jesus was certainly not a Zealot. It has already seemed likely, and will emerge even more clearly, that his praxis was other than that of armed warfare. But it has also become clear that his saying about the imperial tax was not primarily directed against Zealotism but challenged those who had made their peace with existing circumstances. Another saying is evidence that he had nothing to do with the peace of rulers but wanted to work against it.

(c) '... I have not come to bring peace, but a sword...'

According to Matt.10.34f. Jesus said, 'Do not think that I have come to bring peace on earth; I have not come to bring peace, but a sword. For I have come to set a man against his father, and a daughter against her mother, and a daughter-in-law against her mother-in-law.'[25] In this saying, the original context of which has not been handed down to us,[26] the word 'peace' occurs explicitly – and there Jesus resolutely denies that he has come to bring peace. What kind of 'peace' is he thinking of here? That is evident from the second half of this saying. It takes into account the wider family of antiquity, the 'household', the smallest, firmest and most basic unit in society, with a patriarchal and hierarchical structure, at its head the householder as property owner and master, in whom the existing order was most markedly manifest. Strikingly it is not said that Jesus is ushering in a time of decision in which there will be quarrels in the household leading to divisions. That is how Luke interprets the text by reformulating it in 12.51-53.[27] Rather, Jesus says in a quite one-sided way that the alienation only goes from 'below' 'upwards': the son rebels against the father, the daughter and daughter-in-law against the mother-in-law. To understand this saying of Jesus it is important to note that the way in which it is expressed is based on a saying from the book of the prophet Micah (7.6). This passage and its context, and its interpreters in the time of Jesus and beyond, see the rebellion of the young against the old as the clearest mark of the terrors of the end-time.[28] Traditional morality, law and order are dissolved and no longer apply. That is what leads to the terror of the end-time. Jesus takes up this tradition with his quotation of Micah 7.6. But remarkably enough, he does not lament over the terrors of the end-time. As division is the declared purpose of his activity, it must not be seen in negative terms. The dissolution of the existing order is certainly a mark of the end-time, but it is not an expression of evil coming to its climax, nor does it represent any time of terror – which it doubtless is for all those who profit from that order. What terrified those who handed down this tredition is precisely what Jesus described as the goal and purpose of his activity. He does not lament over this division from below; that is precisely what he wants.[29]

When 'peace' is mentioned in this context this term takes on the significance of 'order', of fitting in with the given structures and being inserted into them. So here 'bringing peace' or 'making peace' does not mean the preservation of the existing order in which there is a 'below' and an 'above', in which 'peace' is structured from 'above', in terms of those who have possession and give orders. With this saying Jesus resolutely refuses to give his blessing to and legitimate the *status quo* of an unjust and extremely unpeaceful world. He is not there for that. On the contrary, into such peace, which is only a pseudo-peace, he brings a sword. As the context shows, 'sword' is not to be understood literally, but is a metaphorical expression for division in the household which goes from below; it is a metaphor for the dissolution of the hierarchical structure and rule based on possessions which comes about 'from below', for the unmasking and destruction of a pseudo-peace.

If we recognize this sharp profile of the saying of Jesus, we can also make some inferences about the approximate situation in which it originated. The explicit negation of the expectation that Jesus would bring peace suggests that the occasion for the saying was an attempt to claim his activity for the 'peace party'. This party was made up of those who rejected the approach of the rebellious Zealots who accepted the situation as it had been ordained by Rome and thus wanted to keep the peace.[30] But just as when asked about the tax Jesus did not want to be forced to adopt a Zealot position, so here he emphatically refused to be associated with the peace party. He evidently rejected the alternative of either 'peace' with Rome or armed warfare. But how did he differ from the 'peace party' and the Zealots?

(d) '...for you shall be full...'

Jesus put into practice the virtually programmatic statement in Mark 10.43f. He escaped the claims of his own family by leaving them. They for their part said that he was mad and wanted to get him back under family control: 'Then he went home... And when his friends heard it, they went out to seize him, for they said, "He is beside himself"' (Mark 3.20f.).[31] When Jesus, surrounded in the house with a crowd of people, is told that his family is outside asking for him, he asks, 'Who are my mother and my brothers?' With a reference to those sitting around him he answers this question himself: 'These are my mother and my brothers!' (Mark 3.31-34).[32] Here Jesus presses his denial of his family to the utmost; he completely rejects their claim by declaring that the crowd around him is his family. In this new family the structures of the household have been broken. All are mothers and brothers – and here 'brothers' brings out the aspect of equality and 'mothers' that of mutual service, solidarity.

The continuation of the saying in Mark 10.42 about the rulers who oppress the people matches this exactly. According to Mark 10.43f. Jesus says to his disciples: 'But it shall not be so among you; but whoever would be great among you must be your servant, and whoever would be first among you must be slave of all.'[33] Whereas among those who are regarded as rulers of the people, greatness is manifested in oppression, among Jesus' disciples things are different. There are no rulers among them. So in contrast to the way in which Luke reformulates the saying in 22.26, indicating that there are great men and leaders in the community, here Jesus cannot be asking that such people condescend and act like lesser folk and servants. No great men or leaders are presupposed, but those who want to become such; however, they are told that the greatness and preeminence that they strive for should show themselves in the service of a slave towards the others. The designations 'great' and 'first', like 'servant' and 'slave', are thus robbed of their usual meaning. So 'the present relationships of ruler and ruled are not only reversed; rule of one over another is in fact transcended'.[34] Here the presupposition is one of equality in principle, but an equality which comes alive in mutual service. Being a disciple of Jesus is a specific counter-model to the structure of rule in the world.[35]

The positive practice of Jesus, which goes beyond the alternative of Zealotism or the 'peace party', is also reflected in the composition of the group of disciples, in which there is mention on the one hand of a Zealot (Mark 3.18 par.)[36] and on the other of the call of a publican (Mark 2.14 parr.).[37] But it is particularly evident in his eating with 'publicans and sinners' (Mark 2.15-17 parr.); as a consequence he is accused of being 'a glutton and wine-bibber, a friend of publicans and sinners' (Matt.11.19/Luke 7.34).[38] However the combination of 'publicans and sinners' is defined more closely, it should at least be clear that this is a matter connected with those who are discriminated against in society and for the most part also the socially underprivileged. By turning to them without qualification[39] and entering into fellowship with them, Jesus brings into existence from the periphery something of an alternative society which is aware of itself. In such a praxis the kingdom of God which he proclaims and expects is now already happening. That is evidenced by what is probably the original form of the Beatitudes:

Blessed are you poor,
for the kingdom of God is yours.
Blessed are you who hunger,
for you shall be full.
Blessed are you who weep,
for you shall laugh (Luke 6.20f./Matt.5.3,4,6).[40]

To begin with, these beatitudes must have been a surprise. Here wholeness and well-being is promised to people, here people are called blessed who are certainly not in a situation which could be said to be blessed. The situation of the poor, the hungry and those who weep is certainly not salvation; well-being is specifically denied those who are in distress, who are oppressed and subjugated. When Jesus says that they are the ones who are blessed, one could suppose that he was paradoxically turning the values of the world upside down. But that is not the case. Poverty, hunger and tears are not turned into 'values' by sleight of hand.[41] The fact that this is not the case emerges clearly from the fact that the basis of a beatitude does not lie in those who are praised nor in their present fate. They are not said to be blessed because they are poor, hungry and sorrowful but because, being all those things, they are given a promise which in each case expressly has a reason behind it, namely that their lowly status will be transformed into its exact opposite. That is evident in the second and third beatitudes: the hungry will be full and those who weep will laugh. From this we must assume that the kingdom of God and poverty also form a contrast in the first beatitude. There is evidently an intrinsic connection between the three beatitudes, both in the first clause and in the second: just as in the second and third beatitudes hunger and tears are specific manifestations of the poverty mentioned in the first beatitude, so being full and laughing must be seen as specific manifestations of the kingdom of God. Thus here we are clearly shown one aspect of what the kingdom of God means for Jesus: it is the conquest of poverty and need, the laughter of the liberated, whose oppression and grief has come to an end: 'Here in the face of the circumstances which still exist Jesus discloses the ordinance of God for the world, according to which no one will go short.'[42] Thus the beatitudes prove also to be declarations of war against poverty, hunger and tears: they are concerned for radical change. They look to the coming kingdom of God for this change; the reasons given in the second and third beatitudes are future forms. But this expectation is not just to be waited for; it has a reality in behaviour to match. When Jesus turns to those on the periphery, in his fellowship with his followers, people are already filled, already laugh, who otherwise would be pushed aside and would have nothing to laugh about. So we are to see as an expression of this the way in which the reason given in the first beatitude is put in the present: the kingdom of God is now already an event in symbolic anticipation, in which the hungry are filled and those who weep laugh, in which, in the community of equals, the domination of one person by another has come to an end.

(e) 'If I by the finger of God cast out devils...'

The kingdom of God which is expected and is already being realized is also the context for a further aspect of the activity of Jesus, which has a clear reference to social and political reality. In his saying to Herod Antipas Jesus had described driving out demons as being his task. Gerd Theissen has made some sociological comments on the observation that according to the Gospels and Acts the phenomenon of possession appears prevalent to an enormous degree: 'While possession as such could not be class-specifically conditioned, its mass appearance could be. In a society which expresses its problems in mythical language groups under pressure may interpret their situation as threats from demons.'[43] He had remarked earlier that the stories about the driving out of demons express 'a general social problem, the break-down in interpersonal communication, a profound alienation in social relations'.[44] That can be demonstrated in more detail from the stories about possession in the Gospels. It is a constantly recurrent phenomenon there that the person possessed is dumb; if he does speak it is not as himself.[45] Possession is therefore inability to speak and alienation, alienation from one's fellow human beings and alienation from oneself; it is the crippling of one's own person which can no longer articulate itself. Someone becomes dumb because he or she is dominated by an alien power. The person possessed has been made dumb; his or her capacity for communication has been decisively limited; or he or she is someone in capable of self-expression, who only speaks through the code of those who hold power over them. We can therefore understand how possession appears above all – though not exclusively – among the lower classes: they were most markedly exposed to economic and political pressure. Thus social misery and injustice, oppression and exploitation, are experienced as possession which makes people dumb and speechless.

The connection between possession and occupation appears in the story in Mark 5.1-15 parr. It is evident in the very significant name with which the demon introduces himself. 'My name is Legion, for we are many' (Mark 5.9). Can one conceive of any ancient hearer or reader who would *not* think of Roman troops in connection with the name 'Legion' – in contrast to modern commentators. The narrative is set in the Decapolis, which was under direct Roman rule. Theissen rightly comments: 'The allusion to the Roman occupation is unmistakable. The hostility towards the Roman occupiers is made clear when the demons clearly express their wish to be allowed to remain in the country (5.10). This is precisely what Romans also want.'[46] In the narrative the demons ask to be allowed to go into a herd of swine which then rushes in to the lake. 'In symbolic action the story satisfies the aggressive wish to send them (viz. the Roman occupying forces) into the lake like swine.'[47]

Of course this is not to claim that the narrative in Mark 5.1-15 represents a historical account from the life of Jesus. But it can make clear the political context in which his work of exorcism took place. When we recall his saying about the rulers who subjugate and oppress the people, and his refusal to allow himself to be associated positively with this 'order of peace', and keep alongside it the comment made in his disrespectful saying about Herod Antipas that it is his task to drive out demons, then we can see a context of structural violence which he interrupts with his activities.

According to Mark 3.22ff., Jesus is accused of driving out demons by Beelzebul, their prince. To this, according to Luke 11.19ff./ Matt.12.27f., he is said to have replied: 'And if I cast out demons by

Beelzebul, by whom do your sons cast them out? Therfore they shall be your judges. But if it is by the finger of God that I cast out demons, then the kingdom of God has come upon you.'[48] Those who attack him do not want to assert that their people drive out demons by Beelzebul. So, runs Jesus' unexpressed conclusion, neither does he. There were, then, other exorcists in whose ranks he stood; here he evidently had no anxieties about physical contact. However, by concluding that because he casts out demons by the finger of God the kingdom of God has already arrived, Jesus is making a claim which other exorcists – as far as we know from the tradition – had not made. 'He combines two conceptual worlds which had never been combined in this way before, the apocalyptic expectation of universal salvation and the episodic realization of salvation in the present through miracles... Jesus gives future expectation a root in the present and his miracles become signs of a universal change.'[49] The kingdom of God indicates what is a decisive framework of reference for Jesus. This kingdom is awaited above all from God. Jesus taught his disciples to pray 'Thy kingdom come' (Luke 11.22/Matt.6.10). The kingdom of God certainly represents a counter-reality to the reality experienced in the world, but not by way of a dualistic opposition. By already claiming that his activity indicates the presence of the kingdom of God, Jesus turns this activity into a declaration of war in which God claims his world for himself. The kingdom of God as a counter-reality therefore represents war on the reality of this world by changing it, so that even now it may come to correspond to the kingdom that is expected.

When Jesus claims that the kingdom of God is already present in his action of exorcism, we can see a further aspect of what he understands the content of this kingdom to be. In the stories about the driving out of demons it had emerged that possession makes people dumb and isolates them. Similarly it is shown in Luke 11.14/Matt.12.22; 9.33 that the person from whom the demons has been driven out can speak. He is enabled to speak and to communicate without hindrance. In Mark 5.15 par. it is said of the one who had previously had the demon called Legion, and who was so wild that he had to live outside human habitation, that he was now 'clothed and in his right mind'. He had become capable of social life and communication: he was now in his right mind, whereas previously he had been occupied by an alien power. He had thus gained an identity of his own, a self-awareness. Accordingly the kingdom of God is the community of those who are freed for their own identity, those who have been made capable of speaking and thus put in a position to communicate. Thus Jesus' praxis of the kingdom of God as the interruption of structural power is liberation from alienation:

it consists in giving those who cannot speak a voice, helping those who have been made dumb to articulate themselves.

A consideration of the way in which Jesus drove out demons and the passages in the previous section about the way in which elsewhere he turned to those on the periphery has shown that his saying in Mark 10.43f. in which he resolutely refused to be claimed for the order of violence which was given the name of peace, a saying which indicated that he was more concerned to break it up, is not merely a negative programme but has a positive parallel in what he does. It runs contrary to the rule of domination as it is practised. But it also differs from the way of the Zealots. These understood their armed conflict as a necessary preparation for the coming of the kingdom of God.[50] In this way they were exposed to the pressure of the need to win. Jesus understood what he did differently, namely as a foretaste of what was expected. So, not least, it too is different. He does not wage armed warfare against the powerful authorities but raises up the helpless and lives out with them an alternative to the existing order. The hope for the coming of the kingdom of God and thus for the end of the history of violence therefore already leads to specific interruptions of violence. Some admonitions given by Jesus match that in a very characteristic way.

(f) 'Love your enemies...'

Jesus did not live with his disciples in social isolation, nor did he go with them into a remote place, in order to be able to live out the alternative to the world undisturbed. Nor was he under the illusion that such a praxis could be pursued in society without danger, free from conflicts and the experience of violence. How did the disciples of Jesus preserve their identity as a community of brothers and sisters in solidarity? How did they maintain their claim to be existing in accordance with the kingdom of God, in view of the aggression which they experienced from outside? This question could mark out the area in which the admonitions of Jesus to love one's enemy and not counter violence with violence have their place.[51]

Behind Luke 6.29/Matt.5.39f. it is probable that we have a saying of Jesus to his disciples which went:

> To anyone who strikes you on the cheek
> offer him the other.
> And if anyone takes your cloak,
> give him your garment as well.[52]

First of all we should note carefully the dimension of what is envisaged here. This is a mugging and the theft of a cloak. They are certainly not great matters.[53] The cloak is the most vital possession of the poor man; it serves also to protet him from the coldness of the night.[54] It was probably impossible to rob the disciples of Jesus of more than what they wore on their bodies. Who would embark on a mugging of such people or want to snatch their cloaks? Certainly not rich people, but those of the same social stratum. So the first thing that we must remember is that the dimension within this saying is that of disputes within the lower class.

Secondly, it must be clearly stressed that Jesus here is not talking about mere tolerance and a passivity which accepts injustice. He is requiring activity from the disciple, but a quite unique form of activity: offering the one who hits you the other cheek, giving your garment to the person who robs you of your cloak. Here the one who is hit and robbed takes the initiative. This gives rise to perplexing, indeed absurd situations which should make the aggressor ask, Should I go on hitting? The other person is defenceless! Should I really rob? The other person is in fact naked! The aim of such action can only be to show solidarity with the other. It is not a matter of accepting circumstances passively, but of changing the situations produced by violence by the creation of a new situation. Violence is countered by productive imagination, leading to situations which make it possible for the other person to understand himself as a partner and no longer as an opponent. The disciple of Jesus is encouraged to develop modes of action which interrupt the chain of violence and counter-violence, which bring out the absurdity of injustice in such a way that the other person is invited to show solitdarity. What is asked for here is the practice of love of the enemy which seeks an end of enmity, but not the end of the enemy.

Vögtle claims that the consensus of contemporary exegesis is 'that these statements put in casuistic form are an invitation to the overcoming of the cycle of violence and counter-violence, but are not meant casuistically as regulations which present a literal obligation in individual instances. However, that means that to fulfil these supreme demands of Jesus in a way which does justice to the situation there is need not only of a serious concern for obedience but also for responsible thought and decision.'[55] That is certainly correct – as long as thought and decision really and utterly remain related to the goal and the nature of the admonitions of Jesus and the means mentioned there, and are not shifted on to a supposed awareness of responsibility which simply serves to remove one from the claim of these admonitions. 'Jesus' superlative needs to be translated into a specific mode of behaviour and instructions for action if it is not to become an excuse for leaving everything as it was, for maintaining the *status quo*... It is the way of "short steps". But at the same time we need constantly to remind ourselves of the superlatives of Jesus in order in this way to prevent the comparatives, once arrived at, from becoming hiding places in which we ourselves escape the claims of our fellow men and thus of God himself.'[56] One can often hear people say that the admonitions of Jesus to break through the chain of violence, formulated as they are in the second person singular, apply only to the sphere of personal relationships and at all events are practicable only there, and cannot be transferred into the political sphere. However, Theissen has shown that these admonitions could have been understood by the contemporaries of Jesus against the background of a successful action of non-violent resistance by the Jews against Pilate.[57] Why would a political interpretation not also be appropriate as a possible dimension of the text if it, too, follows the decisive structural elements? If 'these instructions.... in fact demand the involvement of the whole person, especially his creative reason, his wisdom as well as his courage',[58] how could this claim not also be made on the disciples of Jesus in the sphere of political responsibillity? How could it be wrong to compare these instructions with the contemporary discussion of peace? Might they not rather be helpful? If we remember their social dimension, it should first be noted that the majority of our population does not in fact appear here, in that this particular dimension, the struggle for existence among the poor, while largely not local, is nevertheless bitter reality for an extraodinarily large number of people in the so-called developing countries. Should this insight not bring about a change of priority in our perspective, so that we put north-south before east-west? Should it not make us sensitive to the connection between a high degree of armament here and underdevelopment there, so that that becomes the kind of problem to which we cannot and may not any longer close our eyes?

Secondly, when the question arises of the goal in which the other person might possibly be a partner, must not a first step in the present-day question of peace be that we look at the world from the perspective of the Soviet Union, that we perceive and take seriously its historical experiences, what today it feels to be a threat or an encirclement?

And finally, consideration of the relationship between means and ends calls for the creation of a new situation which opens up the way to possible partnership. That the present politics of rearmament and a high degree of armament leads into a *cul-de-sac*, that armament is already killing, without being put into use, is becoming increasingly plain. What else can a healthy 'interruption' mean here if not that we ourselves should take the first credible step towards disarmament?

The hope for the end of enmity but not of the enemy and the conduct mentioned in the admonitions we have discussed are also implied in Jesus' saying about loving one's enemy. The original wording of Matt.5.44f./Luke 6.27f., 35 was probably as follows:

Love your enemy
and pray for those who mistreat you.

And you will be sons of your Father,
for he is gracious to the ungrateful
and the wicked.[59]

'Jesus replaces the manipulative concept of the neighbour with that of the enemy, by which he understands not one's personal opponent, but in general also the national and religious enemy.'[60] Loving one's enemy also contains an aggressive element. Loving one's enemy does not leave the enemy as he is: it wants him not to go on being an enemy for ever, but to change him.[61] By contrast hatred does not seek the end of enmity. It needs a picture of the enemy and must constantly keep it in full view: it wants the enemy as an enemy – but in order finally to make an end of him.

In loving their enemies the disciples of Jesus show themselves to be sons of their Father, who is gracious to those who are ungrateful and evil. In so doing they imitate what they themselves have experienced from God. But from where have they had this experience? The answer can only be, in their encounter with Jesus. Here the extraordinarily lofty claim made by Jesus is made clear. He acts so to speak in God's place: he brings the goodness of God near and makes room for it in the world. In community with him, those who live on the periphery of society have experienced the goodness of God, and so they have become his disciples, In trust in the steadfastness of the goodness of God that they have experienced they are now to act likewise, in order to live as true children of the Father who is at work in Jesus.

Here intercessory prayer is mentioned as the specific embodiment of love of one's enemy. That envisages an extreme situation. Intercessory prayer is the last possibility, but it is still a possibility for one's own initiative, a way of adopting a positive attitude towards the enemy, against injustice and violence, in which room is made for other means. Here it also becomes clear that Jesus does not cherish the illusion that those who overcome violence with non-violent action must at all events be crowned with success. The risk of such action is not simply overlooked – the risk that includes one's own suffering.

Jesus' own career led to suffering and to death, and if one so wishes, one may note his failure. So was his way illusionary, because he did not calculate human behaviour wisely enough? But, were the Zealots more realistic in thinking that they had to counter the military power of Rome with equally military counter-violence? Was the peace-party more realistic when it reconciled itself with the situation as a result of its assessment of the balance of power? It could be shown that Jesus saw the balance of power very clearly, but that he trusted the power of the kingdom of God even more. And he did not think that he had to help on this power by his own violent measures. If hope for the kingdom of God is an illusion, then the way of Jesus was also an illusion. His disciples did not think that. The Easter experience, the faith that God did not abandon Jesus to failure in death, led them to resume Jesus' way and practise discipleship as a community. How this discipleship continued according to various writings of earliest Christianity as far as perceiving the Pax Romana and acting towards it was concerned, we shall see in due course.

2. 'Our citizenship is in heaven...'
The loyalty of those alien and unadapted to the world, according to Paul

Christianity had spread through the urban world of the Roman empire even before missionary activity by the apostle Paul and continued to do so alongside it. However, Paul advanced this process in an extraordinarily powerful way. The origin and growth of Christian communities in cities inevitably led to contacts between Christians and the Roman authorities, so that Christians attracted official notice. But what did Christians look like to the Roman authorities?[1] Tacitus' report on events in Rome under Nero after the burning of the city in 64[2] certainly refer to a point in time later than the death of Paul; however, it is possible to argue back from this report to the previous period. According to Tacitus Nero accused the Christians of starting the fire in order to put an end to the rumour that he himself had caused the burning. The fact that he could pick on them as scapegoats at all presupposes that they were reputed to be enemies of the empire, that they were suspected of political disloyalty. That is also confirmed by Tacitus' report, for according to him they were accused 'not so much on the count of arson as for hatred of the human race'. After Nero had accused them of the burning, they were arrested because they were Christians.[3] Tacitus describes them as 'loathed for their crimes' and though he was probably convinced of their innocence on the charge of having started the fire he says that they were 'criminals who deserved the harshest punishment'.

How could such an impression arise? The essential aspect was certainly the life-style of the Christians, which in many respects differed from the norms and customs of their environment. 'The contemptible withdrawal by Christians from the organizations which were such an integral part of the life and relationships of the pagan world very soon quite universally aroused the hatred of the others.'[4] In addition there is the consideration that 'when the community of the disciples confessed the crucified Messiah Jesus after Easter, they were loaded with a political burden as far as all outsiders were concerned. Someone who had been crucified was perhaps indeed politically suspicious and a rebel against the Roman state!'[5] Finally, mention should be made here of the designation 'Christian' which was attached to this community by outsiders. According to Acts 11.26 the followers of Jesus were called Christians for the first time in Antioch, the capital of the Roman province of Syria. For any Roman this name naturally stood for the political following of a man by the name of Christ. Because the Christians were so suspected of disloyalty in principle, they had to expect denunciations and also official persecutions. This situation of constant latent threat, at times becoming acute, can also be seen from the letters of Paul.[6] They were written at the beginning of the second half of the first century, but they also contain information about the preceding period. We must first investigate the experiences which Paul had had of the Roman empire and its representatives and which he saw in his communities.

(a) '...in blows, in imprisonment, in tumults...'

Numerous passages show that in the fulfilment of his apostolic task of proclaiming the gospel of Jesus Christ to the Gentiles Paul not only found himself in a great variety of unpleasant circumstances but also had to endure the intervention of officials of the Roman empire. In the brief list in II Cor.4.8f. he speaks quite generally of being oppressed and persecuted without naming those responsible for it. In Gal.5.11; 6.12 he makes a connection between the proclamation of the cross of Christ and persecutions which is certainly based on his own experience. Again the possible persecutors are not named. Here he might also be thinking of Jews. Thus in II Cor.11.26 he says that he is threatened with dangers from his people and shortly beforehand in v.24 he has said, 'Five times have I received from the Jews forty lashes save one.'[7] As Paul also appeared in synagogues with his proclamation, he was subject to Jewish religious jurisdiction, and he often had painful experience of this. But in II Cor.11.26 alongside 'danger from my own people' there is 'danger from the Gentiles'. A few verses later, in 32f., Paul reports a plan to arrest him in Damascus. The governor of the Nabataean king Aretas, a Roman vassal, to whom the Romans had evidently entrusted Damascus, had the city watched in order to catch Paul.[8] Paul, however, avoided the threat of arrest by having himself lowered through a window in the wall in a basket. But often the arrests proved successful and Paul had to spend time in prison. The letters to the Philippians and to Philemon were written from prison.[9] Paul thinks it important that he is imprisoned as a Christian, as someone who proclaims the gospel.[10] However, the way in which he puts this suggests that other Christians where he was imprisoned did not want to see things in that light.[11] We should probably suppose that he was imprisoned in Ephesus;[12] according to Phil.1.13 Paul is held prisoner in the praetorium, the residence of the governor, and is therefore being brought before the highest tribunal in the province. According to Phil.1.20 his trial is a matter of life and death.[13]

From I Thess 2.2, in connection with Acts 16.23, it emerges that Paul was also arrested in Philippi, a self-governing Roman colony. So here he must have been arrested on the prompting of the city authorities. Quite apart from his last long imprisonment before his death, this list probably does not give all the places where Paul was imprisoned. In II Cor.11.23 he says in a comparison with his opponents that he has been in prison far more often than they; and in II Cor.6.5 he also mentions 'prisons' in the plural as places where he has stayed.

Flogging was a punishment associated with imprisonment by Roman or city bodies. According to II Cor.11.25 Paul had suffered it three times.[14] Accordingly he puts 'blows' in v.23 alongside 'prisons', and according to II Cor.6.5 he experienced, among other things, 'beatings, imprisonments, tumults'. The last-mentioned point makes it clear that Paul's proclamation was evidently a disruption to public order in that it led to unrest. That may have caused the authorities to intervene and arrest and flog the trouble-maker. In I Thess. 2.2[15] Paul speaks of the flogging that he suffered in Philippi simply as maltreatment.

As the flogging of Roman citizens was not allowed, this raises the question of Paul's legal status. According to Acts he had not only citizenship of Tarsus but also Roman citizenship.[16] He himself says nothing of that in his letters. By his own account he earned his own living as an apostle by a trade, and even worked at it by night.[17] This fact could tell against his actually having had Roman citizenship, since only the rich aristocratic leaders of provincial society could count on getting it. However, Paul need not always have earned his living with his own hands. The way in which he speaks of this makes it clear that he had also seen other days. When in connection with alllusions to his work he says that in it he has made himself a slave and humiliated himself we clearly have the evaluation of someone who had originally had a higher social status.[18] That is also suggested by his powers of linguistic expression and his education as these emerge from his letters, and also from the natural way in which he goes around as a leader with a whole group of fellow workers.[19] There is evidence that individual Jews also had the citizenship of the Hellenistic cities in which they lived, but that presupposes not only great prosperity but also a marked degree of Hellenization, in other words thoroughgoing adaptation to the Gentile environment.[20] This raises a further objection in connection with Paul: by his own testimony, before he became a Christian he was a strict Pharisee;[21] that should have precluded adaptation to the Gentile environment. So it is still possible to assume that Paul had been a citizen of Tarsus and a Roman citizen by birth,[22] but at the same time we would have to note that he evidently attached no importance to it. That would apply completely to the Christian Jew Paul, whose image as a craftsman and itinerant missionary is utterly different from that of a Roman citizen in the provinces. We can well imagine how the authorities would set little store by the law in the case of such a man.[23] Had Paul in fact been a Roman citizen, he would have been able to make his statement in II Cor.11.25 that he has been flogged three times even more telling by mentioning this fact.[24] That he does not do so does not rule out the possibility that he might have been a Roman citizen, but it stresses once again that if he was, he attached no importance to it.[25]

In II Cor.1.8f. Paul speaks of a particularly hard tribulation which had proved more than he could bear, in Asia, by which he probably means Ephesus as the capital of the province.[26] He had already despaired of his life and had already pronounced the death sentence on himself. The use of this legal term points to the context of a trial, so that the Roman authorities are to be regarded as those threatening him with death. He felt the threat to be so strong that according to II Cor.1.9f. he could only understand the preservation of his life which then in fact followed as the help of the God who raises the dead, as deliverance from death. He may possibly be alluding to an early fatal threat in Ephesus in I Cor.15.32, when he speaks of his battle there with wild beasts.[27] At all events, another indication of the fact that at the end of his stay in Ephesus he had an extremely serious clash with the Roman authorities is that he evidently deliberately avoided this city on his last journey to Jerusalem.[28] Unfortunately we have only the tendentious account of Acts to tell us of the arrest which took place during his last stay in Jerusalem and the events which followed it.[29] However, it may be regarded as virtually certain that Paul's arrest and trial eventually led to his execution in Rome.[30]

To sum up, then, we may argue that in exercising his apostolic role Paul had often enough found himself the victim of Roman bodies as well as city authorities and vassal rulers. He did not have these experiences because he had committed some illegalities in the moral and legal sense but because as a Christian his loyalty was suspect and because he continued to propagate being a Christian, which was evidently felt to be a disturbance of public order.

Paul's fate in this respect is not an isolated one, but according to his own perception is a paradigm for Christians in his communities generally. According to Phil.1.30 his readers have the same struggle as he does. Here he expressly points to his own experiences during his stay in Philippi and to his present situation in prison. Earlier, in v.29, he had noted that it had been granted to them not only to believe in Christ but also to suffer for his sake, and in v.28 he had issued the warning not to be 'intimidated by your opponents', In the light of the following context this intimidation may well be the threat of denunciation by fellow citizens to the authorities, and indeed attacks by the authorities themselves. Paul will also be thinking of this in I Thess.2.14 when he mentions the suffering which those to whom he is writing experience from their fellow countrymen. The questions which he puts in Rom.8.33f. are, as the answers show, certinly rhetorical: 'Who can lay charges against God's elect?... Who can condemn?' The context also makes it clear that what is envisaged here is a last judgment which far transcends an earthy tribunal. But should these questions with their legal terminology not be set against the background of the quite specific experience of charges being laid and judgments given specifically against Christians?[31] The answers put such experiences in another relationship and so do violence to it. But at all events it shuld be clear that Paul and his communities experienced the organs of the Roman empire in administration and jurisdiction, along with the legions the guarantees of the Pax Romana, as potential and often also actual persecutors.

Acute perception of the reality shaped by the Pax Romana is also evident in II Cor.11.20. There Paul addresses the Corinthians ironically and describes metaphorically what they have experienced from his opponents. But he has not taken these pictures out of thin air: 'For you bear it if a man makes slaves of you, or preys upon you, or takes advantage of you, or puts on airs, or strikes you in the face. To my shame, I must say, we were too weak for that.' The strong men whose action is described in these pictures stood before the eyes of Paul and his readers and hearers in the form of those with political and social power.

(b) 'When they say "Peace and security"'

It follows from the experiences which Paul was forced to undergo that he did not have very much trust in justice in the Roman empire. His remarks in I Cor.6.1-8 should also be read against this background. He writes in v.1: 'When one of you has a grievance against a brother, does he dare to go to law before the unrighteous instead of the saints?' Here the judges are sweepingly called 'unrighteous' and thus disqualified as judges. This implies a devastating verdict on the practice of law: 'Appealing to the city judge ...is nonsense because it looks for justice among the unjust.' Of course Paul is not 'attacking the law and its norms in general'.[32] The very suggestion that he makes first in vv.4f. that disputes in the community should be settled by its own authorities, presupposes the recognition of law and norms. Thus he declares the community competent in all matters which could have gone before a court and thus removes this concern from 'ordinary judgments'.[33] The second suggestion which Paul makes in vv.7f. and which he considers to be more appropriate, namely to prefer to suffer wrong, in other words to renounce going to law,[34] presupposes the recognition of law. But the way in which he puts it again sheds significant light on his estimation of actual legal practice. Having asked those who go to the courts, 'Why not rather suffer wrong? Why not rather be defrauded?' he immediately continues, 'But you yourselves wrong and defraud; and that even your own brethren.' Going to law here is itself regarded as doing injustice and robbing one's adversary.[35] That injustice and robbery thus appear in the garb of law again makes it clear why Paul can describe the judges as unjust.

As one who is persecuted yet survives,[36] Paul is necessarily at a distance from those who rules. This distance was also created, as far as he was concerned, by the violent death of Jesus. 'The fact... that a Roman governor had Jesus crucified could not escape the notice of Paul if he reflected on the cross.'[37] Paul himself expresses that at another point when he says that the 'rulers of this world' did not recognize the wisdom of God, his plan aimed at the salvation of humanity, and so 'crucified the Lord of glory'.[38] They obviously did not see Jesus as the 'Lord of glory' and did not recognize God's plan in his way of humiliation.[39] They are evidently impressed only by obvious power and authority, and accordingly use their power violently, as is evident in the crucifixion of Jesus. So they pursue their own plans; that is their wisdom – and is in basic contrast to the wisdom of God hidden in the cross of Jesus.

So if Paul thus has the violent character of Roman rule immediately in view at the point which is central for his theological reflection, the cross of Christ, it is not to be expected that he will sing hymns of praise to Roman peace. We must rather acccept that, like his assessment of justice in the Roman empire, so too his assessment of the Pax Romana will generally be very critical. In I Thess. 5.3 he makes it present one of its most important claims. There we read: 'When they say "There is peace and security", then sudden destruction will come upon them as travail comes upon a woman with child'. He quotes 'Peace and security' as a slogan which is general in the world but not used by Christians.[40] As we have seen, the combination of these terms expresses an important claim of the Pax Romana: Roman power brings peace as a permanent state free of wars; it guarantees security from hostile attacks from beyond the bounds of the empire and by preventing armed quarrels within its frontiers; and finally, too, 'inner security', the maintaining of order and the preservation of the security of law is part of that.[41] So 'peace and security' is a conservative slogan which affirms the existing order and wants to see it preserved. Paul takes it up in I Thess.5.3.[42] However, he regards it as a foolish slogan, which Christians will not repeat. He does not refute the claim that the Pax Romana brings 'peace and security' by an empirical analysis, though he could certainly have made some contribution to this as a result of his sufferings. But we may assume that the devaluation of the Pax Romana which he expresses here in the light of quite another dimension will hardly have been made without some feedback from such negative experiences. According to v.2 the other dimension from which the claim to 'peace and security' seems to him to be the 'illusion of peace and security'[43] is 'the day of the Lord', which comes as surprisingly as a 'thief in the night'. Earlier, in 4.13-18, he had spoken of the 'parousia of the Lord', the Lord Jesus who comes to deliver his followers,[44] those who are still alive and also those who are raised from the dead, whereas this day brings destruction for those who delude themselves that they have peace and security. As the Christian apocalyptist which he proves to be here, Paul certainly does not expect a consummation within history. He is radically distinct from those who, like Virgil and Aelius Aristides, associate conceptions of salvation with the Pax Romana. Talk of the 'day of the Lord' causes him to speak in the following verses in contrasting imagery of day and night, light and darkness. Here the words 'peace and security' – and therefore that for which they stand, the Pax Romana – clearly stand on the side of night and darkness. Paul does not count on the continuation of history, on a possible growth to consummation, but expects salvation from the definitive end of history, from the eschatological final coming of Jesus which will radically change the world.

Just as in I Thess.5.1-11 the Pax Romana seems to belong with the night and darkness, so too in I Cor.15.24-26 'every rule, every power and authority' belongs on the side of death. Here Paul is making a comprehensive generalization. How can he not be thinking of the rule, power and authority of Rome, which in its time put its stamp on so many things, which was so clearly before the eyes of the whole world? Here, too, he is concerned with 'the end' as the breaking off of all previous history. According to v.24 the end comes when Christ 'delivers the kingdom to God the Father after destroying every rule and every authority and power'. The exercise of other powers and authorities challenges the Lordship of Christ. So in v.25 they appear as 'enemies' who have to be overcome.[45] According to v.26 death is the 'last enemy' to be annihilated. As long as it rules, Christ and God have not achieved their goal. The term 'enemy' thus combines the powers and authorities with death and makes them its accomplices. That means that for Paul the history shaped here by the Pax Romana stands under the sign of death and on its side; it is the history of death which Christ will break off.

In a similar context, Phil.3.20, Paul formulates in a very evocative way the detachment which Christians have from this history. To other Christians whom he accuses of having their bellies as their gods and being earthy, he stresses: 'Our citizenship is in heaven'. Here he uses a political term which denotes the commonwealth, the state and its constitution, 'the place where people have "rights and a home"',[46] and which therefore also means citizenship. If the citizenship of Christians is in heaven, that makes them strangers on earth. Anyone who talks like this cannot attach any special value to Roman citizenship.[47] Paul combines this detachment from the present world which is in fact the world dominated by Rome with the same expectation that he expresses in I Thess.4.13-5.11 and I Cor.15.20-28: 'and from it we await a Saviour, the Lord Jesus Christ, who will change our lowly body to be like his glorious body, by the power which enables him even to subject all things to himself' (vv.20f.). Only here does Paul use the title 'Saviour'; in this political context it certainly also includes a rejection of expectations of a political saviour of the kind which had already become bound up with Hellenistic kings and then also with the Roman emperors.[48] Christian hope is not focussed on the fulfilment of history but on life from the resurrection[49] under the Lordship of Christ which is no longer infringed by any other rule.

(c) 'Therefore one must be subject...'

The experiences which Paul had to undergo in the world dominated by Rome would not lead us to expect any positive verdict on this rule from him. It was possible to document the critical detachment that was therefore to be assumed. So if we ask in what theological context Paul puts the perceived reality of the Pax Romana and how he evaluates it from that context, our answer on the basis of the texts so far quoted must be: from the perspective of his expectation of God's and Christ's future it is a history of death running on to the point where it is broken off.

But in saying that we have not yet said anything about the way in which Christians are actually to behave in the face of the power still specifically exercised by Rome and its minions. Loyalty in principle is by no means excluded here. That is precisely what Paul admonishes Christians to show in Rom.13.1-7, a text which has become famous. However, this admonition also gives reasons which suggest another valuation of Rome from that which has emerged from previous texts. A certain tension is unmistakable. We shall have to go on to ask how it is to be understood. But the previous remarks about Paul's attitude to Roman power should already have made it clear that we cannot treat Rom.13.1-7 in isolation in connection these questions. Just as discussion in connection with Jesus has always simply or predominantly turned on the story of the 'taxation coin', so in the case of Paul it has turned on Rom.13.1-7. Therefore it is not surprising that this text, too, has become hopelessly overloaded in the history of exegesis and its influence. It is therefore important to bring out what it seeks to say and to put it in relation to the other remarks of Paul:

> Let every person be subject to the governing authorities. For there is no authority except from God, and those that exist have been instituted by God. Therefore he who resists the authorities resists whatever God has appointed and those who resist will incur judgment. For rulers are not a terror to good conduct, but to bad. Would you have no fear of him who is in authority? Then do what is good, and you will receive his approval, for he is God's servant for your good. But if you do wrong, be afraid, for he does not bear the sword in vain; he is the servant of God to execute his wrath on the wrongdoer. Therefore one must be subject, not only to avoid God's wrath but also for the sake of conscience. For the same reason you also pay taxes, for the authorities are ministers of God. Attending to this very thing,[50] pay all of them their dues, taxes to whom taxes are due, revenue to whom revenue is due, respect to whom respect is due, honour to whom honour is due.

August Strobel has shown that all the way through this passage Paul has taken up the terminology of Hellenistic administrative language.[51] Hence he sees in the phrase which is translated above as 'governing authorities' a 'reference to the countless offices in the extensive state apparatus of the world empire'.[52] This observation should be connected with another, that both in the context of this passage and in the passage itself Paul is giving admonitions. That is his intention here, to admonish. Over against that the reasons which he adds merely have an auxiliary function.[53] So Paul is not seeking to give anything like a theory of the state, but advising those whom he is addressing to subordinate themselves to the various people with political power with whom they in fact have to do, to treat them with respect and to do what is asked of them; in other words, he is admonishing them to act loyally.

These admonitions are given by the very man whose bad experiences with Roman instruments of state have just been described. In specific terms, for Paul, to bless when shamed, to hold fast under persecution (I Cor.4.12), not to recompense evil with evil (I Thess.5.15), means to prove loyal to those with political authority. His experiences do not drive him to total opposition and rejection, but the experiences which he is forced to undergo become the testing ground for Christian existence, which is proved precisely where it does not refuse loyalty.

At this point the admonition to loyalty in Rom.13.1-7 has its place in the context of other admonitions. It is also covered by the principle of any admonition to subject Christian life to God in all its expressions, formulated in 12.1f., to serve God in the everyday life of the world, the presupposition of which is a refusal to adapt to this world and change one's thinking, in order as a community to be able to recognize God's will specifically in each occasion. In 12.3-8 Paul primarily has the community in view from the perspective of a multiplicity in unity and unity in multiplicity; each person has his specific endowment as an essential function of the community: it indicates the position which he or she has to fill. Accordingly in 12.9-21 Paul admonishes those to whom he is writing to live as brothers and sisters and then in an almost imperceptible transition talks about relations with people outside the community, which are not to be different from those within the community, despite the aggression with which they meet. As a particular case of behaviour towards such people generally, in 13.1-7 Paul considers attitudes towards those holding power in the state. In 13.8-10 he sums up all that he has said so far in the love command as the fulfilment of the law. The loyalty which was previously required towards those holding power in the state thus appears as a very sober way of making the commandment to love specific in a particular sphere.[54] Finally, in 13.11-14 Paul puts the whole context in an eschatological perspective: the day of the Lord is at hand. Therefore a way of life is called for which matches the day and not the night, a way of life which opposes the prevalent immorality – which means the immorality of the rulers (v.13) – and practises a new life under the 'cloak' of Christ (v.14). This context shows that the admonition to loyalty in Rom.13.1-7 covers only a limited sphere which does not extend to the whole political action of Christians; we shall have to ask later about the public relevance of the action called for in 12.17-21. The context further shows that conflicts are presupposed and that in view of the coming of the Lord the loyalty called for can in no way be understood as an adaptation of Christian identity under pressure. In 13.17, however, there is not even any reflection on possible cases of conflict: here there is merely a strict admonition to loyalty.

It has therefore continually been asked whether this admonition was occasioned by a particular situation in the Roman community. Thus Käsemann, for example, thinks that here Paul is attacking 'the attitude which in virtue of heavenly citizenship views earthly authorities with indifference'.[55] But this 'conjecture' about a 'one-sided front against a feared enthusiasm[56] has all too weak a basis in the text of Rom.12.3 to be in the slightest degree probable.

In a wide-ranging approach Friedrich, Pöhlmann and Stuhlmacher have put forward another thesis. They refer to information in Tacitus and Suetonius according to which in AD 58 the Roman people protested to the emperor Nero against the extortionate practices of the state toll and tax farmers. This led to something like a tax reform which for the moment did away with some abuses. Romans was written before the reform measures, so it still presupposes a situation governed by the malpractices. The authors associate this situation with the alleged return of Jewish Christians to Rome on the repeal of the edict of Claudius which had banned then in 49, probably on the accession of Nero. The Jewish Christians would now have found themselves without the protection of the synagogue in a more difficult economic situation. In vv.6f. Paul is advising them nevertheless to pay their taxes.[57] These scholars see the essential intent of Paul's admonition as follows: 'It was advisable to put up with the burden of taxation because resistance or refusal to pay taxes would threaten the existence of the community, and the world which is moving towards God's judgment needed a state authority to regulate it so that it did not prematurely sink into chaos.'[58] Apart from the fact that there is not even the trace of a hint of the two reasons given here in the text and context of Rom.13.1-7, one main obstacle to this thesis is that it understands the form of the verb in v.6a as an imperative. That is grammatically possible, but improbable as a result of the γὰρ καί ('and indeed'). It is significant that the authors do not say anything about their quite unusual translation, in which the γάρ does not figure at all. We should therefore follow all the more recent commentators in understanding the form of the verb as being indicative. In vv.6a Paul is producing an explanatory subsidiary argument on the basis of the payment of tax. The Roman Christians pay tax as long as that is their duty, and do not need to be admonished to do that,

It might rather be considered that a possible specific occasion for Rom.13.1-7 lay less in a problem that the Roman Christians had with the state authorities than in the fact that Roman Christians suspected Paul himself of having a problem over this question. Ultimately Paul was arrested on several occasions on suspicion of disloyalty.[59] If we further recall that in other passages, too, in Romans Paul is at the same time making an apologia for himself, this assumption does not seem too far from the truth.[60] We should then note that it is rather different if someone who is suspect of disloyalty, who has tangibly felt this suspicion and yet continues acting in the way which makes him incur this suspicion, appeals to loyalty as though loyalty were ordained from above.

Once again, we should remember what can be said with some certainty. Paul admonishes his readers not to resist the political powers with which even Christians have to deal, but to give them what they demand: taxes, duties, reverence and respect. The weight of this passage clearly lies on this admonition to loyalty.

However, extensive reasons are given for the admonition. 'The nub of the problem' lies with them more than in the history of their interpretation.[61] It is certainly right to emphasize that 'we may not overstress the traditional material and reasons given, since these borrowings have primarily functional significance'.[62] Therefore a warning against systematization is needed.[63] But these reasons are given and therefore notice must be taken of them.

In vv.3f. Paul justifies his demand by saying that the rulers praise good deeds and punish evil ones. Here he is taking up a very frequent comment. But we must note how abstract it is compared with his own experiences. That in turn should warn us against drawing conclusions from it for a theory of the state. Paul reinforces both parts of the statement that he has adopted. He describes the state authority as the 'servant of God', which is matched by the way in which it is characterized as an 'ordinance of God' (v.2) and the assertions that it is ordained by God (v.1b) and that those who collect taxes are 'officials of God' (v.6). Here the actual rulers are regarded as the specific ordinance of God, so to speak as those whom he has appointed. Whereas 'in the oriental and Hellenistic world the idea was prominent that earthly rule is of divine origin and that the rulers are therefore sons of God',[64] here the power of the state does not demand subordination in its own right; the real sovereign is God himself. Here Paul is taking up an Old Testament-Jewish tradition.[65] The passage most cited in this connection should also be mentioned here; among the oaths by which the Essenes are bound Josephus mentions the one 'Always to be loyal to all, but especially to the authorities, since no one has a position of rule without God'.[66] Paul takes up this tradition and makes it his own, in order to stress his purpose here. This purpose should be stressed once again. He is concerned with the specific loyalty to be shown to the actual powers which the Christians encounter in the various authorities. The theological basis he gives for this is that there is no such actual power without God, that those in authority are virtually appointed by God to their function. But by doing that without caveat, qualification and dialectic, he at least exposes himself to the danger of providing theological legitimation for *de facto* power no matter how it may have come into being and how it may be used.

The positive evaluation of state power as the 'servant of God', an evaluation which ultimately applies to the Roman imperium, is characteristically different from the evaluations of Rome which have been expressed in the texts we discussed earlier and stand in tension to it. This tension is lessened by the fact that the positive assessment in Rom.13.1-7 is made within the context of the reasons advanced by Paul. Given the purpose of the section, these reasons merely have an auxiliary function. However, that does not do away with the tension altogether. An attempt should be made to read Rom.13.1-7 and the other texts, above all I Thess.5.1-11, in a complementary way.[67] In the images of I Thess.5 – day and night, light and darkness – those who say 'peace and security' are on the side of night and darkness, as too is the power of the state which lies behind this slogan. If we keep Rom.13 in mind in reading I Thess.5, we shall be protected from reading the passage dualistically, as though there were a reality with which God had nothing to do, on which he made no claim, which lay outside his activity and influence.[68] If on the other hand we listen to I Thess.5 on reading Rom.13, we cannot understand this text in a positivistic way, as though all power which had in fact established itself were legitimated by God in its existing form, as though it no longer stood under the judgment of God and as though the history that it shaped were no longer on the way to its radical interruption.

If we look at both passages together it becomes clear that the loyalty which Paul requires towards the power of the state is the loyalty of the one who is alien to the world and a 'citizen of heaven', not the loyalty of the person who is assimilated but that of the one who is not.[69] He and his personal experiences are an impressive example of that. The loyalty to which he admonishes his readers cannot therefore be total; there is the possibility of specific refusal.

(d) '...we have peace with God'

It had become clear that Paul could understand the world history dominated by Rome as a history heading for downfall, in the light of the expectation of Jesus Christ as the coming Lord. But the expectation of downfall is not his only framework of reference, into which he integrates his perception of the Pax Romana. The one whose arrival he expects at the end of this world is Jesus, in other words not an extra-historical figure but a historical individual, albeit a man in whom – as was already attested by the Christian tradition handed down to Paul, and which he also attests himself – God has already acted eschatologically, by raising him from the dead. In the death and resurrection of Jesus God has shown himself to be a love giving itself once and for all, and for all, which opens up and guarantees an imperishable future. This is the connection in which Paul puts the sorry experiences that he has had in and with the Pax Romana. That happens particularly impressively in Rom.8.31-39. I have already pointed out that the rhetorical questions probably include quite specific experiences of accusations, arrests and condemnations.[70] Thus in his list of adverse circumstances in v.35 Paul also speaks of 'persecution' and 'sword', by which he means the sword of judgment.[71] But these experiences are put completely in the shade by the love of Christ which has already been demonstrated, from which nothing can separate the Christian. Paul then goes on to give almost exuberant expression to such certainty in vv.38f. In the real experience of suffering he trusts in the love of God which has been made manifest in Christ as a comprehensive and supportive reality. This trust makes one hold on to something that essentially leads only to yet more experiences of suffering, i.e. for Paul the propagation of faith in Christ and for communities the fact that they are Christians. With this certainty, in v.37 he speaks of a triumphant victory in the midst of experiences of suffering.[72] As these latter partly alluded to the political realities, Paul might deliberately be presenting this 'victory' as an alternative image to the victory of the legions. The future does not belong to the men of violence who impose themselves by their strength at the expense of the weak, but for the sake of Christ it belongs precisely to those weak ones who according to v.36 are 'looked on as sheep for the slaughter'.[73] In exactly the same way, in II Cor.2.14, in the light of God's saving action in Christ Paul can describe his apostolic existence with its many adverse circumstances, caused not least by the power of Rome, as a triumph through God: 'But thanks be to God who makes us triumph in Christ at all times' – a powerful contrast to the triumphal processions in Rome.[74]

While Paul had rejected as a foolish slogan the claim that the Pax Romana offered 'peace and security', on the basis of the action of God in Jesus Christ which has already taken place he can already speak of peace in the present: 'Therefore, since we are justified by faith, we have peace with God through our Lord Jesus Christ' (Rom.5.1).[75] According to this, those who are justified by faith have peace. Immediately before that, in Rom.4.24f., Paul had described them as those 'who believe in him that was raised from the dead, Jesus our Lord, who was put to death for our trespasses and raised for our justification'. So faith relates to the 'victory of God over death disclosed in Jesus Christ'.[76] Accordingly, believers are those who give God the glory by submitting themselves to the crucified Jesus whom God has raised. The resurrection of Jesus from the dead – that is God's eschatological action, the introduction of a new world in which this powerless one rules and in which his power is trusted. So it is no longer a world of death but one of a life filled by God. Thus this world is characterized in Rom.14.17 by 'righteousness, peace and joy'. Paul's hope for the end of the old history of death, to which the Pax Romana also belongs, thus has a subsidiary pledge in the resurrection of Jesus from the dead. This binds together the two different perspectives from which Paul perceives the Pax Romana. Against such a horizon an attempt can now be made to define more closely the peace which in Rom.5.1 is said already to be present. Paul speaks of a 'peace with God', or more exactly 'peace in relation to God'. It is generally recognized today that this is no mere 'peace of the heart'.[77] A comparison with Rom.5.9 shows that the opposite concept to peace with God is the wrath of God[78] in which his eschatological judgment is accomplished,[79] a wrath which also already manifests now itself in perverse life, turned away from God and enslaving the truth in injustice, along with its consequences.[80] Therefore to have peace in relation to God means being absolved from his judgment, which with the arrival of Jesus will interrupt the catastrophic course of history and pronounce an annihilating judgment on it;[81] it also means being removed from the manifestations of this wrath which are evident even now.[82] The believers who participate in this peace therefore stand as it were in the breach which the resurrection of Jesus has made in the old world by marking the appearance of a new world; they hold fast to the interruption of an apparently closed course of history which has taken place in it and so represent the dawn of the new world.[83] Paul shows that this keeping open the breach by standing up for another reality is no triumphal event by the way in which he keeps referring to his tribulations;[84] and so, as I have said above, he can only speak paradoxically of a triumph. The breach made by the resurrection of Jesus as the place of believers is a contested area because the old world will not tolerate this interruption in the immanent cause of its automatic movements, and those who stand for it are regarded as disruptive factors.[85] But for that very reason, according to Rom.3.5 believers can even boast of their tribulations, since these prove necessary as a result of that which brings their peace – though they cannot put that peace with God in question. Therefore the tribulations stand under the perspective of hope: 'More than that (viz., boasting of the hoped-for glory of God), we rejoice in our sufferings; knowing that suffering produces endurance, and endurance produces character, and character produces hope, and hope does not put us to shame,[86] because God's love has been poured into our hearts through the Holy Spirit which has been given us' (Rom.5.3-5). On the one hand already participants in the new world of God, of peace, and on the other hand participants in the tribulations of the old world, as a result of this painful 'at the same time' believers, as Paul explains in Rom.8.18-22, find themselves in solidarity with the suffering and unredeemed creation yet brought with the whole world under the horizon of hope.

(e) '...but overcome evil with good'

Paul explained in Rom.5 that in view of the death and resurrection of Jesus believers already have peace with God; they are removed from the wrath of God, and that means that as far as they are concerned the catastrophic course of history has already been interrupted though they are still involved in tribulations during it. However, they must not become resigned to these experiences; on the contrary, such experiences should make them hopeful, so that in view of their coming Lord they expect the final break and thus also the end of the tribulations. But what does that mean for their actions? Paul has explained the sureness of their hope in Rom.5.5 by saying that the love of God has been poured into their hearts. But that which is in a person's heart, which determines a person at the centre, also moves him or her to act accordingly. Thus real hope is never just mere expectation, but realizes itself symbolically by doing in anticipation what is hoped for. The peace with God that the believers already have and the peace free of all tribulation which they hope for moves them already to look for the realization of peace.

Therefore waiting for the 'day of the Lord' is not a matter of relaxed and inactive waiting; it is expressed, rather, in activity. In I Thess.5.1-11, which contrasts the day of the Lord with the slogan 'peace and security', Paul explains that in metaphorical terms. Those who await the day of the Lord belong to the day and to light; they are not in the darkness; they do not sleep and are not drunk, but are awake and sober. This watchfulness and sobriety consist in the 'breastplate of faith and love, and for a helmet the hope of salvation' (v.8). In speaking in this connection of the 'arming' of the Christian,[87] Paul develops a counter-image to the reality which is described by the slogan 'peace and security', the Pax Romana which is gained and maintained by military might. The slogan 'peace and security' derives from faith in the power of Rome;[88] it rises out of an abyss of hatred and anxiety as the presupposition and at the same time the consequence of force: it is based on the promise of eternal Rome as an infinite extension of the history of violence and is thus simply the expression of deep hopelessness. Over against that, Christian sobriety as faith, love and hope is not to be seen in the calculations of power, in so-called realistic analysis as a projection of the existing situation. Rather, trusting in the crucified Christ it renounces aggressive violence and makes its love specific in the demolition and the overcoming of hatred and anxiety. But Christian sobriety demonstrates itself in particular – and it is here that the stress lies in I Thess.5.1-11 – in a perception of reality which tests it from the perspective of the interruption of history and the coming of Christ. Those who are sober in this way, who do not get drunk with power, will keep possibilities open and already set signs of the new world in the midst of the old. Not least, their hope in the interruption of the course of history experienced as suffering will take shape in the interruption of the negative automatic processes which is already taking place. Paul expresses this in I Thess.5.15 with the formula: 'See that none of you repays evil for evil, but always seek to do good to one another and to all.'

Here the community is the primary consideration: it is itself a sphere of interrupted violence;[89] the most obvious context of the Christian praxis of peace. In I Cor.14.33 Paul ends his comments on the way the community assembly should be organized by saying, 'For God is not a God of disorder but a God of peace.' Immediately before this he had given instructions as to how the assembly was to be held in an ordered way which should protect them from getting into arguments. There is to be room for the spontaneity which was evidently a characteristic mark of the Corinthian assembly,[90] but in such a way that 'all learn and are admonished' (v.31b). As I Cor.14 keeps saying, the community is to be 'built up'.[91] This building up was hindered in Corinth by the fact that individuals who felt that they had particular gifts of the Spirit forced themselves into the foreground, showed off to others and thus produced chaotic conditions. They are kept within limits by Paul. When in such a context he says that God is not a God of disorder but of peace it is clear that peace is not just another word for 'order', although as v.40 again shows, it has elements of order. Order here is not an end in itself; it merely serves the common process of learning in the community. The peace for which Paul claims God thus means the encouraging of one another in the community which is to be practised against the supposed right of the stronger.

In his admonition in I Thess.5.15 not to recompense evil with evil but to look for the good, Paul primarily had in view the sphere of the community, but then immediately adds 'and for all'. The interruption of negative automatic processes thus applies not only to the internal sphere but particularly also to behaviour towards outsiders. In respect of himself as an apostle Paul says in I Cor.4.12: 'When reviled, we bless, when persecuted, we endure; when slandered we try to conciliate.' In Rom.12.14 he asks his hearers and readers to act in the same way: 'Bless those who persecute you, bless them and do not curse them.' This renunciation of retribution, indeed the admonition to respond to negative experience with a positive action, is developed impressively by Paul in the short section Rom.12.17-21. In v.18 he writes: 'So far as it depends upon you, live peaceably with all.' The qualification at the beginning makes it clear that it would be wrong to assume that a Christian concern for peace 'could create peace at any event'. Paul sees that peace does not just rest on the good will of one side. But on the other hand he does not in any way presuppose that on the other side there must from the start be just as great a will for peace if peace is to be achieved. That is evident from the way in which Paul goes on to describe the qualification 'as far as it depends on you'. This phrase is not just a mere gesture for him, with which he resignedly accepts unpeaceful circumstances; rather, it spells things out in detail. He forbids the Christians to take vengence: vengeance is a matter for God (vv.19f.). As in I Thess.5.15 he admonishes his readers and hearers to break through the chain of violence and retribution: 'Do not recompense evil with evil' (v.17a). He immediately balances out a refusal 'to seek any compensation that might be due'[92] with a positive admonition: 'Take thought for what is noble in the sight of all' (v.17b). Others are to be given the advantage, in trust, and action towards them is to be shaped in such a way that it produces positive consequences. So Paul can end by giving as a maxim for Christian peace action which corresponds to the hoped-for interruption of the course of history and life in the dawning of a new world: 'Do not be overcome by evil, but overcome evil with good' (v.21).

3. 'This was not done in a corner' – Orientation on the 'great world' in Luke

Some decades had passed after Paul had written his letters before Luke wrote his double work, the Gospel which stands in third place in the New Testament canon, and the Acts of the Apostles.[1] It is impossible to fix its composition at an exact point in time: it seems most probably to come from a period between 70 and 100; there is more to be said for the second half of this period than for the first. In Luke we have quite a different way of looking at the Pax Romana from what we find in Jesus and Paul. Here we find virtually no negative statements about

Rome and its representatives; rather, they are depicted in an explicitly favourable light.

(a) 'It is not the custom of the Romans to give up anyone...'

In both books by Luke it is striking that soldiers, the primary guarantors of the Pax Romana, repeatedly appear not as manifestations of an aggressive and oppressive military power but rather on the one hand as providing the necessary protection to the legal order – Luke has very considerable interest in this in his positive account of those holding power in the empire – and on the other hand as being well disposed to the indigenous population and active in furthering its interests.

The centurion Cornelius in Caesarea in Acts 10.1f. is shown to be a Roman citizen by the fact that he belongs to the Italian cohort; he is 'a devout man who feared God with all his household, gave alms liberally to the people, and prayed constantly to God'. This model of a pious man who according to v.22 is 'well spoken of by the whole Jewish nation' even becomes a Christian, so that according to Luke one of the first to be converted 'from the Gentiles is a Roman centurion'.[2] The centurion whose child[3] is said by the tradition to have been healed by Jesus in Capernaum is portrayed by Luke in a very similar way to Cornelius.[4] In the passage Luke 7.3-6,[5] which Luke has added, the centurion sends the 'elders of the Jews', i.e. the local leaders, to Jesus. They argue for the centurion with determination for him and say that he is 'worthy, for he loves our people and had our synagogue built for us'.[6] Here Luke virtually gives the impression of warm collaboration between the indigenous population and the foreign occupying forces.

It is also amazing that within a report about the activity of John the Baptist, in the section 3.10-14, the traditional admonition to share which is addressed to 'the crowd' is followed by admonitions which Luke has written himself, to two particular professional groups: to publicans and to soldiers.[7] These are the two supporting pillars of the Roman empire.[8] When they ask what they are to do they are prohibited from misusing the possibilities of their profession; in positive terms they are thus asked to exercise their profession conscientiously.[9] Does not the special mention of these professions presuppose that in Christian communities they were felt to be problematical, indeed incompatible with being a Christian? According to Hans von Campenhausen, 'Until about AD 175, as far as we can see there were still no Christian soldiers and therefore there was no particular "military problem".'[10] When towards the end of the second century an increasing number of soldiers were converted, the question then arose, 'As Christians, may they remain in their former profession?'[11] The fact that Luke makes the first Christian from the Hellenistic Roman Gentile world a Roman centurion and the matter-of-fact way in which in Luke 3.12-14 there is a demand 'not to give up the profession but to practise it rightly'[12] shows how far ahead he is of his time and what a special standpoint he has to adopt in it.

The Lucan portrayal of Roman soldiers in connection with the trial and execution of Jesus is characterized by the fact that they become mere dummies. In the account in the Gospel of Mark the following actions are said to have been carried out by Roman soldiers: the flogging and physical ridicule of Jesus (15.15b-20a), taking him away to be crucified (15.20b), the compelling of Simon of Cyrene to carry Jesus' cross (15.21), the execution (15.22-24a), the sharing of his garments by lot (15.24b), and the execution of two further delinquents (15.27). But according to Luke the Roman soldiers only appear at the point when Jesus is already hanging on the cross; they take part in mocking him by bringing him vinegar to drink and ask him to save himself if he is king of the Jews (Luke 23.36f.). That is all! Comparison with the report by Mark makes Luke's tendency clear, namely to make the Roman soldiers seem relatively uninvolved; they appear only quite peripherally and are merely drawn into the mockery of the others, while their centurion is finally the witness of Jeuss' innocence (23.47).[13] Here Luke has so toned down the negative action of the soldiers which he found in his sources that he can depict them in a markedly positive way in the arrest of Paul in Jerusalem and the subsequent negotiations.[14] When Paul is dragged out of the temple by a raging mob and is on the point of being lynched, news reaches the tribune of the Roman garrison in Jerusalem that the city is in an uproar. The immediate appearance of the tribune with soldiers and centurions saves Paul's life. He is arrested. As the tribune cannot get any reliable information in the turmoil, he has Paul brought to the barracks. Because of the unruly pressure from the crowd the soldiers even have to carry him (Acts 21.30-35). So in Luke's account, Paul's arrest by the Roman army seems virtually to be a protective measure in a threatening situation. In order to be clear about his prisoner the tribune orders that Paul shall be interrogated under torture, as was customary for non-citizens. As the torture is being prepared Paul tells the centurion who leads the squad involved that he is a Roman citizen. The centurion immediately informs the tribune, who thereupon himself asks Paul about his citizenship. Without the need for an order, the soldiers who are to interrogate Paul under torture immediately release Paul, correctly fulfilling the law (22.24-29).[15] The next day the tribune has Paul brought before the Jewish Sanhedrin to learn why he is accused by the Jews. Proceedings here verge on the grotesque. Concerned for Paul's life, the tribune gives the alarm to the troop, which rescues him from the danger and restores him to the safety of the barracks (22.30-23.10).[16] The events described here by Paul 'are historically impossible; the tribune is afraid because he has seized a Roman citizen; but he leaves him in fetters overnight; he does not interrogate Paul himself, but lets the Roman citizen be taken before a Jewish authority.'[17] In this way, however, Luke gives himself the opportunity of again presenting the soldiers of Rome as protection for Paul.[18] In the next scene this happens for a third and final time. When the tribune hears of a planned Jewish attempt on Paul's life, he resolves to send him to the procurator Felix in Caesarea.[19] He offers half his troop for the nocturnal action (23.12-35).[20] In the accompanying letter to the procurator (23.26-30) Luke 'provides the reader with the image he is to retain: the general impression that the Roman State respected Paul's Roman citizenship from the beginning'.[21] Finally, Paul also experiences the protection of Roman soldiers on the journey from Caearea to Rome (Acts 27). Along with other prisoners he is handed over by the procurator to soldiers headed by a centurion called Julius (v.1). The centurion treats Paul kindly and allows him to go ashore to his friends during a stop in Sidon (v.3). When the crew want to leave the ship and passangers in the lurch, Paul and the centurion along with the soldiers work together in trust and thwart the plan (vv.30-32).[22] After the shipwreck the soldiers want to kill the prisoners, because they might escape. But the centurion, who is well-disposed to Paul and wants to save him, prevents them (vv.42-44). In his letter to the Romans Ignatius shows how differently someone who is himself involved depicts such a prison ship: 'All the way from Syria to Rome I am fighting with wild beasts, by land and sea, night and day, chained as I am to ten leopards (I mean a detachment of soldiers), who only get worse the better you treat them. But by their injustices I am becoming a better disciple' (Rom.5.1). This comparison makes it clear that Luke is simply giving a very definite cross-section of reality. There need be no disputing the fact that there were Roman centurions who were kind even towards prisoners, in the way that Julius was towards Paul, and who as members of the occupying forces supported members of the indigenous population like Cornelius, or that there were tribunes strictly concerned to observe the law, like the one who took Paul prisoner. But the extraordinarily positive way in which almost all the Roman soldiers are presented in Luke's account needs to be noted as a first characteristic of his perception of the Pax Romana.

In subsuming the military aspect under the sphere of law Luke accords with Roman self-understanding.[23] So it is no surprise that he puts particularly strong emphasis on the legality and security of the state, which guarantee personal protection – not as a demand but as a fact. That becomes clear above all in his account of the trial of Jesus and the arrest of Paul, and in the subsequent hearings before Roman bodies. Here the presuppositions for such an account were utterly unfavourable, for on the one hand he was presented by the Gospel of Mark with the execution of Jesus by the Romans as a fixed tradition, and on the other hand he knew, albeit not by a comparably stereotyped tradition, that Paul had been similarly executed by Romans.[24] The fate of the 'heroes' of both his books, the Gospel and Acts, thus demonstrates a specifically violent aspect of Roman rule. How does he cope with these facts? It is amazing that precisely at this point he can stress the legality of Roman rule.

According to Luke 23.1 'the whole company' of Jews assembled in the Sanhedrin dragged Jesus before the Roman procurator Pilate and accused him there. But Pilate immediately acknowledged his innocence (23.4). On learning that Jesus was a Galilean he immediately sent him to Herod Antipas, who similarly happened to be in Jerusalem (23.6f.), because Jesus fell within his competence. He would not have been obliged to do that in the case of a non-Roman,[25] but the instruments of Rome act in a remarkable correct way.[26] The writing of a scene which depicted Jesus being interrogated by Herod gave Luke the possibility of shifting to the hearing before Herod two themes which were rooted in the tradition about the hearing before Pilate. I have already observed that he does not mention the flogging and mocking of Jesus by Roman soldiers.[27] Instead of that he says that 'Herod and his soldiers treated him with contempt and mocked him'(23.11). Secondly, he makes Jesus maintain a stubborn silence before Herod (23.9), but not, as is the case in Mark 15.4f., before Pilate. As Herod cannot get anything out of Jesus he sends him back to Pilate (23.11). He in turn says to the accusers that he cannot confirm the charge, nor can Herod (23.13-15); and then yet a third time the representative of Rome stresses the innocence of Jesus (23.22). Here Pilate asks that Jesus should be chastised and then released (23.16,22), as was usual in the case of a warning.[28] So whereas the great men of the world, Pilate and Herod, become witnesses of the innocence of Jesus, the people and their leader press clamorously for his execution, 'and their voices prevailed' (23.18-23), so that Pilate finally 'delivered Jesus up to their will' (23.25).[29] As the procurator has brought out the innocence of Jesus, Luke cannot have Jesus condemned by him. Accordingly in Luke's Gospel the execution, too, is not carried out by Romans. I have already pointed out that in this account Roman soldiers appear only when Jesus has already been hanging on the cross for a long time. Those who carry Jesus away to the place of the hearing before Pilate and to the subsequent crucifixion are the shrieking people and their leaders.[30] The fact that according to Luke the Jews in fact executed Jesus is also evident from the way in which he frequently repeats this statement.[31] However, he does concede that they did it in ignorance.[32]

The same tendency to show the representatives of Rome as carrying out their office correctly and attaching all the blame to the Jews[33] appears in the account of the arrest of Paul and the hearings which follow. I have already commented on the arrest and the immediately subsequent events, in which soldiers play a role.[34] After he has been moved to Caesarea Paul continues to experience correct and considerate treatment. The procurator Felix immediately undertakes a short investigation (23.34f.) in which he enquires after Paul's home province[35] and says that there will be a hearing as soon as Paul's accusers arrive.[36] In this hearing (24.1-23), after speeches for the prosecution and the defence, Felix postpones a decision but at the same time orders that a detailed investigation shall be speeded up to ease Paul's imprisonment. 'What Luke seems to be saying is that the postponement of the affair is against the better judgment of the governor, who really should have released the prisoner.'[37] Luke cannot state this better judgment; he had to content himself with dropping a hint in that direction, as Paul was not in fact freed. So Luke was compelled to explain why on the change of procurators between Felix and Festus Paul still remained in prison. The reason he gave for that was that Felix hoped for a bribe from Paul and that he wanted to do a favour to the Jews (24.24-27).[38] The new procurator Festus immediately shows himself set on rapid action. Only three days after arriving in the residence at Caesarea he goes to Jerusalem, but remains there only eight to ten days and takes up proceedings in Paul's case the morning after his return (25.1-6). Without himself becoming aware of the fact, in Jerusalem he proves to be Paul's guardian, as he refuses the request of the Jews that the prisoner should be sent to Jerusalem, planning an ambush to kill him on the way (25.2-5). By taking up this theme, which was already used in 23.12-22, Luke is making a literary preparation for the rest of the story. He must explain why despite Paul's innocence and despite the correctness with which the Roman authorities act Paul is still not free. So after the accusation and defence have been presented, he makes Festus suggest that the hearing should be continued in Jerusalem (25.9), wanting to do the Jews a favour. Here he does not know to what danger he is thus exposing Paul. 'But first the reader knows of the Jewish attack';[39] and secondly,

Paul had been informed about the first such attempt (23.16) and could therefore guess what to expect in this case, too. So Luke has created a situation in which Paul is virtually compelled to appeal to Caesar (25.10f.). After Festus has allowed the appeal to Caesar (25.12), in the Lucan account he is relieved of the necessity of making a verdict. But that gives Luke the possibility of making Festus quite openly a witness to the innocence of Paul. He creates a great scene in which this is done (25.13-26.32). King Agrippa II and his sister Berenice come to Caesarea to welcome the new procurator. Festus tells the king about the case of the prisoner Paul. Here Luke does not let slip a chance of making Festus stress the high quality of Roman law:'It is not the custom of the Romans to give up anyone before the accused has met the accusers face to face; and had opportunity to make his defence concerning the charge laid against him' (25.16). As Agrippa wants to see Paul, Paul has a lofty forum for a defence speech. Even before the prisoner is introduced to the assembly Festus declares his innocence (25.25), and after the speech all those involved in the assembly agree even more (26.31), so that Agrippa finally observes: 'This man could have been set free if he had not appealed to Caesar' (26.32). Thus Luke has stylized as a tragic event the fact that Paul continues to remain in prison: Festus, who wanted to do the Jews a favour but did not suspect that carrying it out would provoke an attack on the life of Paul, which he had also unwittingly prevented shortly before, forced Paul to appeal; and this now compels him to leave Paul in prison and send him to Rome. It is only consistent that Luke should conclude Acts by announcing that Paul preached in Rome for two years 'without hindrance' (28.31). How could he have gone on also to tell of his execution, having earlier stressed to such a degree the legal correctness of the Roman authorities and their assertion of Paul's innocence?

When it comes to considering the legal aspect of the Pax Romana in Acts the account of Paul's arrest in Jerusalem and his subsequent imprisonment in Caesarea is certainly the most illuminating part. But this same tendency to depict the correctness of Roman organs and to eliminate or tone down their acts of violence is also evident elsewhere. In Acts 16.11-40 Luke tells of Paul's mission in Philippi. This city was a Roman colony and thus had a Roman constitution. Paul himself writes in I Thess. 2.2 that he had suffered and had been maltreated there; he adds that those to whom he is writing already know that. Luke also knew it. If he wanted to describe the beginning of the Pauline mission in Europe, which took place in Philippi, he evidently could not avoid also mentioning that Paul was flogged, arrested and expelled from there. But the way in which he does that is significant. Paul and Silas are dragged before the city authorities on the charge of causing unrest; they are said to be Jews and to have proclaimed customs unlawful to the Romans (v.19-21). As Luke presents it, the accusation is thus based on a false presupposition; those accused are later shown to be Romans and therefore also rehabilitated as Christians. When the mob turns against them, the authorities have them whipped and arrested (v.22f.). The next morning they send lictors with instructions to let the prisoners go (v.35). Only now does Paul appeal to his citizenship: 'They have beaten us publicly, uncondemned, men who are Roman citizens; and have thrown us into prison; and do they now cast us out secretly? No, let them come themselves and take us out' (v.37) It is no answer that an earlier appeal to the civic authorities will have 'hardly been possible in the tumult'.[40] Luke could not mention it earlier as he had to report the beating. But after the authorities have heard that the missionaries are Roman citizens they are terrified and immediately meet Paul's demands (v.38f.). Thus the fact that they were expelled, which was also there before Paul, is changed 'into a request to depart peacefully'.[41]

Luke can paint a 'picture of the ideal conduct of the organs of state'[42] in Acts 18.12-17. During the proconsulate of Gallio in Achaea 'the Jews' drag Paul before his judgment seat in Corinth and accuse him. But 'Gallio acts as Luke wishes Roman authorities to act towards Christians'.[43] He rejects the accusation as being incapable of substantiation under the law because it does not relate to any offence or crime.

According to Acts 19.23-40 two fellow-workers of Paul get into difficulties as a result of the uproar provoked by Demetrius the silversmith. No less a figure than the town clerk takes their side by confirming that there has neither been sacrilege nor blasphemy of the goddess Artemis (v.37). Moreover, he reminds Demetrius and his followers that orderly conduct is possible and necessary if they have a charge to make: 'The courts are open; and there are proconsuls; let them bring charges against one another. But if you seek anything further; it shall be settled in the regular assembly' (v.38f.). Luke has the town clerk say precisely what the prefect of Egypt is to say rather later in an edict on anti-Jewish demonstrations in Alexandria.[44] That shows once again how much he is stressing state law and state security as elements of the Pax Romana.

Luke can only succeed in presenting this peaceful image of soldiers who benevolently support the indigenous population and guarantee the existence of law and order and of Roman officials and local authorities who are strictly concerned with the law because he almost completely leaves aside the corruptness and the violent character of Roman rule. He only indicates this where it seems to be unavoidable. That is first the case in the goings-on in Philippi, but he deals with them in such a way that at the end the authorities in no way appear in a bad light. Elsewhere he does not indicate a single adverse circumstance in which Paul was involved by non-Jews. Rather, 'the representatives and authorities of the empire stand out for their impartial, indeed favourable, treatment of Paul'.[45] Luke has suppressed the fact that Paul deliberately avoids Ephesus on his last journey to Jerusalem and the events which led to that. However, this view, which transforms what actually happened, is seen less through the eyes of faith than through those of political calculation. Secondly, Luke criticizes the procurator Felix gently by mentioning his corruptibility, which has to be the reason why he continues to keep Paul in prison. Otherwise, however, the picture which Luke gives of Felix is positive. It stands out all the more clearly against the negative description of him by Tacitus who calls him 'a man with the soul of a slave who exercised kingly authority with cruelty and arbitrariness'.[46] According to Acts 24.2, however, the Jewish people was given 'much peace' through the concern of this procurator and he had introduced 'reforms'.[47] The fact that Paul was sent as a prisoner to Rome and not set free was historically solely the result of Roman actions; Luke, however, has turned this into a tragic complex of circumstances. In his account Romans often appear as those who save Paul's life; in reality Romans eventually executed him. The most amazing thing is the elimination of the violent expression of Roman rule in the report on the death of Jesus, which in view of the existing tradition can only be said to have been a violent one. Luke could not simply pass over the death of Jesus as he did that of Paul. As he wanted to write a Gospel he had to portray this death. In literary terms, the way which he relieves the Roman authorities of responsibility for the execution of Jesus and the carrying out of the crucifixion, using others instead, is a *tour de force*; in historical and theological terms, however, it is a monstrosity.

The shift in perspective in the perception of the Pax Romana which is evident in all this can be followed very closely in Luke's reformulation of the saying of Jesus handed down in Mark 10.42, about those (apparent) rulers who subject the peoples and oppress them violently. Luke 22.25 reads: 'The kings of the Gentiles exercise lordship over them; and those in authority over them are called benefactors.' The detachment expressed in the Marcan version which talks of those who 'are supposed to' or 'seem to' rule is removed; instead of that, the language has the style of an objective description. Even more important, however, the elements which stress the violence of the rule which is exercised are consistently deleted. In this way Luke has neutralized the saying. Hence it is quite improbable that the second part of it, about those in authority who are called 'benefactors', can be meant 'critically or ironically and sarcastically'.[48] The conclusion has to be that 'Luke has carefully corrected the Marcan vocabulary in order to put the *imperium* in a favourable light.'[49] Consequently the second part of the statement means, 'Those who rule in the secular sphere are not oppressors of the people but are in a position to bestow divine benefits on them.'[50] Thus the comparison between Mark 10.42 and Luke 22.25 can largely be summed up by saying that a perception 'from below', which is critically detached from the existing exercise of power and its violence, has become a neutral statement which points to another position.

(b) '...nor committed any crime against the emperor'

The positive description of Roman bodies by Luke is of course matched by the view that Christians should show loyalty towards them. But again the way in which Luke expresses this loyalty is significant. He 'contents himself with demonstrating that the Christian proclamation does not affect the empire. It is primarily proclamation of the resurrection, and that is a matter which does not affect Roman penal justice.'[51] Luke stresses that Jesus and the Christians are virtually harmless politically. That first emerges particularly clearly in the account of the hearing before Pilate against Jesus. No evangelist puts the accusation in such emphatic political terms as Luke. According to Luke 23.2 Jesus is accused as follows: 'We found this man perverting our nation, and forbidding us to give tribute to Caesar, and saying that he himself is Christ a King.' The accusation is given a political focus, however, only so that it may be decisively rejected as false. That then happens three times, each time through Pilate (23.4,14,22). The same thing is repeated in Acts. The Jewish orator Tertullus accuses Paul before the procurator Felix: 'This man is a pestilent fellow, an agitator among all the Jews throughout the world, and a ringleader of the sect of the Nazarenes' (24.5). According to 17.6f. the Jews of Thessalonica had spoken even more pointedly before the city authorities about Paul and Silas and their followers: 'These men who have turned the world upside down have come here also...; and they are all acting against the decrees of Caesar saying that there is another king, Jesus.' But the reader of Acts has been told several times, and indeed by Romans, that the emperor in no way need fear 'king Jesus' as a competitor, 'that Christianity has nothing to do with political Messianism, and is also immediately recognized in this its non-political character',[52] and therefore that this is a matter of religious questions, not of politics. This is said by the proconsul Gallio in Corinth (18.14f.); it is said by the Roman tribune immediately after

Paul's arrest when he notes that his prisoner is not the 'Egyptian' agitator he supposes him to be (21.37-40).[53] It is said by the tribune in his letter to the procurator Felix that the case concerns 'questions' about Jewish law but that there is no accusation worthy of death (23.29). The procurator Festus talks in precisely this way to King Agrippa (25.18f.) and finally also to all the high society whom Paul is allowed to address in the procurator's residence in Caesarea (26.31). He denies having stirred up a crowd (24.12): 'Neither against the law of the Jews nor against the temple, nor against Caesar have I offended at all' (25.8). Instead of this, in the hearing before the Sanhedrin arranged by the Roman tribune he asserts that he is being judged 'for the hope of the resurrection of the dead' (23.6; 24.21).

So whereas Luke on the one hand continually stresses that the church does not endanger the peace and security of the state,[54] on the other he depicts 'the unbelieving part of Judaism as politically rebellious'.[55] In the farewell speech to the presbyters at Ephesus he makes Paul remark sweepingly in this respect that the tears and trials which he has had to endure are based on 'accusations of the Jews' (20.19).[56]

Even before the final arrest in Jerusalem Luke has Paul constantly in difficulties as a result of Jewish activists: the Jews of Damascus resolve to murder Paul and make preparations to do so (9.23f.). Hellenistic Jews in Jerusalem attempt to murder Paul (9.29). In Pisidian Antioch Jews stir up influential women sympathizers and the leaders of the city so that Paul and Barnabas are driven out (13.50). The Jews in Iconium cause a stir and embitter the Gentiles against the Christians there, so that the Gentiles and Jews along with the city authorities take joint action against the missionaries to maltreat them and stone them (14.2,5). The Jews from Antioch and Iconium address the crowd in Lystra and this time actually manage to have Paul stoned (14.19). The Jews in Thessalonica get the city in an uproar in order to mobilize it against the missionaries (17.5). The Jews from Thessalonica stir up the crowd in Beroea against Paul (17.13). The Jews in Corinth drag Paul before the seat of the consul (18.12). Jews in Greece plan an attack on Paul (20.3). In this way Luke gives the impression 'that it is the Jews who are constantly causing public disturbances. It is they who need to be watched by the authorities, not the Christians.'[57]

It cannot be disputed that there is also a particular historical experience behind this account. Paul himself reports the sufferings he has experienced at the hands of his fellow Jews in a similar way,[58] but the reality may have been rather more varied than Luke suggests. We can easily understand how the Christian mission which appeared in the synagogues of the diaspora would lead to disputes there. That would be all the more likely to happen if it were particularly successful among the godfearers, who were more or less firm members of the synagogue, acknowledged its ethical monotheism and observed certain ritual rules, but were not prepared to become full members of the Jewish community by accepting circumcision.[59] Godfearers consisted above all of those in a better social position, for whom the demand for circumcision represented too great a barrier if they wanted to retain their social status.[60] The Christian mission did away with this barrier. By winning over the godfearers, however, it drew well-to-do and influential sympathizers away from the synagogue. It is all too understandable how that inevitably led to disputes. Probably the disturbances among the Jews of Rome which led to an expulsion of Jews from the city by an edict of Claudius[61] was caused by Christian preaching. In the period after the putting down of the Jewish revolt of 66-70 by Rome the synagogues must have had an added interest in avoiding such disturbances. So we can see how Jews would want to dissociate themselves from Christian missionaries and occasionally even denounce them to the authorities as troublemakers before they had official attention drawn to themselves by unrest. Luke for his part now turns the tables on the Jews: they did not keep to the religious questions which were the issue but denounced the Christian mission as political, thereby provoking unrest. However, by its schematic generalization this accusation becomes a distortion of reality. At two places what Luke says can be checked by Paul's own statements, and in each case it proves false. In Damascus Paul was not persecuted by Jews (thus Acts 9.23f.) but by the tetrarch of Aretas (thus II Cor.11.32f.).[62] Contrary to Acts 17.5 the persecutors in Thessalonica were not Jews but, according to I Thess.2.14, the fellow countrymen of the Christians there, who were explicitly different from Jews. Therefore we need to be sceptical about what Luke says elsewhere.

While Luke everywhere stresses the unpolitical character of the Christian proclamation and thus at the same time the natural loyalty of Christians to Rome, according to him this loyalty is not unconditional but has a limit. But again it is very significant that in his extensive work he never demonstrates this limit in connection with Roman bodies, but only with Jewish authorites. Thus Jesus is silent before Herod but not before Pilate.[63] Thus Luke says of the apostles in Jerusalem that after their flogging before the Sanhedrin they rejoiced 'that they were counted worthy to suffer dishonour for the name (viz. of Jesus)' (Acts 5.40f.); where Luke cannot avoid speaking of a flogging of Paul by Roman authorities in connection with his activity in Philippi he has him appeal to his Roman citizenship and demand satisfaction (Acts 16.37f.) As 'the basic Christian attitude in cases of conflict',[64] which is certainly also meant to apply towards Romans, he takes an 'often repeated commonplace'[65] from the time of Plato which 'Peter and the apostles' state to the Sanhedrin: 'We must obey God rather than men' (Acts 5.29).[66]

(c) 'I was born a Roman...'

It is thus characteristic of Luke's perception of the Pax Romana that he should give a positive account of life controlled by Rome and in so doing stress that it is not affected by Christian proclamation. What are the conditions for this perspective? From what standpoint does it come about?

It is significant that each of Luke's two volumes has a preface and dedication.[67] This means that they lay claim to be literature.[68] The address 'most excellent Theophilus' characterizes the recipient of the dedication as a person in a high position.[69] The function of the dedication is to ensure that the person whom it honours sees to the public circulation of the work.[70] It follows from this that Luke 'intended his work for a wider public'.[71] Beyond the church he is addressing 'sympathizers and interested non-Christians'.[72] He therefore seeks – as this course implies – an educated public, which in antiquity was also socially privileged. It is in keeping with this that he has in view as an audience above all well-to-do Christians in groups within the church.[73] In the account in Acts, that is also reflected in his stresses on the way in which prominent people in high positions become members of the church. In 17.4,12 he asserts summarily that 'not a few' well-to-do women were won over by Paul and Silas in Thessalonica and Beroea. For Philippi, Lydia (16.14), who is mentioned by name, might be included in this group because she is a dealer in purple.[74] Philip baptizes a senior official of the Queen of Ethiopia (8.27,38). Through Paul, Dionysius the Areopagite in Athens comes to believe (17.34),[75] and so indeed does the Roman proconsul of Cyprus, Sergius Paulus (13.12). Luke will have known why he notes this sensation so drily and does not develop it further. As a historical fact the conversion of a proconsul would have had quite a different influence in forming tradition. For Luke the apologetic aim which he can thus already pursue 'at the beginning of the Pauline mission' is an important one.[76] The fact that he can actually conceive of the conversion of a Roman proconsul is even more amazing than the story he tells about the centurion Cornelius.[77] He is more restrained when it comes to the procurator Felix and King Agrippa. But at any rate the one has a 'rather accurate' knowledge of Christianity and is further instructed by Paul (24.22,24) and the other exclaims, 'You almost persuade me to be a Christian' (26.28).[78]

The almost matter-of-course way in which according to 9.15 Luke shows Paul among the great of the world belongs in the same context.[79] I have just mentioned the procurator Felix, the proconsul Sergius Paulus and King Agrippa. Paul makes a great entrance before Agrippa and his sister Berenice, with all the court, the procurator Festus and his tribunes and the most prominent men of the city of Caesarea (25.23).[80] He is friendly with Asiarchs[81] in Ephesus; when they believe him to be in danger, these great men, who in all probability will also have had obligations in the state cult, have nothing more urgent to do than to warn the Christian missionary (19.31)![82]

According to Luke, this missionary, shown respect and consideration by the highest representatives of society, also has a right to be in the great world in which he can move in so sovereign a way. He is not only a citizen of his home town of Tarsus (21.39) but also one of Rome (16.37f.; 22.25-29; 23.27). What Paul actually says in his letters does not exclude the possibility that he did in fact have the Roman citizenship he claimed, but can hardly make it probable. If Paul really was a Roman citizen, then he himself attached no weight to the fact.[83] But that is what the Lucan Paul does emphatically. He proudly replies to the tribune who asks him about his citizenship and who himself has purchased it for a good deal of money: 'I was born a Roman' (22.28). The way in which Luke depicts Paul as a Roman citizen who is protected by this law makes us ask whether – however things may have been with Paul in this respect – Luke himself might not have had this privilege. Luke could evidently be a Roman citizen and a Christian at the same time. All the points cited in this section so far at least indicate that the author of the Gospel and Acts had a high social status.[84] His perspective on the great world is also attested by the notes with which he inserts the events he is describing into world history,[85] and by his claim about the passion and resurrection of the Messiah Jesus and the beginnings of the church: 'This was not done in a corner' (26.26).[86]

According to Ernst Haenchen it was true of ancient historiography that: 'What is significant for world history demanded as its framework high society, the world of the high and mighty.'[87] However, the whole of primitive Christianity was permeated by the decisive significance for the whole world of Jesus and the proclamation related to his fate; the only question was to whom this was to be made clear and by what means. By 'seeking to achieve the heights of ancient historiography',[88] Luke has to adapt to the norms of the great world from which he is not too far removed as a result of his social status. So he comes to occupy a standpoint which makes him consider reality more from a perspective 'from above'. This quite evidently leads him to suppress violence which originated from the centre and to see only the 'sunny side' of the reality of Rome.[89] Thus the dominating power is left to the field which it controls, in that conflicts are as far as possible ruled out in principle by the constantly repeated declaration that Christianity has no say there. That is the price which Luke has to pay for his ticket to the great world.

However, this price is even higher, in so far as the reality perceived has a feedback effect on the picture of the community which Luke puts forward. That can be seen most clearly by the reformulation of Mark 10.43f. which he presents in 22.26.[90] In the previous verse he had neutralized those sayings in his source which were critical of authority by 'objectively' stating that the kings of the Gentiles rule over them and those in authority are called benefactors. The transition which then follows is already illuminating. While according to the Marcan text Jesus says, 'But it is not so among you', in other words envisages a different structure for his disciples, Luke personalizes the remark by addressing it to the disciples, 'But not so with you!'[91] Accordingly he is not concerned to do away with conditions of rule but with 'the right use of authority and power in the community'.[92] 'Rather let the greatest among you become the youngest, and the leader as one who serves.' The existence of 'great' and 'leading' figures in the community is here taken for granted and recognized; it is no longer put in question. All that matters is *how* the great figures perform their task of leadership.[93] So a structural question[94] has been made a mere 'matter of style'.[95]

(d) 'Peace in heaven...'

But does not the Gospel of Luke also contain statements which are explicitly critical of authority? One might recall Mary's Magnificat, in which God is praised as the one who 'casts down the mighty from his seat and exalts the humble' (1.52). In 2.11 it is the child in the manger and not the emperor Augustus who is spoken of as Saviour and Lord; and again it is of the child and not the emperor that in 2.14 the whole heavenly host sings, 'Glory to God in the highest, and on earth peace among men with whom he is pleased.' But the angel's song of praise has a clear parallel within the Gospel of Luke. So it must not be seen in isolation, but must be understood alongside that passage. The parallel is the praise of the disciples with which they escort Jesus as he enters Jerusalem: 'Blessed is the King who comes in the name of the Lord! Peace in heaven and glory in the highest' (19.38). Here, too, Luke has characteristically altered his source.[96] As the Markan narrative of the entry of Jesus into Jerusalem shows, the hope for the messianic kingdom was bound up with this. In Mark the crowd hails Jesus as he enters: 'Hosanna! Blessed is he who comes in the name of the Lord! Blessed is the kingdom of our father David that is coming! Hosanna in the highest!' Luke has deleted the cry of Hosanna which expresses messianic hope[97] along with the mention of the kingdom of David. It is not the crowd that praises Jesus as he enters but his disciples.[98] For Luke, too, Jesus is king and he even explicitly adds this designation. But the kingdom of Jesus is expressed for the moment only in the heavenly world: 'Peace in heaven and glory in the highest.' Whereas in Mark the second cry of Hosanna, 'Hosanna in the Highest', also includes the world above,[99] in Luke the sole accent is on it. For him the entry of Jesus into Jerusalem is the beginning of a heavenly enthronement which has nothing to do with a present manifestation of the kingdom of God.[100] Because Jesus, we are told in a redactional note in 19.11, 'was near to Jerusalem, and because they supposed that the kingdom of God was to appear immmediately', he told the parable of the talents to dismiss this view. The journey to Jerusalem, which right at the beginning, in 9.51, had been said to be motivated by the fact that the time of his 'being received up', namely ascension, had come, served towards the heavenly enthronement of Jesus. After that Luke also revised the parable of the talents (19.12-17). The ascension indeed enthrones Jesus as king, but he only enters upon his rule on earth at his return, at the parousia. It is not a matter of setting up a kingdom but of testimony to the king in heaven.[101] This framework marks out the period of the earthly Jesus in a special way: the kingdom appears in his person. 'Jesus' call to discipleship is a call to the present kingdom which – as we can carefully put it – is present with Jeus on earth.'[102] But as he is no longer dwelling on earth but is enthroned in heaven, where 'salvation is now present and gained',[103] Luke depicts 'the time of the activity of Jesus first as a time of anticipatory description... From the limited period of the activity of Jesus the church is to be given an idea of what believers may hope for from the future rule of God.'[104] But that means that despite all the continuity and analogy[105] the time of the church is fundamentally different from the time of Jesus. At one point Luke makes that vividly clear by making Jesus contradict an instruction given to the disciples. According to 22.35 he asks them, 'When I sent you out with no purse or bag or sandals, did you lack anything?' The wording here refers directly to 10.4, the sending out of the seventy-two, the content to 9.3, the sending out of the twelve. After the disciples say 'No' to his question Jesus continues in v.36: 'But now, let him who has a purse take it, and likewise a bag. And let him who has no sword sell his mantle and buy one.' The reason he gives for these demands in v.37 is that his end is near.[106] So they relate to the time after the passion of Jesus. Then, in the time of the church, conditions will obviously be different from what they used to be. Now the disciples have to provide for themselves to the point of self-defence, though according to v.38 this is modest.[107] The distinction between the times allows Luke to collect 'various primitive Christian traditions'. So it comes about that 'his account in detail does not always coincide with the general drift'.[108]

The other perception of the Pax Romana by Luke can be explained by the social position which he occupies. He certainly also had other experiences which made him treasure the Roman peace. According to Paul Walaskay, Luke affirms 'that the positive advantages of the empire by far outweigh the occasional pressure from an errant ruler'.[109] An incidental feature in the presentation of the Gospel also indicates other experiences. Whereas according to Mark and Matthew Jesus occasionally withdraws in order to escape the grasp of the powerful,[110] in Luke he always withdraws to pray.[111]

Secondly, the positive description of aspects of the Pax Romana by Luke becomes understandable in terms of the readers he has in view and his purpose in addressing them. Whereas according to Hans Conzelmann the substance of Luke's political apologetic is that he 'appeals to the insight of the state by demonstrating that the Christian proclamation does not affect the empire',[112] Paul Walaskay by contrast argues that Luke offers the early church an *apologia pro imperio*:[113] he opposes an anti-Roman attitude 'in order to help the church to survive in a given political order'.[114] If we see that he is looking for readers in the church and beyond,[115] we may not understand these as alternatives.

But whatever positive experiences and whatever good intentions Luke may have had, the reproduction of the reality of the Pax Romana which he offers in the Gospel and in Acts is possible only by leaving out the violence that is practised in it. So violence is not interrupted, but painted over.[116]

4. 'Peace and concord' – Parallels between the church and the empire in Clement of Rome

In investigating the way in which the Pax Romana was seen in earliest Christianity we must consider a work which is not in the New Testament canon but is one of the group of 'Apostolic Fathers',[1] the so-called First Letter of Clement. This work, written in Rome, not only mentions the peace which emanates from this city, but also shows itself to be largely shaped by it. At the beginning the writer is said to be 'the church of God, living in exile in Rome', and it is addressed to 'the church of God, exiled in Corinth'. The work, which also has 'the distinguishing marks of a real letter' elsewhere,[2] is thus meant to be composed by the Roman community as a whole; accordingly the sender always speaks in the first person plural. However, the language and style of the letter and its content show such uniformity that we must assume it to have been written by an individual. The superscriptions and subscriptions to the manuscript give his name as Clement. About 170 Bishop Dionysius of Corinth mentions in a letter to Bishop Soter of Rome not only a letter which he has recently received from there but also 'the letter which Clement formerly sent us'.[3] About ten years later Hegesippus mentions 'the letter of Clement to the Corinthians'.[4] Above all, the evidence of Dionysius from Corinth, the community to which the letter was sent, makes it probable that the individual who must have composed the letter from Rome bore the name Clement. That may probably be connected with the information in the Shepherd of Hermas (Vis.II, 43) according to which a Clement was entrusted with corresponding from the Roman community abroad. It seems likely that he is to be regarded as the author of the letter to the Corinthians.[5]

As to the time of composition, Eusebius cites Hegesippus as evidence that during the reign of the emperor Domitian (81-96) there had been a revolt in the Corinthian community, and he associates the letter with this. The remark in 1.1 in which the Roman community explains its late intervention in the conflict in Corinth with a reference to misfortunes which have suddenly come upon it is often identified with the 'persecution under Domitian' at the end of his reign, which is often mentioned by later church authors.[6] However, the sources which are closer to this time provide no evidence of such a persecution. Still, local persecutions were always possible, also, of course, under Domitian.[7] Further considerations, though, make the time immediately after the death of Domitian a probable period for the composition of I Clement. In chapters 5 and 6 the author regards the Neronian persecution in Rome as an event which already lies some time in the past.[8] On the other hand, however, the martyrdoms of Peter and Paul are, according to 5.1, still regarded as 'examples of our generation'. If we date I Clement to the time following the death of Domitian this extensive work appears in a wider context, since that period – especially in Rome – marked the beginning of considerable literary productivity.[9] This letter would thus have been written at the same time as the writings of Luke and Revelation.

(a) 'If we consider the soldiers in the service of our leader...'

Towards the end of his letter Clement has a long prayer, in the formulation of which he may be following the liturgical usage of the Roman community.[10] In this prayer there is also a petition for peace: 'Give us and all who live on the earth concord and peace' (60.4). If this is peace for all the inhabitants of the earth, then it is political peace;

and for the time of Clement that must mean the peace which actually exists, the Pax Romana. That is stressed by the fact that in addition to peace the petition also mentions concord. 'Peace and concord' is typical political terminology.[11] So when Clement prays here for concord and peace he is praying God to sustain the Pax Romana. That is stressed by the prayer in 61.1 for the 'leaders and rulers' who exercise imperial power: 'Grant them health, peace, concord and stability'. Here again the terms 'peace' and 'concord' are used; they cannot refer to the personal well-being of the emperor and his senior officials but must refer to the security of the Roman empire which these individuals represent, and peace and order in it. The same goes for the term 'stability' which appears at the end. In this context the 'health' mentioned in the first place can similarly only be understood in political terms, in that the health of the ruler is the necessary presupposition for the general well-being of the kingdom. So this intercession proves to be a precise Christian parallel to the public vows for the well-being of the emperor.[12] Clement is concerned for the peaceful and secure existence of the Roman empire.

The extraordinaily positive view of existing political reality which emerges here also appears in the way in which God and the rulers are put in parallel. In 60.2 the prayer runs: 'Guide our steps so that we walk with holy hearts and do what is good and pleasing to you and to your rulers.' The natural way in which what is well-pleasing to rulers runs parallel to what is well-pleasing to God is very striking in comparison with the primitive Christian terminology which is used elsewhere.[13] This parallelism occurs again only a little later, in 60.4: 'Grant that we may be obedient to your almighty and glorious name, and to our rulers and governors on earth.' Obedience to God and obedience to rulers correspond. That means, however, that the latter is the specific form of the former in the political sphere.[14] It should also be noted that the petition for obedience directly follows the petition for 'concord and peace'. The connection between the two petitions is thus to be understood as an indication that peace is gained by being obedient to rulers. Thus at this point the prayer clearly reflects the structure of the Pax Romana as subjection to Roman authority.

Clement is a long way from questioning the rule of Rome in any way. On the contrary, the parallel between God and the ruler is an indication that he gives theological legitimation to this rule. That even becomes explicit in 61.1: 'You, Master, gave them (viz. our rulers and leaders) imperial power through your majestic and indescribable might, so that we, recognizing it was you who gave them the glory and honour, might submit to them, and in no way oppose your will.' That goes beyond what Paul says in Romans 13. The exalted and indescribable power of God has so to speak its extended arm in the power, glory and honour of the emperor and his senior officials. Therefore obedience to them is synonymous with obedience to God, and disobedience would be a violation of the divine will.[15] Clement emphatically stresses that anyone who obeys the rulers is in no way opposed to the will of God.[16] So it is not surprising that he regards Roman rule as a good thing; it is virtually a gift of God. Immediately after the petition for the ruler in 61.3 there is praise of God as the one 'who alone is able to do this and still better things for us'.

However, we see Clement dissociating himself from the prevalent ideology when he speaks of rulers and leaders as 'sons of men', whereas the emperor of the time is regarded as the 'son of the deified' (*divi filius*).[17] 61.2 reads: 'For it is you, Master, the heavenly King of Eternity, who give the sons of men glory and honour and authority over the earth's people.' Taken by itself, this general statement that God gives the sons of men power to rule could even be understood as a criticism of the rule of particular individuals. But the context in which it stands leaves no doubt that Clement understands this *a priori* in the context of existing rule. Nor can one infer a critical attitude towards it on his part from the conclusion of 61.1. There the petition for 'health, peace, concord and stability' for the rulers and leaders is concluded with the statement 'that they may administer the authority you have given them without blemish'. It had become clear that the petition for the rulers related to their person only as it served the empire, and that substantially the prayer was for the preservation of the empire. Not the least sign of this is the blameless way in which they exercise their rule.[18] The orientation on existing power is unmistakable. Peace is defined in terms of the existing order. Here Clement shows himself to be a theological apologist for the Pax Romana.

The way in which he speaks of Roman soldiers also shows that he values the order of peace in his time in a positive way. In 37.2-4 he writes: 'Let us note with what discipline, readiness, and obedience those who serve under our generals carry out orders. Not everyone is a legate or a tribune or a centurion or a quinquagenarian and so on, but each in his own rank carries out the orders of the emperor and of the generals. The great cannot exist without the small, neither can the small exist without the great. All are linked together; and this has an advantage.' Clement does not have the least problem here; he speaks quite openly, indeed in wonderment, not of soldiers generally, but of Roman soldiers. In his wonderment, which stresses the military as an obedient instrument of political leadership and above all emphasizes the hierarchical order within the army, he agrees completely with Aelius Aristides, who says: 'If one wanted to begin with the one person who controls all and watches over all, over provinces, cities, armies, even over the generals, and to end with the one who has command of four or two men – I have left aside all the grades in between – how should that not surpass any human order?'[19] By mentioning *quinquagenarii* (leaders of groups of fifty) Clement betrays the fact that he does not have a very accurate knowledge of the Roman army as it is, since there was no such rank. He may have taken over the term from the Greek Bible with which he was familiar.[20] His detachment from the army as it was – nor does he have any experience of battle – combined with his wonderment at it suggests that he saw it as a beneficial power of order.

(b) 'For love of the fatherland...'

The unconditionally positive view of the Pax Romana and the Roman legions as its prime guarantors which we find in Clement raises questions about his position. He writes on behalf of the Roman community and therefore lives in Rome. But Clement not only lives in Rome but is a Roman who can identify with Rome's superiority. That is evident from the assurance with which he speaks of those who rule, the emperor and his senior officials, as '*our* rulers and leaders' (60.4)[21] and of the soldiers as being in the service of '*our* rulers'.[22] Even if in the initial greetings at the beginning of his letter he describes the Christian community in Rome as being in exile, 'he feels completely at home in Rome'.[23] He is 'loyal to the bottom of his heart',[24] that is, out of inner conviction rather than tactical considerations. His attitude to the state is also illuminated by his short account of the story of Judith (55.4f.), who during a siege gains entry into the camp of the enemies of Israel by a stratagem and kills the general Holophernes.[25] According to the Jewish book her motive is the glory of God, to whose covenant fidelity she appeals; according to Clement she does it 'for love of the fatherland and her besieged people'. Could he put it like that if he himself did not feel love for his fatherland Rome?

If in Rome his position is at the centre of the then world, it should also be pointed out that in Rome he was not a member of the lower classes; all the indications point, rather, to a higher social status. The prime evidence for that is his extensive knowlege and his capacity for expressing himself in writing. Secondly, it is clear that he is writing from the perspective of the rich when in 38.2 he says: 'The rich must provide for the poor; the poor must thank God for giving him someone to meet his needs.' The only active person here is the rich man, whereas the poor man is considered solely as someone who reacts to his beneficence.

Clement also writes in 55.2 from the perspective of the free man and in 1.3; 3.3 and 21.6 from that of the older man;[26] in 34.1 he considers the worker from the perspective of the employer: 'The good labourer accepts the bread he has earned with his head held high; the lax and negligent workman cannot look his employer in the face.' Finally, his name shows that he is a male; that he consistently thinks in patriarchalist terms is evident from 1.3 and 21.6f., according to which wives are to be subordinate to their husbands, to look after the house, and be respectful and silent in the community.[27]

So in I Clement we are listening to a Roman in a good position; in that position he evidently experienced the Pax Romana as a good thing. So in his work existing reality was there as a 'whole world'.

(c) 'Who thinks of everything with benevolence'

Clement of Rome, who regards Roman rule as a good thing and is therefore interested in the preservation of the empire, has no questions about the reality which he encounters and as he experiences it. The oppressive prayer 'How long, Lord?', which refuses to be content with things as they are and which therefore appeals to the promise of God, is deeply alien to him. That is immediately clear from the way in which Clement uses the book of Job, from which he quotes quite often. In the speeches of Job this book is full of complaints about a painful reality, and even more it is directed against a way of thinking articulated in the speeches of the friends, according to whom meaning and justification lies in what is the case in any situation.[28] Thus Job's friends infer from his sufferings that he has transgressed, whereas Job uses his uprightness as a basis for challenging his fate so that 'the world order itself becomes questionable to him'.[29]

Now it is significant that Clement does not even echo Job's questions and complaints. From Job's speech in 26.3 he quotes an expression of trust at the prospect of the resurrection,[30] and in 17.3f he alters a complaint about human destiny into a self-accusation by Job about his own sinfulness,[31] by which he again restores 'order'. In 20.7 he cites a quotation from the speeches of God which in context express the way in which chaos is limited by the divine,[32] but for Clement stress the order of the world. Above all, however, Clement cites extensive passages from the speeches of Job's friends,[33] which forbid questioning because everything has its order against which men may not rebel. What they offer is an 'accumulation of right solutions... the only problem of which is that they are right solutions which do not work out'.[34] Clement is evidently as little affected by suffering in the world and suffering for the world as are Job's friends. He indicates 'from what dark grave he who fashioned and created us brought us into his world' (38.3).[35]

In 20.1-10 Clement describes how the whole cosmos is 'in order' in an almost hymnic way. He makes his reader look at the heavens, at day and night, sun, moon and stars, at the earth and the underworld, the sea, the ocean and the worlds beyond, at the seasons, winds and springs, indeed at the smallest animals. Everywhere a harmonious regularity prevails under the Father and Creator.[36] All these are God's 'magnificent and excellent gifts of peace and kindness' (19.2); 'All those things the great Creator and Master of the universe ordained to exist in peace and concord' (20.11).[37] What Clement does not note in considering this creation – any more than he does when considering the Roman army – are war and conflicts. He is concerned solely with the ordering of cosmic and natural processes which he then transfers to the sphere of society and the church. The frequent occurrence of the terms peace and concord already indicate his interest in the latter.[38] Conversely, however, interest in social harmony in an order gradated by functions allows Clement to see only the parallel structures in the cosmos and nature. Thus peace is defined as order and harmony on the basis of divine power. Can we not see this as the Pax Romana under its imperial ruler?

It naturally follows from this picture of a comprehensive, well-ordered world as presented by Clement that one has to fit oneself into these pre-existing structures. The benefaction of cosmic order calls for behaviour to match (21.1), above all subordination to those who have produced the order of the world and continue to guarantee its ongoing existence: God and the rulers. In 21.6-8 Clement describes the behaviour required, in more detail, as revering the Lord Jesus, having reverent fear for 'our rulers', respecting the old, bringing up the young in the fear of God, showing women what is good, and teaching children humility. He had already described what was good the state of the Corinthian community in a very similar way, in 1.3.[39] Thus it corresponds to a world in which 'most things are in order'.[40]

However, there are also irritations in this 'whole world'; there are persecutions instigated by the rulers and directed against Christians. How does Clement cope with them? He describes the persecutions at proportionate length in 5.1-6.2. That the confession of Christians can lead to death is shown there by Peter (5.4) and Paul (5.5). In addition, Clement mentions a great mass of unnamed men and women who had to share their fate. So here he clearly has the Neronian persecution in view. But the persecutions are not even hinted at anywhere.[41]

So the first thing to note when one considers how Clement copes with the experience of the persecutions is that he keeps quiet about the persecutors. Secondly, he seems to play down the persecutions as misfortunes. That follows from 1.1, where he excuses the tardiness of his letter by mentioning 'the sudden and successive misfortunes and accidents we have encountered'.[42] The most probable explanation of this is that he is referring to persecutions survived by the Roman community. The terms that he uses both describe an event that has taken place and characterize it above all as an accident.[43] This corresponds to the request in 60.3: 'Save us from those who hate us without good reason.' As in Diognetus 5.17[44] the persecution rests on a misunderstanding.[45]

Finally and above all Clement cites the Christians' own misdemeanour as the cause of persecutions. In 5.2 he sums it up as follows: 'By reason of rivalry and envy the greatest and most righteous pillars were persecuted, and battled to the death.' He goes on to mention Peter and Paul in particular, each time stressing clearly that their martyrdom was 'by reason of wicked jealousy' and 'by reason of rivalry and contention' (5.4,5). He also twice stresses that the other men and women who were persecuted suffered torture and death 'by reason of rivalry' (6.1). So in 3.2 also, alongside events within the community he may also have persecutions in mind when he describes the point at which the vigorous growth of the Corinthian community became negative by saying: 'From this there arose rivalry and envy, strife and sedition, persecution and anarchy, war and captivity.' With all this Clement is suggesting that the persecutions are caused by misbehaviour in the community.[46] Unlike Paul he does not understand this misbehaviour as an expression of Christian existence; on the contrary, he sees it as unnecessary disruption. At any rate it cannot disturb his clear picture of reality.

(d) *'To bow the neck and adopt the attitude of obedience'*

So far I have attempted to bring out the perception of the Pax Romana expressed in I Clement and describe the context which is evident from it and its political attitude. However, the primary intention of the letter is certainly not political;[47] it is concerned with the church. Its occasion emerges clearly from two passages. In 44.6 Clement writes in respect of presbyters who have become bishops: 'But you, we see, have removed a number of people, despite their good conduct, from a ministry they have fulfilled with honour and integrity.' He assesses this in 47.6 with the words: 'It is disgraceful, exceeding disgraceful, and unworthy of your Christian upbringing to have it reported that because of one or two individuals the solid and ancient Corinthian church is in revolt against its presbyters.' So what has happened in Corinth is that at the prompting of a few people – we may infer from 3.3 that these were young people – the community has deposed some of its own presbyters.[48] The Roman community intervenes in this conflict with Clement's letter. In so doing it is pursuing the aim of having the deposed presbyters reinstated, and those who prompted the deposition going voluntary into exile. This, then, is a conflict in the community with an aim related to the community. It is particularly important for understanding the letter to note that the very perception of this conflict by Clement, not to mention the solution he suggests, are determined completely by this political attitude.

The mere description of the situation in Corinth by Clement, which at the same time contains his assessment, is a precise analogy to the political sphere and is derived from that. Clement describes what happened in Corinth, the deposition of some presbyters by the community, as 'rebellion', as 'revolution'. As early as 1.1 he speaks of 'abominable and unholy rebellion'.[49] According to 2.6 rebellion is an abomination.[50] Thus Clement uses political terminology to describe events in Corinth and also shares the official assessment of them. Only someone who regards Roman rule as a good thing and who therefore must regard revolt against it as a bad thing can act in this way.[51] In accordance with the idea that the benefits of the Pax Romana are being destroyed by rebellions, in 14.2 he points out that those in the community 'who aim at dispute and rebellions' thus want to bring about alienation 'from the good state', from the right ordering of the *status quo*,[52] which is in accord with the will of God.[53]

Therefore 'the enemies' – questions are specifically asked about them in 36.6 – are, 'those who are wicked and resist his will'.[54] There are 'those who turn away', as Clement puts in connection with the story of the deliverance of Lot from Sodom in 11.1f. Here it is very illuminating to see how the sin of Lot's wife, without any support from the biblical text, is said to be that she had a difference of opinion with her husband and did not agree with him. That this interpretation leads to imperialist and patriarchalist thought is clear, and is further stressed by the use of the term 'concord'.[55] Anyone who does not toe the line incurs punishment and chastisement. Rome has no room for non-conformists.

If the situation is to be described in this way, then in positive terms the solution must be a restoration of the *status quo ante*,[56] as is also the case with a disruption of the Pax Romana. Thus the general Cerialis calls on the Treveri and Lingones, after their revolt has been put down, to devote themselves heart and soul to 'peace and the capital'. Significantly, what he says is also bound up with a warning against stubbornness and an admonition to obedience.[57] Similarly, Clement asks his readers 'to return to the goal of peace which was handed down to us from the beginning' (19.2). So if peace is the opposite to rebellion,[58] it is clear that its content is to be defined in terms of the existing order, and that the existing circumstances are said to be peace. Therefore according to Clement, in Corinth only those piously keep the peace who want to restores the *status quo ante*, whereas he dismisses as hypocritical the concern of others for peace of of which he must obviously take note (15.1).[59] Since in this way he becomes clear about the meaning of peace, he can continually admonish his readers to peace, indeed he virtually describes his whole work as a 'plea... for peace and concord' (63.2).[60] Thus he takes up the phrase 'peace and concord', with which he had described the Pax Romana in 60.4 and which obscures the fine colouring of its tendency to impose subjection, and uses it as a description of his intended aim for Corinth. He does that once again, explicitly, at the end of his letter, in 65.1, when he describes the peace and concord in Corinth as desired and longed for.[61] According to 54.2 he means by it specifically 'keeping peace with the presbyters who have been appointed', and that is then spelt out clearly – as in the case of the Pax Romana, in 57.1, for those 'who began the revolt': 'Be subject to the presbyters.'[62]

So it can be shown that both Clement's perception of the conflict in Corinth and the aim that he seeks to achieve with his letter are indissolubly bound up with his Roman political perspective. That is equally true of the method of solving the conflict which he adopts, which proves to be dependent on the Roman model of lordship. Assumptions about the unasked-for intervention of the Roman community in Corinth should also be on similar lines. Theoretically, any other community could have done this. But is it a coincidence that the Roman community is the one that acts? Does it not model itself directly on the political central power which at a time of unrest in a province or an allied kingdom intervenes to restore order? It does not (yet) have the powers of an empire; it has to content itself with an admonitory letter, brought by a three-man delegation (65.1). Here, too, the political model could have had an effect on the delegation.[63]

Clement now sees the solution of the conflict in Corinth above all as being that those who caused the deposition of the presbyters, people who in his eyes are authors of a rebellion and disturbers of the peace, should voluntarily go into exile. In the political sphere rebellion could be punished with exile as well as death.[64] Of course for Clement there is no possibility of a death sentence.[65] He cannot impose exile, but he can suggest it skilfully and urgently: 'Who of your number is noble, large-hearted and full of love? Let him say: If it is my fault that revolt, strife and schism have arisen, I will leave, I will go away wherever you wish, and do what the congregation orders' (54.1).[66] This advice is by no means 'remarkable',[67] but represents the closest imaginable parallel for Clement to the usual political practice.[68]

What Clement is suggesting is, fundamentally, simply subjection to the already existing order. In 63.1 he expresses that as clearly as can be desired when he explains what he thinks is appropriate, namely, 'To bow the neck and adopt the attitude of obedience. Thus by giving up this futile revolt we may be free from all reproach and gain the true goal ahead of us.' In this demand for order and subordination we meet the same 'Roman spirit'[69] as is also expressed in the speech of Cerialis[70] or the famous passage in the Aeneid about the Roman mission,[71] a spirit concerned with subjection which has created an impressive testimony to itself in the Pax Romana.

(e) 'Each ... in his order'

It is only logical that the way in which Clement perceives political reality should also determine his picture of the community and that there should be parallels between empire and church. Here it should be observed as it were in passing that the petition for the rulers for 'stability', which means the continued good order of the empire,[72] also recurs in 65.1 as a wish for the community in Corinth. However, the imperial influence emerges in an extraordinarily evocative way in the fact that Clement can understand the community in terms of the Roman army. I have already explained to what extent he identifies the two.[73] But in the context his admiration of the hierarchical military order in 37.2-4 has the aim of serving the Christian community as a model. This model decisively shapes Clement's understanding of the church as the body of Christ and the simile of the body and its members associated with it, which Clement takes over from Paul.

The description of the hierarchy of military ranks ends in 37.4 with the comment that its usefulness – Clement does not, of course, go into the question 'for whom?' – lies particularly in the interplay of greater and lesser. Immediately after that he picks up the image of the body and its members: 'Take our body, for instance. The head cannot get along without the feet. Nor, similarly, can the feet get along without the head. The tiniest parts of our body are essential to it, and are valuable to the total body. Yes, they all act in concord, and are united in a single obedience to preserve the whole body' (37.5). This recalls what Paul says in I Cor.12.12-27.[74] There he is concerned to stress the equality of the members in their difference; he demonstrates how ridiculous it is for individual members to put themselves above others. In Clement there is a substantial reinterpretation in precisely this respect. It arises specifically out of the military imagery which has gone before, but it is also expressed in v.5 itself in the exclusive contrast between head and feet, and in the stress on subordination. Here Clement is in fact closer than is Paul to an earlier Roman use of the imagery of the body and its members, namely the famous parable by Menenius Agrippa of the belly and the limbs, with which this patrician is said to have moved the plebeians who had left Rome to return to it.[75]

In 38.1 Clement draws the conclusion from the picture he has painted: 'Following this out we must preserve our Christian body too in its entirety. Each must be subject to his neighbour, according to his special gifts.' Here, too, he shows himself to be influenced by Paul in so far as, like Paul, he does not make a purely metaphorical comparison, but speaks of the community as the 'body in Jesus Christ'. Jesus Christ makes up this body, which represents the community. In I Cor.12.27 Paul calls the community the 'body of Christ'; Christ is represented by the community of equal brothers and sisters who serve one another with different gifts.[76] In a very similar way, it seems, Clement writes of mutual subordination which is orientated on particular gifts of grace. However, the first specific instances which he then gives in v.2 demonstrates that there can be no question of real mutuality in his case, and that, rather, social structures of rule are left unquestioned within the community. 'The strong must take care of the weak: the weak must look up to the strong. The rich must provide for the poor; the poor must thank God for giving him someone to meet his needs.' Here social status is seen as a gift of grace. That could be Pauline, to the degree that even a person's social existence is claimed for Christ and thus for fellowship in the community. However, in Clement's explanation the weak and the poor are no longer considered as subjects in their own right; they evidently have no gift of grace of their own with which they contribute towards building up the community, but are merely considered the objects of the good deeds of the strong and the weak and have to react gratefully to them.

So it is certainly no coincidence that the term 'layman' appears for the first time in a Christian work in I Clement. In 40.5 we have: 'The layman is bound by the layman's code.'[77] Immediately after that Clement continues in 41.1; 'Each of us, brothers, in his own rank must win God's approval and have a clear conscience. We must not transgress the rules laid down for our ministry, but must perform it reverently.' Instead of charismatic functions in which all are involved, here we have fixed offices which largely rob the majority of the community of their functions.[78] Instead of the community of equals in accordance with the military model we have the structure of command and obedience in a hierarchical order. The orientation on the Pax Romana which Clement takes for granted, namely on a peace won and safeguarded by military force, thus also militarizes his conception of peace within the church. Peace in the community arises through subordination to one of the 'officials' who have been appointed. As this 'peace' has been put in question by the deposition of presbyters, with an eye to the leaders of the community Clement is not least interested in safeguarding rule. In the political sphere he had set God and the rulers side by side; in this way, as also with the comment that the power to rule was given by God to the rulers, he had legitimated them. He now acts in a very similar way in the church sphere. It already emerged from 41.1 that for Clement obedience to God is synonymous with obedience to the presbytyers who have been appointed. He substantiates this authority in 42.1-4; 44.1-3 above all by claiming that a line runs backwards through them which is said to go through their predecessors, through the first converts who were appointed by the apostles to bear office, through the apostles and Christ, back to God himself.[79]

Both the political and ecclesiastical concept of peace in Clement thus have the same pattern: the existing order is presented as peace; anyone who acts against it is a rebel. So no questions are asked about it; on the contrary, it is legitimated and thus removed from the level of possible discussion.[80]

In Clement's view, the community has largely lost the dimension of being part of the alternative world which already becomes event in the symbolic anticipation of the expected kingdom of God. Rather, in essential points it reflects society.[81] Similarly, Clement is concerned that the authorities should not be provoked by the behaviour of Christians. Several times he suggests that the rebellion in Corinth might bring on the danger of a persecution.[82] It may be true that Christians should not draw attention to themselves by folly and foolish actions – but does that mean that they should not draw attention to themselves at all? What are the criteria? Can it be a criterion that no offence is given to the authorities and that they 'get through' with as little danger as possible? Clement does not engage in any argument on matters of substance; he is looking for 'ringleaders' in order to eliminate them and thus suppress conflict. So in his work, too, the humiliated and suffering Christ depicted in terms of Isa.53 serves as an example of humility, for the disciplining of the community (16.1-17).[83]

According to Harnack, Clement's attitude was 'the basis of the attitude of the church to the Roman state which led to the victory of the church'.[84] If we consider instead Paul's 'inability' to speak of a triumph of Christians other than in broken and paradoxical terms, the question arises whether what Harnack calls a victory is not a matter of changing the symbols while keeping the basic structure the same.[85]

5. 'The lamb will conquer...' – The preservation of Christian identity in suffering and resistance: the Revelation of John

The Revelation of John shows quite a different perspective from I Clement,[1] though both works were written at about the same time. It is still the most probable hypothesis that Revelation was written about the end of the reign of Domitian, i.e. about AD 95.[2] There is no direct mention of Rome at any point. Nevertheless controversy with the *imperium* runs through the whole book.[3] The reality governed by the Pax Romana is seen very clearly. That happens in an unprecedentedly one-sided way. There is not a single positive statement, nor even a neutral one; Rome and its actions are only depicted in the darkest colours.[4] so first of all we must investigate the situation of the writer of this work and the experiences that he had in it.

(a) '...beheaded for the testimony of Jesus and the word of God'

The author gives his name as John.[5] Without explicitly terming himself a prophet he makes it clear that he is one.[6] As he shows knowledge of the specific situation of each of seven different communities in the province of Asia to which the letters at the beginning of his work are sent, he may have been an itinerant prophet working in the sphere of western Asia Minor.[7] He calls himself a 'brother and colleague' of Christians, whom he addresses as 'brothers who share in Jesus the tribulation and the kingdom and the patient endurance...' When he immediately goes on to say that he was on the island of Patmos 'on account of the word of God and the testimony of Jesus' (1.9) it seems reasonable to assume that he had been exiled there because he was a Christian.[8] So he is writing from a distressing and oppressive situation. The fact that he describes his readers as brothers who 'share with him in tribulation' means that he does not understand his situation as an isolated individual fate, but connects it with their own. He tries to point this out by citing the suffering of Christians which has already come about and is to be expected. In particular, he mentions just one Christian who has been executed, and whose martyrdom seems already to have taken place some time ago, when in the letter to Pergamon he speaks of the 'days of Antipas,[9] my faithful one, who was killed among you' (2.13).[10] Alongside this one victim of Roman violence who was probably singled out because of his 'prominence'[11] there are many anonymous victims. Thus in 6.9, when the fifth seal is opened John sees 'under the altar the souls[12] of those who had been slain for the word of God and the witness that they had borne'.[13] In the vision of the thousand-year kingdom in 20.4 he sees sitting on thrones the souls of those 'who had been beheaded for their testimony to Jesus and for the word of God'. According to him, Rome wages war against all those 'who keep the commandments of God and bear testimony to Jesus' (12.17). Rome is 'drunk with the blood of the saints and the blood of the martyrs of Jesus' (17.6). He can go even further and say that in Rome 'was found the blood of prophets and of saints, and of all who have been slain on earth' (18.24). Here the perspective goes beyond the Christian martyrs and takes in the other victims of Rome's murderous rule.

With this further involvement of other victims, with the characterization of Rome as lusting for war and out for the blood of the Christian community, and with the repeated indication of the reasons why in his view Christians have been executed, John makes it clear that the executions which have taken place are not fortuitous occurrences – regrettable, but avoidable in principle. In his view, rather, given the character of Rome, Christians must reckon with this fate if Christian life is to be lived out consistently. In the communities addressed by John it was possible to consider the executions which had taken place as individual instances. We shall have to go into this in more detail later. We are not to suppose that towards the end of the reign of Domitian there was a world-wide persecution with a systematic tracking down of Christians. There is no evidence for this,[14] nor can it be inferred from Revelation. Rather, what we have is evidence of a situation of persecution in which Christian communities had to undergo oppressive experiences even going so far as executions.[15] But that does not mean that this situation was felt and assessed by all Christians with the same clear-sightedness.[16] Rather, it is the aim of John that his readers should understand what has already happened as a sign of the times indicating the fundamental opposition between the community and Rome, and between Christ and the emperor, and that they should accept and demonstrate this opposition in a consistent Christian existence.[17]

So we must ask what John sees as the reason for the persecutions and how his understanding matches up with historical events. He says that the persecutions take place on account of the word of God and the testimony of Jesus.[18] At all events, this makes it clear that he sees the persecutions as being caused by the existence of Christians. But do these definitions relate to being a Christian generally, or do they stress quite specific ways in which being a Christian is expressed?

In 20.4 those who are beheaded are defined more closely as those who 'had not worshipped the beast or its image'.[19] Doubtless this is a reference to the Roman cult of the state and the emperor. As refusal to worship them results in execution, the situation described by Pliny in his letter about the Christians may be meant here.[20] Those accused of being Christians were asked before the governor, as judge, whether the accusation was true. Anyone who denied it had to substantiate the denial by a ritual sacrifice before statues of the gods and the image of the emperor and curse Christ. Anyone who admitted being a Christian was asked a second and third time with the threat of the death penalty. Those who persisted were condemned.[21] This treatment by Pliny was no innovation. Granted, at the beginning of his letter to the emperor Trajan he acknowledges his uncertainty.[22] But that did not prevent him from carrying out the process of condemning to death or acquitting. In his answer the emperor essentially approves the procedure adopted by his governor. He simply asks him only to proceed against Christians if they are denounced as such, but not to take official steps to search them out; and he forbids Pliny to take account of anonymous accusations because that is not appropriate to his age.[23] These qualifications by Trajan are evidently new; the procedure adopted by Pliny was already well-tried and certainly already practised during the time of Domitian. Against this background, 'holding fast to the testimony of Jesus' has a very precise sense. It is a matter of holding fast to the confession of Jesus in a trial despite the condemnation to death that is certainly to be expected.[24]

Hence the question arises whether the definition 'on account of the word of God' does not also have a specific meaning. This formula is replaced in 12.17 and 14.12 by another one which is probably understood to be synonymous; there alongside bearing testimony to Jesus or keeping the faith of Jesus there is mention of 'keeping the commandments of God'. And in 3.8 the community in Philadelphia is not only praised for not having denied the name of Jesus, which might again be an allusion to the legal situation, but also praised before that for keeping his word. On the other hand mention of specific blame attaches only to a single point. In 2.14 the community in Pergamon is blamed because in it there are people who 'observe the teaching of Balaam', which includes 'eating food sacrificed to idols'. Similarly, the letter to Thyatira censures the prophetess Jezebel who teaches 'eating food sacrificed to idols' (2.20). That suggests that we should assume that 'observing the commandments of God' is a matter of observing the prohibition against food sacrificed to idols. That will also be in mind in 2.10 when in the letter to Smyrna we read: 'Do not fear what you are about to suffer. Behold the devil is about to throw some of you into prison, that you may be tested, and for ten days you will have tribulation.' Here John is clearly alluding to Dan.1.12,14, the narrative about the four Jewish young men at the court of Nebuchadnezzar who do not want to make themselves unclean by eating and drinking at the royal table. John evidently expects 'that Christians will be arrested and forced to eat food sacrificed to idols',[25] and thus proclaim their apostasy. But how could he have such an expectation and refer back to the passage in Daniel if he has not already heard of such cases?

Eating food sacrificed to idols – all the meat offered for sale came from the ritual slaughtering in the temples – was not an isolated religious problem but raised general questions of social communication and integration. Members of the lower classes in whose diet meat played no part could eat meat at public festivals which were associated with temples and also with gods. Festivals of associations and family festivals took place in the context of sacrificial meals at the temple.[26] Anyone who as a Christian withdrew from them was alienated from the world and made himself an outsider. Pliny's letter about the Christians again shows that such conduct, if it was not just an isolated occasion, had political and economic consequences. At the end of his letter the governor expresses his hope that 'the contagion of that superstition' which is already widespread, 'can be stopped and set right. At any rate it is certain enough that the almost deserted temples begin to be resorted to, that long disused ceremonies of religion are restored, and that fodder for victims finds a market, whereas buyers until now were very few.'[27]

This makes it clear that both the points which John has in view – the refusal to eat meat sacrificed to idols and the refusal to sacrifice before the image of the emperor and the statues of the gods and to curse Christ – belong closely together. The conduct of Christians which is alien to the ways of the world and makes Christians stand out arouses the suspicion of disloyalty. That leads to denunciations and arrests, in which loyalty is then tested in the way described.[28]

In two passages, 2.14, 20, in addition to eating meat sacrificed to idols, there is mention of 'immorality'. That is certainly not understood in the sexual sense.[29] The word 'immorality' here might be taken up from the Old Testament Jewish tradition and denote idolatry as 'going astray' after other gods, which in a society with a religious stamp involved a wide sphere of public and indeed private life.[30]

The situation at the time of the composition of Revelation was decisively stamped by the fact that emperor worship under Domitian had been heightened to an unprecedented degree.[31] It was particularly flourishing in the province of Asia, 'the classical land of the imperial cult'. In Ephesus, for example, there was a temple to the emperor with the image of Domitian.[32] The second 'beast' of 13.11-14, which John identifies with 'the false prophets',[33] is probably to be understood as the senior priesthood of the imperial cult.[34] These 'great animals' are therefore the guardians of 'the ideology and metaphysics, the cult and symbolism of the state'.[35] So if there were influential circles in the provinces which to an extraordinary degree propagated the cult of the emperor as a natural expression of loyalty towards Rome, so that it played a prominent role in public awareness, and if Christians kept clear of it and the festivals associated with it, their behaviour must have been all the more likely to provoke the suspicion of disloyalty.[36] In such a context arrests and indeed executions could lead to heightened enmity towards the Christians, with further accusations, trials and executions. That is the situation in which John writes and in which he expects such a dramatic intensification of the conflict as to make 'the history of the church end in the graves of the saints and the people shrivelled up in the wilderness'.[37] So he focusses the experience he has had on a reflection on the basic choice between the emperor or Christ,[38] which then also determines his portrayal of Rome.

(b) 'Who is like the beast...?'

The situation which is experienced as threatening and the expectation of far greater oppression give John the perspective from which he looks at and evaluates the Roman empire and puts some aspects of the Pax Romana into sharp focus. He stresses the all-embracing power of Rome. It is 'the great city, which has dominon over the kings of the earth' (17.18). It has 'power over all races, peoples, languages and nations' (13.7).[39] So it is not surprising that all the inhabitants of the earth pay homage to it as the victorious and all compelling power[40] and ask in amazement, 'Who is like the beast and who can wage war against it?' (13.4). Evidently no one; the power of violence is impressive and automatically finds its supporters, participants and propagandists. So the kings of the earth have come to an arrangement with Rome, carry on its business and thus live in luxury.[41] But above all Rome itself lives in splendour and luxury.[42] The merchants of the earth and the shipholders have grown rich on the great luxury of the city.[43] They have brought just about everything to Rome: 'cargo of gold, silver, jewels and pearls, fine linen, purple, silk and scarlet, all kinds of scented wood, all articles of ivory, all articles of costly wood, bronze, iron and marble, cinnamon, spice, incense, myrrh. frankincense, wine, oil, fine flour and wheat, cattle and sheep, horses and chariots, and slaves, that is, human souls.'[44] So whereas Rome and its vassals live in abundance, like those who do business with them, and make profits, famine prevails in the province: 'A measure of wheat for a denarius and three measures of barley for a denarius' (6.6). Prices for basic foods climb so high that for a great part of the population that means hunger.[45]

Emperor worship, which is regarded as idolatry, and the extraordinary luxury are branded in the image of Rome as the great harlot which John paints impressively with powerful strokes:

> And I saw a woman sitting on a scarlet beast which was full of blasphemous names, and it had seven heads and ten horns. The woman was arrayed in purple and scarlet, and bedecked with gold and jewels and pearls, holding in her hand a golden cup full of abominations and the impurities of her fornication; and on her forehead was written a name of mystery: 'Babylon the great, mother of harlots and of earth's abominations.'[46]

The name Babylon provides a further negative qualification. The fact that it is introduced as a 'mystery' indicates that it is a code name. Of course it refers to Rome.[47] But it is more than just a code name: Babylon is the city hostile to the people of God on which God's judgment has come. In all the passages in Revelation in which Rome appears as Babylon it does so in connection with pronouncements of judgment.[48] As surely as Babylon provoked the judgment of God, so surely does that apply to Rome.

There is also an extraordinarily negative assessment of Rome when John depicts it as 'the beast which arises from the abyss'.[49] It is the power of chaos. The creation was wrested from it, and continues to be threatened by it. But that means that the rule of Rome does not make the world the creation that God wants it to be. The order produced by Rome's compelling power and the world administered by it which Aristides praises in such lofty tones[50] is, on the contrary, a perversion of God's creation: in truth it is the utmost disorder, chaos.

The abundance of Roman power, towering above all that has existed previously, and its fearful rule of terror, leads John to describe a further beast: 'And I saw a beast rising out of the sea, with ten horns and ten heads, with ten diadems upon its horns and a blasphemous name upon its heads. And the beast that I saw was like a leopard, its feet were like a bear's and its mouth was like a lion's mouth' (13.1f.). The world kingdoms of Daniel which are symbolized by a succession of dangerous beasts are here united in a single monster: 'That means that the *imperium Romanum* is the accumulation of all the monstrosities and anti-godly powers of earlier empires. It has become a single wild animal.'[51]

John regards the power of Rome in its ultimate intensification which he has described in this way as being satanic. That becomes clearest when after the description of the monster in 13.2 he immediately adds: 'And to it the dragon gave his power and his throne and great authority.' The dragon mentioned here is twice explicitly identified with Satan, the devil.[52] He has been driven out of heaven on to the earth; there he rages, embodied in Rome, in awareness that he has only a short time left.[53] It might seem that here John was thinking in dualistic terms.[54] But alongside this statement that the dragon has given the beast his power, we have four times another statement that 'it has been given him' to do what he does, a statement the logical subject of which is God.[55] This makes it clear that a limit is set to the power of the beast.[56] John does not attempt to achieve a logical balance between the two statements. Absence of logical contradiction could be had only at the price of either leaving the world to the devil or introducing God to legitimate a diabolical reality. In view of John's experiences, and in view of the bloody suffering under the rule of Rome, how could faith in God as creator and Lord of the world be maintained other than in contradiction? This logical contradiction is none other than the consequence of the fact that God himself is involved in the contradictory reality, suffers in it and contradicts it and thus leaves room for contradictions.

(c) 'How long?...'

This contradiction is articulated in John not only in the description of the power of Rome as satanic but also in the fact that he announces the imminent end of Roman rule, which claims to be eternal; thus Revelation is full of imagery which denotes the downfall of Rome. According to 18.21, in a symbolic action a mighty angel throws a great millstone into the sea saying, 'So shall Babylon the great city be overthrown with violence, and shall be found no more.'[57] The desire for the annihilation of Roman power is expressed similarly when in the image of the decisive battle the birds of the air are summoned to 'eat the flesh of kings, the flesh of captains, the flesh of mighty men, the flesh of horses and their riders, and the flesh of all men, both free and slave, both small and great'.[58] This is the great banquet of God, when the vultures sate themselves on the refuse of Rome and all its allies.

John depicts the downfall of Rome in the most imposing way in 18.9-15, not by giving his readers and hearers a direct picture of it, but by looking at Rome indirectly with the eyes of those who were bound up with it, who had become powerful and rich through it and with it:

> And the kings of the earth, who committed fornication and were wanton with her (viz. the city of Babylon), will weep and wail over

her when they see the smoke of her burning: they will stand far off, in fear of her torment, and say, 'Alas, alas, that great city, thou mighty city Babylon! In one hour has thy judgment come.'

And the merchants of the earth weep and mourn for her, since no one buys their cargo any more... The merchants of these wares who gained wealth from her, will stand far off, in fear of her torment, weeping and mourning aloud, 'Alas, alas for the great city that was clothed in fine linen, in purple and scarlet, bedecked with gold, with jewels, and with pearls! In one hour all this wealth has been laid waste.'

And all shipmakers and seafaring men, sailors and all whose trade is on the sea, stood far off and cried out as they saw the smoke of her burning, 'What city was like the great city?' And they threw dust on thir heads, as they wept and mourned, crying out, 'Alas, alas for the great city where all who had ships at sea grew rich by her wealth. In one hour she has been laid waste.'[59]

The kings, merchants and seafarers gaze spellbound on the smoking ruins of Rome and break out in lamentation. They, who were bound up with Rome, also remain bound up with her in her downfall. John will direct the gaze of those who are not bound up with Rome beyond the downfall to the new Jerusalem, so that their sight of the downfall is only a passing one.

This passing glance at the downfall of the mighty city is not superfluous. It expresses the hope that the acts of violence, the victors of history, will not always be able to triumph over their victims. So in 6.10 it is those who have been killed whom John makes to cry out in a loud voice, 'O Sovereign Lord, holy and true, how long before thou wilt judge and avenge our blood on those who dwell upon the earth?' With this cry they protest[60] against the history of violence whose victims they have become, and call for its end;[61] at the same time they defend themselves against any attempt to make sense of their death. That is also made clear by the answer that they are given immediately after their question, 'Then they were told to rest a little longer, until the number of their fellow servants and their brethren should be complete, who were to be killed as they themselves had been.'[62] Here 'the measure of time is determined by the number of the martyrs'.[63] The achievement of their number, appointed by God, brings in the end. With this idea John encourages his readers to accept suffering for the sake of their being Christians, and he consoles them by connecting this suffering with the end for which they hope. As the further context and the context of the whole of Revelation shows, all the stress is on this end and not on the way in which it is achieved.[64] Therefore there can be no question of suffering being given a meaning. It is not a matter of subsequently adding meaning to cruel events, sheer meaninglessness, but of removing what produces such meaninglessness, breaking off the history of violence.

Before the martyrs in 6.11 are given an answer to their question they are given white robes, an act which is certainly to be understood as one of 'heavenly transfiguration'.[65] But these white garments are not a 'reward', in the sense that now meaning is given to their suffering;[66] rather, this is to equip them for the time of waiting which is announced immediately afterwards.[67] They have still not reached the goal as long as the history of violence continues unceasingly, as long as their murderers can still continue their work under the guise of justice. Only when those who are fixed on the city of 'Babylon', looking at its downfall with spellbound gaze, break out in cries of lament, does the invitation to rejoicing ring out for them: 'Rejoice over her, O heaven, O saints and apostles and prophets, for God has given judgment for you against her.'[68] Here John is fundamentally different from Ignatius of Antioch, who about twenty years later went almost eagerly as a prisoner on a transport to Rome for his martyrdom, as is indicated by his letter to the community there. Ignatius thinks in individual and personal terms. His question is, When will I finally get to God? And he hopes to do so through his martyrdom. By contrast John's thought is far more comprehensive. His question is: How long will this catastrophic history continue to run as it is doing? Will it never come to an end? By making the martyrs cry out 'How long?' he maintains that their death remains a protest, as it was a contradiction which led to their condemnation: rejection of idolatry and the emperor cult, a refusal to adapt to the rulers. Their death remains a protest against a reality which calls for such victims and at the same time is evidence of another reality, of a better world of God's righteousness.

We are to understand in this sense, that their own evil doings must catch up with the perpetrators, the way in which according to 11.18 the twenty-four elders before the throne of God ask at the end of their prayer for 'the destruction of the destroyers of the earth'. That with which it has conquered the earth will rebound on Rome:

> 'Render to her (viz. the harlot Babylon) as she herself has rendered, and repay her double for her deeds; mix a double draught for her in the cup she mixed. As she glorified herself and played the wanton, so give her a like measure of torment and mourning. Since in her heart she says, "A queen I sit, I am now a widow, mourning I shall

never see," so shall her plagues come in a single day, pestilence and mourning and famine, and she shall be burned with fire; for mighty is the Lord God who judges her' (18.6-8). Luxurious Rome, the great city, will be desolate. 'And the sound of harpers and minstrels, of flute players and trumpeters, shall be heard in thee no more: and a craftsman of any craft shall be found in thee no more; and the sound of the millstone shall be heard in thee no more; and the voice of the bridegroom and bride shall be heard in thee no more' (18.22f.).

The hope for the downfall of Rome is not free from a lust for vengeance. That is shown, for example, by the desire for double retribution; it is also shown by the passages which speak of the 'lake of fire and brimstone'. Not only are the devil, death and Hades thrown into it (20.10,13) but also Rome and its propagandists, 'and they will be tortured day and night to all eternity' (20.10). Moreover all those are thrown into it who do not stand in the Book of Life (20.15): that is, all those who have not perjured themselves before the beast (13.8)[69] and thus also those among the Christians who were too cowardly to confess.[70]

An article on Isaiah 11 and Virgil's Fourth Eclogue finally reduces a comparison between these two texts to the illuminating quintessential statement: 'By their wishes you shall know them.'[71] What is indicated by the wish of eternal torment for one's enemies? Does it not indicate the whole extent of a bad situation as John experiences it? That could be demonstrated by a comparison with Luke. In Acts 3.21 Luke formulates the attractive notion of the restoration of all things, of which Karl Barth is said to have said that one must have it in one's head but may not dogmatize about it. 'The restoration of all things' over against the eternal torment of those who do not stand in the book of life? But it has also become clear that Luke depicts the Roman empire in a very positive way, and that he himself seems to have social privileges and to be integrated into society. The wish, too, is evidently not completely independent of the social and political situation of a person. Are those who are privileged perhaps also privileged for a 'higher' ethos of which the victims are deprived by their situation? However, the idea of the restoration of all things could at any rate also 'fit' the privileged to the degree that it can now make a matter of indifference injustices that have become familiar, wrong that is present now. The wishes of Revelation for retribution and justice, however, remain a protest against that which cannot be overlooked.

(d) 'The kingdom of the world has become the kingdom of our God...'

The reason why John can hope for an imminent downfall of Rome is that the devil who appears in the Roman empire has already been conquered in heaven. After the birth of a child who symbolizes the Messiah he depicts in mythical imagery a battle in heaven the result of which is clear, 'And the great dragon was thrown down, that ancient serpent, who is called the Devil and Satan, the deceiver of the whole world[72] – he was thrown down to the earth, and his angels were thrown down with him.'[73] There he carries on his 'last fight'[74] which has now basically already been lost. So the seer already hears an angel crying out, thus anticipating the final defeat of Rome, 'Fallen, fallen is Babylon the great, for all nations have drunk the wine of her impure passion.'[75]

Therefore it is already possible to speak of the fall of Rome in the perfect, because God already holds sway. The prayer of the twenty-four elders before the throne of God begins with a thanksgiving, 'We give thanks to thee, Lord God almighty, who art and who wast, that thou hast taken thy great power and begun to reign.'[76] Again and again in almost hymnic fashion it is stressed that praise, honour and glory, saving help and lordship, power and authority, might and strength belong to God.[77] It is not due to the Roman emperor, who claims all this for himself, but to God and his anointed: 'The kingdom of the world has become the kingdom of our Lord and of his Christ and he shall reign for ever and ever.'[78] God's anointed, the Christ, the Messiah, is the one who is the cornerstone of all these statements. In the vision of the book with the seven seals an angel cries out asking who is worthy to open the book and loose its seals. When no one can be found the seer John weeps. For only when the seals are loosed can the course of final events described in the book begin (5.1-4). But then one of the elders before the throne of God says to John, 'Weep not, for lo, the lion of the tribe of Judah, the Root of David, has conquered, so that he can open the scroll and its seven seals' (5.5). As in IV Ezra 4.11 the lion stands for the Messiah. There he emerges roaring from the wood and announces the end of the Roman eagle. Here, too, the lion from the tribe of Judah is the victor.[79] But then the picture changes in a unique way when John immediately goes on to write, 'And between the throne and the four living creatures and among the elders, I saw a lamb standing, as though it had been slain, with seven horns and with seven eyes, which are the seven spirits of God sent out into all the earth' (5.6). The victorious lion is - a lamb, and indeed a slain lamb, slain like the witnesses to Jesus who stood fast in trial. Nevertheless this lamb has power, indeed complete power, as is shown by the fact that it has seven horns.[80] The

Spirit of God goes forth from it, which inspires the whole earth to steadfast resistance against Rome; that is indicated by its seven eyes, which are interpreted as the spirits of God which are sent out everywhere. Here John is reinterpreting the message of the death and resurrection of Jesus. With the word 'slain' he connects the death of Jesus with the death of his witnesses (6.9), indeed with all the victims of Rome (18.24). So the death of Jesus, too, is a protest against a murderous reality. At the same time, however, John makes a distinction by saying of the lamb 'as though it had been slain'. The fatal wound is evidently not the last thing that must be noted in looking at it. It is at the same time the lion from the tribe of Judah which has conquered; it is 'worthy to receive power and wealth and wisdom and might and honour and glory and blessing' (5.12). Therefore it can be said with certainty, with a view to the final messianic struggle, 'The lamb will conquer; he is the lord of lords and king of kings.'[81] Nowhere does John say that Jesus has been raised or exalted, that he is risen. Naturally he presupposes this message when he talks of the power of the lamb, but by using political terminology he interprets it in political terms and thus draws a direct contrast between Christ and the emperor. If the lamb is lord of lords and king of kings, then the protest represented by its death is no longer just an impotent protest but a protest which has achieved its aim, which has already broken off the history of violence culminating in the rule of Rome and will soon put a definitive end to it. It is evidence of a counter-reality. The future is not with the violent victors of history but with their victims. The images in Revelation of the victory of the lamb contradict the experience of reality in which lambs do not conquer, but rather are slaughtered. These images therefore form a potential for resistance, for resisting this reality and thus bearing witness to another reality, a counter-reality of peace and justice, which is stronger. In the certainty that here God himself intervenes, with Christ as the lamb which is slain, John not only depicts the coming downfall of Rome but also outlines positive pictures of hope.

(e) 'A new heaven and a new earth...'

The images of hope in Revelation are also stamped by the situation of elemental threat as John senses it. He experiences reality as so threatening that the continuity of the world and history seems incomprehensible; here there can only be a complete break. Nevertheless he does not want to be away from the earth; he does not dream of being transported into heaven.[82] The new thing that he hopes for is not unimaginably different, but elements of the old creation permeate the new.[83] In them, however, there is no manifestation of historical continuity, but resistance against it. Historical continuity is posed by the power of Rome; continuity over the break can only be expected from the creative action of God, who will make a new heaven and a new earth: 'Then I saw a new heaven and a new earth; for the first heaven and the first earth had passed away, and the sea was no more' (21.1). In the context of a completely negative experience of reality John can only maintain his faith in God as creator by taking up and reshaping the promise of Isa.65.17. There the new comes into being from the old; here the old is replaced by the new. The old is not origin, but contrast. According to Genesis 1 the initial creation of the world consists in the ordering of chaos into cosmos. The threatening chaos is limited but not conquered. Here, however the threat is felt to be so great that deliverance seems conceivable only by its complete removal. Heaven and earth must be new, but the sea can no longer exist. This is the chaotic element from which, according to Genesis 1, heaven and earth emerged.[84] For John, however, it is the element from which the fearful beast emerged, which symbolizes the Roman *imperium*. The Roman legions who fought for and claimed victory came over the sea; the cargo ships which delivered the fruits of work in the provinces to the victors go over the sea.[85] The Mediterranean, which has become *nostrum mare*, namely the Roman sea,[86] is so alien to provincials like John that the sight of it triggers off anxiety and the wish arises that it might be no more.

The new Jerusalem comes out of the newly created heaven. 'Any idea of a transfiguration and renewal of the earthly Jerusalem is ruled out.'[87] There is creativity here only in the creative action of God.

> And I saw the holy city, new Jerusalem, coming down out of heaven from God, like a bride adorned for her husband; and I heard a great voice from the throne, saying, 'Behold, the dwelling of God is with men. He will dwell with them, and they shall be his people, and God himself will be with them; he will wipe away every tear from their eyes, and death shall be no more, neither shall there be mourning nor crying nor pain any more, for the former things have passed away. And he who sat upon the throne said, 'Behold, I make all things new' (21.2-5).

Here John presents a collage of Old Testament quotations and allusions.[88] In so doing he is relying on the faithfulness of the promise of God and thus on the expectation of the breaking off of the history of disaster which at the same time represents a breach in any historical continuity of the constancy of hopes and the certainty of deliverance. However, comprehensive though the hope expressed in this collage may be, it should at the same time be noted that it is a specific protest against the tears and sufferings of the oppressed, the cries and griefs of those who have been tortured and killed, caused by the rule of Rome. And the passage disputes Rome's rule when it says that men and women will be God's people. That the people of Rome are subjects was a Roman claim and largely corresponded to the reality which is also noted by Revelation.[89] But this reality will not continue but be radically broken off.[90]

The new Jerusalem which comes down from heaven, as John describes it at length in 21.10-22.5, 'is the counterpart to Rome, the capital of the world, the city of all cities at the time of John'.[91] But in the description of this city one can also see the 'legacy of power'[92] in the background. In order to bring out its greatness and unique beauty and perfection, John has it built of gold, precious stones and pearls.[93] These are the very things with which the great harlot, Rome personified as a luxurious woman, is adorned in 17.4. They are the same things that, according to 18.12, the merchants first mention in their list of cargoes to Rome. The values of the victors as expressed in their luxury[94] have also found their way into the consciousness of the victims.[95] That still has no immediate effect on John and the communities of his time. But once 'the visible church wants to represent something of the harmony, splendour and glory of the new Jerusalem',[96] and not merely in a symbolic sense but in the literal sense of the description given there – what will be the effect of this legacy?

'The legacy of power' shows itself once again when the suffering experienced under Roman rule turns into the wish for rule for oneself. At the end of 22.5 it is said of the servants of God in the new Jerusalem 'And they will reign for ever.'[97] But that raises the question: Over whom? According to v.2 the 'peoples' mentioned shortly beforehand are healed by the leaves of the tree of life and thus belong among the 'servants of God'. The ruling which is mentioned of them is therefore in the truest sense of the word without an object, a relic of the experience and language of the old time.[98] The fact that despite the term he adopts John is not concerned to reestablish structures for ruling also emerges from the fact that he puts forward a community structure which is one for brothers and sisters. He therefore regards the community as the sphere of interrupted power. In this way it corresponds to an aspect of his account of the new Jerusalem which similarly shows interrupted power: John does not seem to be able to imagine even the eternal city coming from heaven as being without walls[99] – but its gates are never shut.

(f) 'Here is a call for the endurance of the saints'

So John does not only paint negative pictures of hope but also positive ones. He depicts the imminent downfall of Rome, but also the new Jerusalem coming down from the new heaven. The question as to what he himself is now doing in the face of the ardent expectation of the end which is evident here can therefore be answered quite simply: he is writing. He is writing a very extensive work which takes a good deal of time not only to write but to read, and he evidently thinks that reading it will help people to recognize and to survive the time which still remains. This work is 'underground literature';[100] it speaks in code. Rome is not mentioned, but rather Babylon and strange animals, and mythical images are depicted. Yet this is not mere encipherment; it is not only nor even primarily translating what is meant into a secret languagae which is incomprehensible to outsiders. The encipherment is at the same time also a very clear and eloquent symbolization with which John snatches the masks off the lofty claims of Rome and shows its murderous aspect. In addition the symbolization lifts the conflict with Rome to a higher level and there decides it in the overcoming of Satan by God and his Messiah.[101] But is not all this the mere daydream of a downtrodden individual with which he consoles those like him?

There is no doubt at all that the images of hope depicted by John are also meant to give comfort. But as he does this does he not actually *dis*comfort? Does he not make people unfitted for the present by promising a better future? What are his readers and hearers to do now? He asks them to stand fast, by persevering and enduring:[102] 'Here is a call for the endurance and faith of the saints'. At first sight that may seem precious little, but for John this is no small matter, but rather everything; he is concerned for a consistent life in Christian identity as testimony to the Lordship of Christ. What 'endurance' means for him can be spelt out in more detail by considering another possibility which he rejects. He shows that it was also practised in the communities to which he writes. According to 2.14,20 there were Christians who taught that food sacrificed to idols should be eaten. I have already indicated that this was not an isolated religious question but that participation in the customs of the dominant Gentile environment raised questions of social communication and participation generally.[103] As it is explicitly said that the other Christians actually taught the eating of sacrificial meat, they will have gone over to the offensive in arguing for their adaptation to the environment and will have given it a theological basis. The thesis quoted in 2.24 that they 'have learned the deep things of Satan' points to that. This is 'probably to be understood as meaning that for them Satan and idols no longer have power'.[104] Therefore without hesitation they can take part in the religious phenomena of life in a pagan society.[105] Anyone who acts in this way will hardly be suspected of disloyalty and denounced; if it came to denunciation, such a person could be more inclined than others even in this state of confession to perform the cultic actions required and to rescue himself by making a mental reservation. Between on the one hand those who taught that food sacrificed to idols could be eaten and on the other John, who categorically rejected any compromise at all with the pagan environment, there may have been a majority in the community who took a middle line, rejecting food sacrificed to idols in principle yet not necessarily demonstrating their own Christianity but rather allowing tactical caution to play a role.[106]

According to John the decisive question with which he sees the Christians of his time confronted is not 'How can I survive this situation with the least possible harm? Have I a realistic understanding of the power situation with a view to coming through it?' Nor does he show any longing for martyrdom, as the comparison with Ignatius of Antioch made clear.[107] Rather, the question of the possibility of his own survival is completely put in the shade by the one question which is important to him: In this situation, how can I bear witness to the rule of Christ, his claim to the whole world?[108] If the question is put in this way, his answer can only be one of refusal in the face of the exaggerated and veiled 'world power', Rome. Hence the rejection of eating food sacrificed to idols represents the *status confessionis*. So he calls for an 'exodus', 'Come out of her (viz.Babylon), my people, lest you take part in her sins' (18.4). As 'joining in', life along the usual lines, necessarily means complicity with Rome, the consequence is 'social separation'.[109] Those who boast of their lofty theological knowledge, claiming that the idols are nothing and therefore 'joining in' without thinking, where that seems necessary, do not note that by coming to terms with existing circumstances they deny the Lordship of Christ, corrupt their own identity as Christians and surrender the world to its supposed lords.[110] Against this, by refusing to 'join in', by contradicting and resisting, they dispute that the world belongs to those who claim the rule over it; enduring resistance is a testimony to the rule of God and Christ.[111] 'Here is a call for the endurance of the saints, those who keep the commandments of God and the faith of Jesus' (14.12). This sentence can be regarded as a summary of all that John wants to say.

This endurance puts Christian life into the role of the outsider and will heighten the danger to the physical existence of Christians. John is clearly aware of this:[112] 'If anyone is to be taken captive, to captivity he goes; if any one slays with the sword, with the sword must he be slain.'[113] But anyone who suffers this fate for the commandments of God and faith in Jesus by so doing also stands up for Jesus' power in powerlessness; he does not bow to the realities imposed by the powerful but challenges their absolute validity as a witness to the reality of the Lordship of Christ.[114] John calls him the 'victor'[115] who endures, who is 'faithful to the end' (2.20), and who thus trusts in the living power of Jesus even in the face of the threat of violent death by not yielding to this death which he could have avoided by adaptation. To someone who in this way conforms to the lamb which is slain and yet has conquered and will conquer John promises God's future. As this 'victory' is achieved in defeat and thus represents a clear contrast to the Roman *victoria*, it is once again clear that John's hope is not that now the right people will gain power but that the history of the rulers which has caused so much suffering will finally come to an end.[116]

(g) '...and sing a new song'

Though John has depicted the suffering experienced in the present so harshly and expects so much worse before the last time which is immediately ahead, his book is not utterly dominated by gloom and hopelessness but is full of certainty at God's presence in the midst of all tribulation and full of confidence in respect of God's future.[117] He also communicates this impression above all by the way in which at important points he produces hymnic passages which celebrate the power of God and Christ.[118] Thus according to 5.8f. the four beings around God's throne and the twenty-four elders before the Lamb fall down and sing a new song in which according to v.11 the hosts of angels join, and finally according to v.13, 'every creature in heaven and on earth and under the earth and in the sea, and all therein saying, "To him who sits upon the throne and to the lamb be blessing and honour and glory and might for ever and ever."'[119] Even if John has written all these passages himself for their place in the book of Revelation,[120] they are full of traditional elements[121] and probably also contain phrases that were used in worship.[122] At any event, they remind the communities of their worship, and particularly of the hymns they sing there.[123] This recollection is all the more likely since the place of worship is the place at which the book of Revelation is presented to the assembled community.[124] In the solemnity of the liturgy the community hymns the power and glory of Christ; there it assures itself of this glory and anticipates a life under it which is free from the damage and oppression of the lordship exercised by others.[125] By continually recalling the liturgy, by putting the power of God and Christ celebrated in hymns in the liturgy in direct contrast to the power of Rome and thus giving a reason for endurance and resistance, John also defines the liturgy as a place of learning: acknowledgment of the rule of God and Christ is to be understood as testimony before the world and thus at the same time as a protest against all the rule which runs contrary to it. Recollection of the liturgy therefore becomes a subversive recollection. So the reading of the book of Revelation leads not least to celebrating the liturgy as training in resistance. Should that not be a specifically Christian contribution to a peace which includes justice?[126]

IV CONCLUSION

Breaking Through

How was the structure of power in the Pax Romana conceived of by Jesus and the early community? How was it evaluated? How did people react to it? The second part of this book investigated this kind of question. It emerged that the answers are not uniform but place the accents differently even to the point of contradiction. The two most widely divergent positions, those of the Revelation of John and I Clement, are hardly separated in time and are connected with similar events, with persecutions under the emperor Domitian. But whereas the seer John sees the actions of Rome as expressing such a murderous rage that he can understand Rome only as the incarnation of Satan and cries out for this history of violence to be broken off, Clement the Roman only looks back in passing at the time of persecution which has just been withstood as at a storm that has passed over. For him this was a 'state of emergency' which has nothing to do with normal conditions; for John, however, these normal conditions are one long 'state of emergency'.[1] So he fortifies those who would resist and hold out; the other approach, however, not only stresses the need for loyalty but in addition also gives theological legitimation to *de facto* political power.

Among the New Testament writers, Luke with his two-volume work, the Gospel and Acts, comes closest to Clement of Rome. He too shows clearly and emphatically a positive attitude to the reality controlled by Rome and puts particular stress on the correct legal procedure adopted by the Roman authorities, so that loyalty is something to be taken for granted. If we isolate the section Rom.13.1-7 from the overall context of Paul's remarks which relate to the Pax Romana, even he differs only in degree from similar remarks by Clement. The contrast between Romans 13 and Revelation 13 almost cries out to be expressed in newspaper headlines: 'The servant of God for your good' stands over against the 'beast from the sea', the embodiment of bestiality. One cannot say that in the time of Paul what is said in Revelation 13 was not yet relevant. That is not even true for the time of Clement, who is contemporaneous with the apocalyptist John. On the other hand, even in the time of Paul persecutions were an ever-possible threat for Christians and Christian communities. Moreover the system of the principate could continually produce phenomena like Domitian, as Caligula and Nero before him indicate. Taking political life as a whole, however, Domitian's reign was not an extraordinary change. Its distinctive feature consisted above all in the fact that he led murder run riot even in the highest circles. So Pliny and Tacitus could breathe again after his death and count themselves lucky to have reached the time of Nerva and Trajan. However, for Christians in Bithynia and Pontus whom Pliny had executed, it was irrelevant who ruled in Rome: the dark Domitian, under whom their fellow believers had died a martyr death in Asia, or the gentle Trajan, under whom they suffered the same fate.

The contrast between Revelation 13 and Romans 13, and even more that between Clement and John, thus cannot be removed or even relativized by a reference to the circumstances of the time. However, it should be noted that Rom.13.1-7 is far from saying all that can be said about Paul's perception of the Pax Romana. In this respect it represents only a cross-section, and in no way stands in the centre of an overall context which is not free from contradiction. It describes the loyal acceptance of the political environment within which the community lives a life that runs contrary to the Pax Romana. By contrast in Luke the accepted framework even affects the structure of the community, and in Clement even the force which guarantees its external order, the military, virtually becomes a model for the community. It needs no further demonstration that Clement thus also presents a fundamental contrast with Jesus himself and his disciples.

These brief comments do not attempt to be a summary of the results achieved in Part Two, but merely indicate the problem that we must now investigate. Granted, I Clement is not part of the New Testament canon, but its position becomes increasingly influential in the later history of the church. Within the New Testament it finds the strongest support in the writings of Luke and in the isolated statement in Rom.13.1-7. Even without introducing Clement, therefore, the differences and indeed oppositions are still clear enough. How do we deal with them in connection with the question of peace? May we make use of some passaages here and others there? In that way reference back to the New Testament would be a matter of whim and not take us any further. Given the differences, what is the significance of the Reformation scriptural principle (*sola scriptura*) 'that the Christian community has to regard the holy scriptures of the Old Testament and the New Testament as the decisive source and norm of its (*a*) proclamation, (*b*) experience and (*c*) knowledge'?[2] In the New Testament is there anything like a guideline, a criterion or criteria, which allows us to assess the differences as well as noting them and thus avoid just any use of them?

Our investigations in the second part have not only shown that there are very different answers in the New Testament, even on the question of peace, but have especially brought out that what is said in the different writings and groups of writings in the New Testament is connected with the reality out of which they have grown and to which they are related – which for us is a historical reality. Therefore historical reconstruction can make an essential contribution to the understanding of New Testament texts. But it has become clear above all that these statements are bound up with the particular experience of reality had by those who made them. They were in different situations which were connected with different experiences and interests. Different interests and experiences in turn gave rise to different perceptions and different evaluations. So it has also proved that particular standpoints and perspectives determine perception and evaluation. Virtually no one can do anything about his or her place and situation, but some have the possibility of extending and changing the perspectives of their perception. The question which arises in view of the different statements which the New Testament makes about peace should therefore be put like this: does the testimony of the New Testament indicate a binding standpoint from which we must perceive reality?

The New Testament texts which contain perceptions of the Pax Romana do not provide any analysis of the Roman system of rule, though they also offer acute observations. They address Christians who live in the context of this rule. They address Christians on the basis of, and with a view to, what marks them out and commits them as Christians, namely that they have come to believe in Jesus. That is their primary reference to reality, within which their perceptions of the Pax Romana are made. It is the reference to the reality of God which has emerged in the resurrection of the crucified Jesus, to his love which empties itself to the uttermost. Thus the way of Jesus on the cross is God's own movement downwards and to the periphery, his unconditional solidarity with those who have nothing, those who suffer, the humiliated and injured.[3] The God who comes in the crucified Jesus does not behave in the way in which the great Caesar thinks the divine should behave, as he is once said to have said to his mutinous soldiers: 'Do you believe that you were of crucial importance for me? Divine providence will never stoop so low that fate troubles itself whether the like of you live or die: as the great ordain, so the affairs of this world are directed – the life of humanity is determined by a few.'[4] In the crucified Jesus God has not allied himself with the great, but on the contrary with those on the periphery. He did not do this to glorify marginal existence or to claim that ' those on the margin' are 'better people', but in the power of the resurrection to bring out the separation of margin and centre, to make a new creation, to endorse the death of Jesus as a permanent and effective protest against those structures which continually bring about separation at the centre and at the margin.

But if that is the case, does not then the periphery, the margin and the marginalized, become an important hermeneutical category? That at any rate must be the case in the reality of a world which to an increasing degree is falling apart into the centre and the margin. If the conviction of the crucified Jesus who is risen, if the testimony of the revelation of the love of God in the cross of Jesus, is the centre of the content of the New Testament, then is not the consequence a clear indication that reality is to be seen from the periphery? It is not a matter of legitimating what the marginalized do, far less idealizing it; it is a matter of nothing more nor less than the perspective from which reality is perceived – a perspective given by the cross of Jesus.[5] Anyone who attempts to follow this pointer towards a standpoint will accept the accusation that he is not sufficiently aware of the magnitude of a supposedly overall context and the splendour of the great; but he or she will find it impossible to overlook the cries of the oppressed.[6] That is the standpoint from which we must look at the perception of the Pax Romana by Luke and Clement. However, the question arises even more strongly for ourselves, for in the reading of the New Testament the important thing would be to think and act along the lines of the perspective which the cross of Jesus provides on our own reality and thus also to see our own involvement in the profits produced by a peace controlled by force from a power centre.[7] In this perspective the objection that one cannot just leap over two thousand years of history proves to be an attempt to neutralize radical New Testament statements.

To rediscover our own present in the past when reading scripture, to draw from this discovery hope in the prospect of a future disclosed by God, and thus to endure the present is a kind of reading of scripture which we find in scripture itself. As an example of this, let me quote some verses from the letter to the Hebrews.[8] In Chapter 11, in which the author seeks to demonstrate by figures from scripture how faith is lived as Christian experience, vv.23-27 run:

> By faith Moses, when he was born, was hid for three months by his parents, because they saw that the child was beautiful; and they were not afraid of the king's edict. By faith Moses, when he was grown up, refused to be called the son of Pharaoh's daughter, choosing rather to share ill treatment with the people of God than to enjoy the fleeting pleasures of sin. He considered abuse suffered for the Christ greater wealth than the treasures of Egypt, for he looked to the reward. By faith he left Egypt, not being afraid of the anger of the king; for he endured as seeing him who is invisible.

The author rediscovers the conflict of his own time in the stories of Moses. It is the conflict in which the community is involved, between loyalty towards Roman authorities and holding fast to the confession of Jesus. In 10.32 he reminds his readers and hearers of 'the former days' immediately after their baptism,[9] which immediately involved them in this conflict and thus in a battle which brought suffering. According to vv.33f. this affected all those in the community, some directly affected by imprisonment and public shame, others by solidarity with those directly involved[10] and through consequences which arose from this like the confiscation of property.[11] This time of suffering is probably recalled[12] because the threat is always there under the surface,[13] and the author does not want it to be avoided through adaptation. Therefore in v.35 he calls on Christians not to give up their confidence, their boldness.[14] Accordingly, looking back on the stories of Moses in 11.23-27 he twice mentions fearlessness towards Pharaoh,[15] who in connection with this theme is called 'the king' in both v.23 and v.27. The Greek word underlying this often denotes the Roman emperor. Moses' parents acted 'by faith' against an official 'decree of the king'.[16] Faith is shown by them, as also by the Christians addressed, in a lack of fear about being convicted of illegality.[17] The author wants to see the lack of fear with which Moses gave up his privileges and entered into solidarity with the tormented people of God (11.24-26) and in which those not affected by persecution show solidarity with those who are affected, among the Christians whom he is addressing. Any other behaviour here would be sin. Moses chose 'rather to share ill treatment with the people of God than to enjoy the fleeting pleasures of sin' (11.25). 'Sin' here is refusing to show solidarity with the suffering people of God.[18] Unconditional loyalty offers security, allows one to enjoy life; holding fast to the confession in the way which is manifested in practical solidarity always exposes a person to possible persecution. The discovery of this situation and the way in which it is overcome in scripture strengthens one's own weak position so that it becomes endurance, remaining in solidarity in the community of those who are oppressed, not giving up, resisting.

The author sees the basis of this behaviour, even by Moses, in a decision for the abuse suffered by Christ (11.26),[19] who for his part counted as nothing the shame he incurred as the crucified one (12.2).[20] The abuse shown to Christ on the cross thus provides the perspective for the discovery of one's own situation in scripture and with that the way in which it can be dealt with. Just as Moses left the ties of Egypt which offered him security and pleasure to suffer abuse with Christ by sharing suffering with his people, so, continuing this line, the author also summons his readers and hearers to a similar exodus. After saying in 13.12 that Jesus 'suffered before the gate', he writes in vv.13f.: 'Therefore let us go forth to him outside the camp bearing abuse for him. For here we have no lasting city, but we seek the city which is to come.' He issues a summons out of the assimilation which conceals the Christian confession, which promises security without danger and the peaceful enjoyment of life, but which rejects solidarity with the oppressed and thus denies the abused Christ; he calls his people to join 'the secular public with its danger and threat, to the point of being open to abuse and persecution'.[21] Finally, he justifies that by saying that on earth there is no abiding city for Christians. In saying this he is clearly opposed to the claim of 'eternal Rome'.[22] Christians have nothing to do with the fortress mentality of the Pax Romana.[23] Because they belong to God's coming city,[24] they are now on their way to this city unprotected and full of expectation.

Do we not rediscover our own situation here? A policy of security which threatens God's creation with annihilation; playing at sandcastles which take coolly into account megadeaths and infected and destroyed continents; a constantly escalating level of armaments which to an unimaginable degree makes claims on invention, fantasy, productivity and money whereas elsewhere countless people live in misery, in inhuman living conditions which are also a result of such a high level of armament. Is that not supreme irrationality in the garb of perfected technical rationality? Certainly we must note the facts. It is a fact that there is violence in the world, violence which also threatens us. But if the threat of violence holds us spellbound, an unlimited quest for security is not the inevitable consequence. Does not the abused Christ release us from this spell? Does he not also show us the violence which emanates from us as a fact, and above all the needs of the least of his brothers and sisters?[25] Does he not direct us towards solidarity with the suffering people of God whose ecumenical dimensions we may no longer suppress? From what perspective do we perceive facts? What is our primary problem: the connection between a high level of armament here and need there or our own security at any price? Can Christians have any other alternative than to go out from the fortress of a policy of security which is already fatal? Should not the confession of Jesus Christ really be at stake here?

Out of the fortress! Jesus cannot be found in it. The abused Christ executed on the cross encounters us in the open air and in unprotected, open space. He calls on us to set out. The way is not the goal; but the way pointed out and marked by the cross of Jesus is the place of the people of God at which it waits for and seeks the coming city. It has 'expectations which are capable of disappointment'.[26] In the outlines of the coming city which are already taking preliminary shape in being on the way, it continually looks, against all hardness of heart and full of hope, for a way of breaking through and moving forward.

Chronological Table of the Roman Emperors from Augustus to Commodus

31 BC – AD 14	Augustus
14-37	Tiberius
37-41	Caligula
41-54	Claudius
54-68	Nero
68-69	Galba, Otho, Vitellius
69-79	Vespasian
79-81	Titus
81-96	Domitian
96-98	Nerva
98-117	Trajan
117-138	Hadrian
138-161	Antoninus Pius
161-180	Marcus Aurelius (161-169 co-regency with Lucius Verus)
180-192	Commodus

Short Biographies of the Ancient Non-Christian Authors Cited

Apuleius

Born AD 125 in Madaura, Numidia, brought up in Carthage, studied in Athens, travelled in the East, lawyer in Rome, then again later in Africa, finally priest of the emperor cult in Carthage.

Aristides, Aelius

Born AD 117 son of a priest of Zeus in Asia Minor, educated in rhetoric by the most famous teachers of his time, 142/3 travelled to Egypt, 143/4 visited Rome, returned home, taught rhetoric and lectured in various places. Died about 187.

Augustus

Born 63 BC, died AD 14. Shortly before his death the emperor wrote an account of his acts.

Caesar

Born 100 BC, died 44 BC. This politician and general was also an active writer; we have his accounts of the Gallic War and the Civil War.

Dio Chrysostom

Born about AD 40 in Prusa in Bithynia, the most famous orator of his time, exiled under Domitian (an itinerant life in accordance with the Cynic ideal of hardening oneself and doing without); under Nerva and Trajan travellled to Rome in the service of his home town. The last report on him comes from the time when Pliny was proconsul in Bithynia (110/111).

Epictetus

Born about AD 55 in Hierapolis, Phrygia, a slave, who with the permission of his master went to hear the Stoic philosopher Rufus. After being freed he was a philosophical teacher in Rome. Expelled with all the philosophers in 89, he was active as a philosopher in Nicomedia; he died about 135.

Gellius, Aulus

Dates of birth and death unknown; he lived in the second century AD, and was probably born in Rome. Trained in grammar and rhetoric, he spent a year studying in Athens when he was thirty, and before or after that was appointed a judge.

Horace

Born 68 BC in Venusia (Apulia) the son of a freeman and freeborn mother, he grew up in Rome and from about 45 studied in Athens. He was a supporter of Brutus and took part in the battle of Philippi. He returned to Rome and in 38 was accepted into the circle around Maecenas. He was a friendly of Augustus, and died 8 BC.

Josephus

Born AD 37/38 of the Jewish priestly nobility; grew up within Palestinian Judaism, from 64-66 in Rome, 66/67 leader of the Jewish rebels in Galilee. Taken prisoner by Vespasian in 67 and spared because he prophesied that Vespasian would become emperor; freed by Vespasian after he had been made emperor. In Titus' entourage at the capture of Jerusalem and then writing in Rome, died after 100.

Juvenal

Born AD 67 in Aquinum (Campania), first active as a declamator, main creative period as a satyrical poet in the reign of Hadrian, perhaps died under Antoninus Pius.

Livy

Born 59 BC (?) in Padua, from a well-to-do family, a historian without any political or military activity; acquainted with Augustus, died AD 17 (?) in Padua.

Lucan

Born AD 39 in Cordoba, Spain, nephew of the philosopher Seneca. Educated in Rome, active as an epic poet; among Nero's friends, took part in Piso's conspiracy and committed suicide in 65 on the orders of Nero.

Marcus Aurelius

Born AD 121, died 180. The emperor, trained in philosophy, emerged as a Stoic writer in his *Meditations*, which were written after 168/169.

Martial

Born about AD 40 in Bilbilis, Spain, went to Rome about 64, the client of a rich patron. Wrote epigrams, elevated to the equestrian order, returned to Spain in 98 (or later) to a property given by friends, died 103/104.

Ovid

Born 43 BC in Sulmo the son of a Roman *eques*, studied rhetoric in Rome. Educational travelling to Greece and Asia Minor, career interrupted to write poetry, banished to Tomis on the Black Sea in AD 8, died 18.

Pausanias

Born between AD 111 and 115, presumably came from Asia Minor (Lydia), travelled to Greece, Rome, Syria, Palestine and Egypt. Wrote a description of Greece between about 160 and 180.

Petronius

Proconsul of Bithynia, a consul closely associated with Nero, who valued him as an arbiter in matters of taste, but ordered him to commit suicide in 66 because of an intrigue.

Philostratus

Born between AD 160 and 170, in possession of rights as an Attic citizen, studied in Athens, Ephesus and Hierapolis, active as a Sophist in Athens, travelled in Greece and Asia Minor, summoned to the imperial court and accepted into the circle of Julia Domna, the wife of the emperor Septimius Severus; after 217 returned to the East, where he stayed above all in Athens. Died under Philip Arabs (244-249). At the wish of Julia Domna Philostratus wrote the biography of Apollonius of Tyana, a Pythagoraean miracle worker and philosopher from the first century (died under Nerva).

Pliny the Elder

Born AD 23/24 in Como the son of a member of the equestrian order, 47-52 military career, withdrew into grammatical and rhetorical studies in the last decade of Nero's rule, 67/68 representative of the army prefect in Judaea, 68/69 sub-procurator of Syria, 69/70 a tribune of the legion in Egypt. Under Vespasian he held several procuratorships, in 76 he was given a high office at court and finally was a naval prefect in Misenum. He died in 79 when Vesuvius erupted.

Pliny the Younger

Born 61 or 62 in Como, nephew of Pliny the Elder, with whom he grew up after the early death of his father. Studied rhetoric in Rome, active as a lawyer, official career, consul in 100, imperial legate in Bithynia from 100-c.112, probably died there.

Plutarch

Born AD 45 of an eminent family from Chaironeia (Greece), studied philosophy in Athens, travelled to Greece, Egypt, Asia Minor, Italy and Rome, communal honorary offices in his ancestral city, from about 95 priest of Apollo in Delphi, close connection with the great men of Rome, died after 120.

Pompeius Trogus

Historian of the Augustan period from Gaul, whose grandfather had received Roman citizenship from Pompey.

Propertius

Born 47 BC in Assisi; in 41/40 some of the family's land was confiscated. Renounced a public career and turned to elegaic poetry, accepted into the circle around Maecenas, died 2 BC.

Seneca

Born 4 BC (?) in Cordoba, Spain, from the equestrian order; rhetorical and philosophical training in Rome. Preparation for a political career, elevation to become a senator; exiled to Corsica 41-48 because of an intrigue. Tutor of the young Nero and an influential director of imperial policy in the first years of his reign, after 62 he lost his influence and withdrew into literary work. On suspicion of being privy to the Piso conspiracy he was forced to commit suicide in 65.

Suetonius

Born about AD 70, of the equestrian order, probably from Hippo Regius in Numidia; rhetorical training (in Rome?), involvement as a lawyer, friendly with Pliny the Younger and furthered by him; high offices at the imperial court under Trajan (from about 114) and Hadrian. Retired 121.

Tacitus

Born about AD 55-56, rhetorical training in Rome, public career, consul 97, proconsul in Asia about 112/113.

Tibullus

Born about 50 BC, of the equestrian order, family's possessions partly confiscated in 41/40; representative of the circle of poets encouraged by Messalla, died probably about 17 BC.

Velleius Paterculus

Born c.20 BC, of the equestrian order, an officer; between AD 4 and 12 took part in the German-Pannonian campaigns of Tiberius; wrote a Roman history, died after AD 30.

Virgil

Born 70 BC in Mantua, educated in Cremona and Mediolanum, after 55 studied rhetoric in Rome (probably a Roman *eques*), broke off his studies because of a lack of aptitude. Studied philosophy in Naples, introduced to Octavian and Maecenas, died 19 BC.

Sources

(a) Works of non-Christian ancient authors

Where possible I have cited bi-lingual editions (the original with an English translation).

Apuleius, *The Golden Ass. Metamorphoses*, translated by W. Adlington, revised S.Gaselee, LCL, London and Cambridge, Mass. 1915

Aristides, *Die Romrede des Aelius Aristides*, ed.Richard Klein (with a German translation), Darmstadt 1983

Augustus, *Res gestae* (with Velleius Paterculus), translated by Frederick W.Shipley, LCL, 1924

Caesar, C.Julius, *The Gallic War*, translated by H.J.Edwards, LCL, 1917

Caesar, C.Julius, *The Civil Wars*, translated by A.G.Peskett, LCL, 1914

Dio Chrysostom, translated: I, II by J.W.Cohoon, III by J.W.Cohoon and H.Lama Crosby, IV, V by H.Lama Crosby, LCL, 1932-1951

Epictetus, *The Discourses as reported by Arrian, the Manual, and Fragments*, translated I, II by W.A.Oldfather, LCL, 1925, 1928

Gellius, Aulus, *The Attic Nights*, translated, I-III by John C.Rolfe, LCL, 1927

Horace, *Satires, Epistles, Ars Poetica*, translated by H.Ruston Fairclough, LCL, 1926

Horace, *Odes and Epodes*, translated by C.E.Bennett, LCL, 1924

Josephus, I, *The Life. Against Apion*, translated by H.St J. Thackeray, LCL, 1926

Josephus, II-III, *The Jewish War*, translated by H. St J. Thackeray, LCL, 1927-28

Josephus, IV-IX, *Jewish Antiquities*, translated: IV,V by H.St J.Thackeray, VI,VII by Ralph Marcus, VIII by Ralph Marcus and Allen Wikgren, IX by Louis H.Feldmann, LCL, 1930-1965

Juvenal (and Persius), *Satires*, translated by G.Ramsay, LCL, 1940

Livy, *Ab urbe condita*, translated: I-V by B.O.Forster, VI-VIII by Frank Gardner Moore, IX-XI by Evan T.Sage, XII by Evan T.Sage and Alfred C.Schlesinger, XIII by Alfred C.Schlesinger, LCL, 1919-1951

Lucan, *The Civil War*, translated by J.D.Duff, LCL, 1928

Marcus Aurelius Antoninus, *The Communing with Himself; together with his Speeches and Sayings*, translated by G.R.Haines, LCL, 1916

Martial, *Epigrams*, I,II translated by Walter C.A.Ker, LCL, 1919, 1920

Ovid, *Metamorphoses*, I, II translated by F.J.Miller, LCL, 1916

Pausanias, *Description of Greece*, I-IV, translated by W.H.S.Jones, LCL, 1918-1935

Petronius, *Satyricon* (with Seneca, *Apocolocyntosis*), translated by M.Heseltine, LCL, 1916
Philostratus, *The Life of Apollonius of Tyana, the Epistles of Apollonius and the Treatise of Eusebius*, I, II, translated by F.C.Conybeare, LCL, 1912
Pliny the Elder, *Natural History*, translated: I-V, IX by H.Rockham, VI-VIII by W.H.S.Jones, X by D.E.Eichholz, LCL, (1938) 1949-1962
Pliny the Younger, *Letters and Panegyricus*, I, II, translated by Betty Radice, LCL, 1969
Plutarch, *Moralia*, translated: I-V by Frank Cole Babbitt, VI by W.C.Helmbold, VII by Phillip H.de Lacy and Benedict Einarson, VIII by Paul A.Clement and Herbert B.Hoffleit, IX by F.H.Sandbach and W.C.Helmbold, X by Harold North Fowler, XI by Lionel Pearson and F.H.Sandbach, XII by Harold Cherniss and William C.Helmbold, XIII 1,2 by Harold Cherniss, XIV by Benedict Einarson and Phillip H.de Lacy, XV by F.H.Sandbach, LCL, 1927-1976
Plutarch, *Lives*, I-XI, translated by Bernadotte Perrin, LCL, 1914-1926
Pompeius Trogus, *M.Iuniani Iustini epitoma historiarum Philippicarum Pompeii Trogi*, ed. Otto Seel, Stuttgart 1972
Propertius, translated H.E.Butler, LCL, 1912
Seneca, *Ad Lucilium Epistulae Morales*, I-III, translated by Richard M.Gummere, LCL, 1917, 1920, 1925
Seneca, *Apocolocyntosis* (see Petronius, *Satyricon*), translated W.H.D.Rouse, LCL, 1916
Seneca, *Tragedies*, I,II, translated by F.J.Miller, LCL, 1917
Suetonius, I,II, translated by J.C.Rolfe, LCL, 1914
Tacitus, I-IV, *Annals*, translated by John Jackson, LCL 1931, 1937; *Histories*, translated by Clifford H.Moore, LCL 1925, 1931
Tacitus, *Dialogus de Oratoribus, Agricola, Germania*, translated by William Peterson, LCL, 1914
Tibullus, *Carmina* (with Catullus), translated by J.P.Postgate, LCL, 1912
Velleius Paterculus, *Compendium of Roman History*, translated by Frederick W.Shipley, LCL, 1924
Virgil, *Eclogues, Georgics, Aeneid I-VI*, translated by H.Ruston Fairclough (1916), LCL, revised 1947
Virgil, *Aeneid VII-XII*, translated by H.Ruston Fairclough, LCL, 1918

(b) Collections of non-Christian texts from antiquity

Billerbeck, Paul (Hermann L.Strack), *Kommentar zum Neuen Testament aus Talmud und Midrasch* I-IV 1,2, Munich [5]1969
Charlesworth, John T. (ed.), *Old Testament Pseudepigrapha* (two vols), New York and London 1983, 1985
Corpus Iuris. Eine Auswahl der Rechtsgrundsätze der Antike, translated into German and edited by Rudolf Düll, Munich 1939
Dittenberger, Wilhelm (ed.), *Orientis Graeci Inscriptiones Selectae. Supplementum Sylloges Inscriptionum Graecarum* I,II, Leipzig 1903, 1905
Dittenberger, Wilhelm (ed.), *Sylloge Inscriptionum Graecarum* I-III, Leipzig [3]1915-1920

Freids, Helmut (ed.), *Historische Inschriften zur römischen Kaiserzeit von Augustus bis Konstantin* (German translations), Texte zur Forschung 49, Darmstadt 1984

Hengstl, Joachim (ed.), *Griechische Papyri aus Ägypten als Zeugnisse des öffentlichen und privaten Lebens* (German and Greek texts), Munich 1978

Horsley, G.H.R (ed.), *New Documents illustrating Early Christianity. A Review of the Greek Inscriptions and Papyri published in 1976*, Macquarie University 1981

Maehler, Herwig (ed.), *Urkunden römischer Zeit*, ÄgU.G XI, 1, Berlin 1966

(c) Collections of texts from earliest Christianity and works by early Christian authors

Nestle-Aland, *Novum Testamentum Graece*, post Eberhard Nestle et Erwin Nestle communiter ed. Kurt Aland/MatthewBlack/Carlo M.Martini/Bruce M.Metzger/Allen Wikgren, apparatum criticum recensuerunt et editionem novis curis elaboraverunt Kurt Aland et Barbara Aland, Stuttgart [26]1979

Huck, Albert, *Synopse der drei ersten Evangelien mit Beigabe der johanneischen Parallelstellen*, new edition by Heinrich Greeven, Tübingen [13]1981; English translation of the text published as Burton H.Throckmorton, *Gospel Parallels*, Nashville [4]1979

Synopsis Quattuor Evangeliorum, ed. Kurt Aland, Stuttgart [8]1973

The Apostolic Fathers (including Didache, Barnabas, II Clement, Diognetus, Shepherd of Hermas), translated by Kirsopp Lake, I, II, LCL, 1912-13

Irenaeus, *Libros quinque adversus haereses*, I,II, ed. W.Wigan Harvey, Cambridge (1857) 1965

Tertullian, *Opera*, ed. August Reifferscheid and Georg Wissowa, CSEL XX, 1, Prague 1890; *Works*, The Ante-Nicene Fathers (two vols.), translated by A.Cleveland Coxe, reissued Grand Rapids 1980

Origen, *Contra Celsum*, ed. H.Chadwick, Cambridge 1953

Eusebius, *The Ecclesiastical History*, translated by Kirsopp Lake and J.E.L.Oulton, LCL, I,II, 1926, 1932

Bibliography

All the works given here are cited in the footnotes simply by the author's name. Where there is more than one work by the same author, in addition to the name a key word from the title is given; in commentaries on books of the New Testament the abbreviation of the work in question. Works cited once or twice which have only an indirect bearing on the subject are cited at the place where they are quoted with full bibliographical details. There are inevitably inconsistencies.

Agnoli, Johannes, 'Von der pax romana zur pax Christiana. Zum institutionellen Scheitern zweier Weltfriedensversuche', in *Systemwandel und Demokratisierung, FS Ossip K.Flechtheim*, ed. C.Fenner and B.Blanke, Frankfurt and Cologne 1975, 81-108

Aland, Kurt, 'Das Verhältnis von Kirche und Staat nach dem Neuen Testament und den Aussagen des 2.Jahrhunderts', in id., *Neutestamentliche Entwürfe*, ThB 63, Munich 1979, 26-123

Applebaum, Shimon, 'The Legal Status of the Jewish Communities in the Diaspora', in *The Jewish People in the First Century. Historical Geography, Political History, Social, Cultural, and Religious Life and Institutions*, ed. S.Safrai and M.Stern, Assen [2]1974, 420-63

Aune, David E., 'The Social Matrix of the Apocalypse of John', *BR* 26, 1981, 16-32

Bammel, Ernst, 'The Poor and the Zealots', in *Jesus and the Politics of His Day*, ed. id. and C.F.D.Moule, Cambridge 1984, 109-28

– , 'The Revolution Theory from Reimarus to Brandon', in ibid., 11-68

– , 'Romans 13', in ibid., 365-83

– , 'The Trial before Pilate', in ibid., 415-51

Bartsch, Hans-Werner, 'Die neutestamentlichen Aussagen über den Staat. Zu Karl Barths Brief an einen Pfarrer in der DDR', *EvTh* 19, 1959, 375-90

Baumbach, Günther, 'Das Verständnis von *eirene* im Neuen Testament', in *Theologische Versuche* 5, ed.Joachim Rogge and Gottfried Schille, Berlin 1975, 33-44, 49-52

Bechert, Tilmann, *PAX ROMANA. Friedenspolitik in römischer Zeit, Texte und Bilder zur Ausstellung 2. Mai bis 27.Juni 1982*, Niederrheinisches Museum der Stadt Duisburg

Beck, Herbert, and Peter C.Bol (eds.), *Spätantike und frühes Christentum. Ausstellung im Liebighaus, Museum alter Plastik, Frankfurt am Main, 16.Dezember 1983 bis 11.März 1984*, Frankfurt am Main 1983

Benjamin, Walter, 'Über den Begriff der Geschichte', in id., *Gesammelte*

Schriften I.2, ed. Rolf Tiedemann and Hermann Schweppenhauser, Frankfurt am Main 1974, 691-704

Bergmeier, Roland, 'Jerusalem, du hochgebaute Stadt', *ZNW* 75, 1984, 86-106

Beyschlag, Karlmann, *Clemens Romanus und der Frühkatholizismus. Untersuchungen zu I Clemens 1-7*, BHT 35, Tübingen 1966

– , 'Christentum und Veränderung in der Alten Kirche', *KuD* 18, 1972, 26-55

– , 'Zur ΕΙΡΗΝΗ ΒΑΘΕΙΑ (I Clem 2.2)', *VigChr* 26, 1972, 18-23

Bietenhard, Hans, and J.J.Stamm, *Der Weltfriede im Alten und Neuen Testament*, Zurich 1959

Bindemann, Walther, 'Materialistische Bibelinterpretation am Beispiel von Römer 13,1-7', *ZdZ* 35, 1981, 136-45

Blank, Josef, *Im Dienst der Versöhnung. Friedenspraxis aus christlicher Sicht*, Munich 1984

– , 'Kirche und Staat im Urchristentum', in *Kirche und Staat auf Distanz. Historische und aktuelle Perspektiven*, ed. Georg Denzler, Munich 1977, 9-28.

Bleicken, Jochen, *Verfassungs- und Sozialgeschichte des römischen Kaiserreiches* 1, 2, UTB 838, 839, Paderborn etc. ²1981

Böcher, Otto, *Die Johannesapokalypse*, EdF 41, Darmstadt ²1980

– , *Kirche in Zeit und Endzeit. Aufsätze zur Offenbarung des Johannes*, Neukirchen-Vluyn 1983

Borbein, Adolf H., 'Die Ara Pacis Augustae. Geschichtliche Wirklichkeit und Programm', *JdI* 90, 1975, 242-66

Bornkamm, Günther, *Jesus of Nazareth*, London and New York 1960

Bousset, Wilhelm, *Die Offenbarung Johannis*, KEK 16, Göttingen ⁶1906, reprinted 1968

Brandenburger, Egon, *Frieden im Neuen Testament. Grundlinien urchristlichen Friedensverständnisses*, Gütersloh 1973

Braun, Herbert, *An die Hebräer*, HNT 14, Tübingen 1984

Bringmann, Klaus, 'Christentum und römischer Staat im ersten und zweiten Jahrhundert n.Chr.', *GWU* 29, 1978, 1-18

Brunner, Gerbert, *Die theologische Mitte des ersten Klemensbriefs. Ein Beitrag zur Hermeneutik frühchristlicher Texte*, FTS 11, Frankfurt 1972

Budde, Ludwig, *Ara pacis Augustae. Der Friedensaltar des Augustus*, Hanover 1957

Bultmann, Rudolf, *The History of the Synoptic Tradition*, Oxford and New York 1968

Burr, Viktor, *Nostrum mare. Ursprung und Geschichte der Namen des Mittelmeeres und seine Teilmeere im Altertum*, Würzburger Studien zur Altertumswissenschaft 4, Stuttgart 1932

Cadbury, Henry J., *The Book of Acts in History*, London 1955

Campenhausen, Hans von, 'Zur Auslegung von Röm 13. Die dämonistische Deutung des *exousia*-Begriffs', in id., *Aus der Frühzeit des Christentums. Studien zur Kirchengeschichte des ersten und zweiten Jahrhunderts*, Tübingen 1963, 81-101

– , 'Der Kriegsdienst der Christen in der Kirche des Altertums', in id., *Tradition und Leben. Kräfte der Kirchengeschichte. Aufsätze und Vorträge*, Tübingen 1960, 203-15

Carr, Wesley, *Angels and Principalities. The Background, Meaning and Development of the Pauline Phrase* hai archai kai exousiai, MSSNTS, Cambridge 1981

– , ' "The Rulers of This Age" ' – I Corinthians II.6-8', *NTS* 23, 1977, 20-35

Cassidy, Richard J., *Jesus, Politics and Society. A Study of St Luke's Gospel*, Maryknoll, NY [3]1980

Chantraine, Heinrich, Response to Z.Rubin, 'Pax als politisches Schlagwort im alten Rom', in *Frieden und Friedenssicherung in Vergangenheit und Gegenwart, Symposium der Universitäten Tel Aviv und Mannheim 12-21 January 1978*, ed.Manfred Schlunke and Klaus-Jürgen Martin, Munich 1984, 35-40

Christensen, Torben, *Christus oder Jupiter. Der Kampf um die geistigen Grundlagen des römischen Reiches*, Göttingen 1981

Collins, Adela Yarbro, *Crisis and Catharsis: The Power of the Apocalypse*, Philadelphia 1984

– , 'Myth and History in the Book of Revelation: The Problem of its Date', in *Traditions in Transformation: Turning Points in Biblical Faith, FS Frank Moore Cross*, ed. Baruch Halpern and Jon D.Levenson, Indiana 1981, 377-403

– , 'Persecution and Vengeance in the Book of Revelation', in *Apocalypticism in the Mediterranean World and the Near East*, ed. David Hellholm, Tübingen 1983, 729-49

– , 'The Political Perspective of the Revelation to John', *JBL* 96, 1977, 241-56

– , 'The Revelation of John: An Apocalyptic Response to a Social Crisis', *CTM* 8, 1981, 4-12

– , 'Revelation 18: Taunt Song or Dirge?', in *L'Apocalypse johannique et l'Apocalyptique dans le Nouveau Testament*, ed.J.Lambrecht, BETL LIII, Gembloux/Leuven 1980, 185-204

Conzelmann, Hans, *Die Apostelgeschichte*, HNT 7, Tübingen 1963, English translation: *Acts*, Hermeneia, Philadelphia 1987 (forthcoming; page references in the notes are to the German edition)

– , *I Corinthians*, Hermeneia, Philadelphia 1975

– , *Heiden, Juden, Christen*, BHT 62, Tübingen 1981

– , *The Theology of St Luke*, London and New York 1960, reissued 1982

Cullmann, Oscar, *The State in the New Testament*, London 1957

Delling, Gerhard, 'Frieden IV', *TRE* 11, Berlin and New York 1983, 613-18

Dibelius, Martin, *Studies in the Acts of the Apostles*, London 1957

– , 'Rom und die Christen im ersten Jahrhundert', in *Botschaft und Geschichte. Gesammelte Aufsätze II. Zum Urchristentum und zur hellenistischen Religionsgeschichte*, with H.Kraft, ed. G.Bornkamm, Tübingen 1956, 177-228 (= SHAW.PH 2/1941, Heidelberg 1942)

Dinkler, Erich, *Eirene. Der urchristliche Friedensgedanke*, SHAW 1973/1, Heidelberg 1973

– and Erika Dinkler-von Schubert, 'Friede', *RAC* VIII, Stuttgart 1972, 434-505

Ebach, Jürgen, 'Apokalypse. Zum Ursprung einer Stimmung', in *Einwürfe* 2, ed. Friedrich-Wilhelm Marquardt, Dieter Schellong and Michael Weinrich, Munich 1985, 5-61.

– , *Das Erbe der Gewalt. Eine biblische Realität und ihre Wirkungsgeschichte*, Gütersloh 1980
– , 'Konversion oder Vertilgung. Utopie und Politik im Motiv des Tierfriedens bei Jesaja und Vergil', in *Spiegel und Gleichnis. FS Jacob Taubes*, ed. N.W.Bolz and W.Hübener, Würzburg 1983, 23-39.
– , *Leviathan und Behemoth. Eine biblische Erinnerung wider die Kolonisierung der Lebenswelt durch das Prinzip der Zweckrationalität*, Paderborn, etc. 1984
Eggenberger, Christian, *Die Quellen der politischen Ethik der 1. Klemensbriefes*, Zurich 1951
Ehrhardt, Arnold A.T., *Politische Metaphysik von Solon bis Augustin I. Die Gottesstadt der Griechen und Römer*, II. *Die christliche Revolution*, Tübingen 1959
Eisler, Robert, Ἰησοῦς βασιλεὺς οὐ βασιλεύσας. *Die messianische Unabhängigkeitsbewegung vom Auftreten Johannes des Täufers bis zum Untergang Jakobs des Gerechten II*, Heidelberg 1930.
Ellul, Jacques, *Apocalypse. Die Offenbarung des Johannes - Enthüllung der Wirklichkeit*, Neukirchen-Vluyn 1981
Schüssler-Fiorenza, Elisabeth, *Priester für Gott. Studien zum Herrschaft und Priestermotiv in der Apokalypse*, NTA 7, Munich 1972
– , 'Religion und Politik in der Offenbarung des Johannes', in *Biblische Randbemerkungen, Schüler-FS Rudolf Schnackenburg*, ed. Helmut Merklein and Joachim Lange, Würzburg 1974
Fischer, see Sources (c)
Foerster, Werner, εἰρήνη κτλ., *TDNT* 2, (398-400), 405-18
Franke, Peter Robert, *Kleinasien zur Römerzeit. Griechisches Leben im Spiegel der Münzen*, Munich 1968
Frankemölle, Hubert, *Friede und Schwert. Frieden schaffen nach dem Neuen Testament*, Mainz 1983
Freis, see Sources (b)
Fritz, Kurt von, 'Tacitus, Agricola, Domitian und das Problem des Prinzipates', in *Prinzipat und Freiheit*, ed. Richard Klein, WdF 135, Darmstadt 1969, 421-63
Fuchs, Harald, *Augustin und der antike Friedensgedanke. Untersuchungen zum neunzehnten Buch der* civitas dei, Berlin and Zurich [2]1965
– , *Der geistige Widerstand gegen Rom in der antiken Welt*, Berlin 1964
Gauger, Jörg-Dieter, 'Der Rom-Hymnos der Melinno (Anth.Lyr II[2] 6, 209f.) und die Vorstellung von der "Ewigkeit" Roms', *Chiron* 14, 1984, 267-99
Georgi, Dieter, 'Die Visionen vom himmlischen Jerusalem in Apk 21 und 22', *Kirche. FS Günther Bornkamm*, ed. Dieter Luhrmann and Georg Strecker, Tübingen 1980, 351-72
Gnilka, Joachim, *Das Evangelium nach Markus*, EKK II, 1,2, Zurich, etc. and Neukirchen-Vluyn 1978, 1979
– , *Der Kolosserbrief*, HTK X,1, Freiburg, etc. 1980
– , *Der Philipperbrief*, HTK X,3, Freiburg, etc. 1976
Goppelt, Leonhard, *Theology of the New Testament* (two vols.), Grand Rapids and London 1982, 1983
Gross, Karl, 'Domitianus', *RAC* 4, Stuttgart 1959, 91-109

Haenchen, Ernst, *The Acts of the Apostles*, Oxford and Philadelphia 1971

Harnack, Adolf von, *Einführung in die Kirchengeschichte. Das Schreiben der römischen Kirche an die korinthische aus der Zeit Domitians (I. Clemensbrief)*, Leipzig 1929

– , *Geschichte der altchristlichen Literatur bis Eusebius* II 1, Leipzig 1897

– , *Militia Christi. The Christian Religion and the Military in the First Three Centuries*, Philadelphia 1981

Hart, H.St J., 'The Coin of "Render to Caesar..." (A note on some aspects of Mark 12:13-17; Matt.22:15-22; Luke 20:20-26)', in *Jesus and the Politics of His Day*, ed. Ernst Bammel and C.F.D.Moule, Cambridge 1984, 214-18

Hegermann, Harald, 'Die Bedeutung des eschatologischen Friedens in Christus für den Weltfrieden heute nach dem Zeugnis des Neuen Testament', in *Der Friedensdienst der Christen. Beiträge zu einer Ethik des Friedens*, ed. Werner Danielsmeyer, Gütersloh 1970, 17-39

Heinze, Richard, *Die augusteische Kultur*, ed. Alfred Korte, Darmstadt [4]1983 (= Leipzig [2]1933)

Hengel, M., *Crucifixion*, London and Philadelphia 1977

– , *Die Zeloten. Untersuchungen zur jüdischen Freiheitsbewegung in der Zeit von Herodes I bis 70 n.Chr*, AGJU 1, Leiden and Cologne [2]1976

Hengstl, see Sources (b)

Hock, Ronald F., 'Paul's Tentmaking and the Problem of his Social Class', *JBL* 97, 1978, 555-64

Hoffmann, Paul, 'Eschatologie und Friedenshandeln in der Jesusüberlieferung', in *Eschatologie und Friedenshandeln. Exegetische Beiträge zur Frage christlicher Friedensverantwortung*, SBS 101, Stuttgart 1981, 115-52

– and Volker Eid, *Jesus von Nazareth und eine christliche Moral. Sittliche Perspektiven der Verkündigung Jesu*, QD 66, Freiburg [3]1979

– , 'Zur Verbindlichkeit des Gebots der Feindesliebe in der synoptischen Überlieferung und in der gegenwärtigen Friedensdiskussion', in *Ethik im Neuen Testament*, ed.Karl Kertelge, Freiburg, etc. 1984, 50-118

Horsley, see Sources (b)

Jaubert, Annie, 'Les sources de la conception militaire de l'église en 1 Clement 37', *VigChr* 18, 1964, 74-85

Jens, Walter, 'Libertas bei Tacitus', in *Prinzipat und Freiheit*, ed. Richard Klein, WdF 135, Darmstadt 1969, 391-420

Jewett, Robert, *Dating Paul's Life*, Philadelphia and London 1979

Jörns, Klaus-Peter, *Das hymnische Evangelium. Untersuchungen zu Aufbau, Funktion und Herkunft der hymnischen Stücke in der Johannesoffenbarung*, StNT 5, Gütersloh 1971

Käsemann, Ernst, 'Principles of the Interpretation of Romans 13', in *Religious Questions of Today*, London and Philadelphia 1969, 196-216

– , *Commentary on Romans*, Grand Rapids and London 1980

– , 'Römer 13,1-7 in unserer Generation', *ZTK* 56, 1959, 316-76

– , *Jesus Means Freedom*, London and Philadelphia 1969

Karpp, Heinrich, 'Christennamen C II 2, Christiani', *RAC* 2, Stuttgart 1954, 1131-7

Kent, John P.C., Bernhard Overbeck and Armin Stylow, *Die römische Münze*, Munich 1973

Kippenberg, Hans G. ' "Dann wird der Orient herrschen und der Okzident dienen". Zur Begründung eines gesamtvorderasiatischen Standpunktes im Kampf gegen Rom', in *Spiegel und Gleichnis, FS Jacob Taubes*, ed. N.W.Bolz and W.Hübener, Würzburg 1983, 40-8

Klein, Richard, Introduction to *Prinzipat und Freiheit*, ed. id., WdF 135, Darmstadt 1969, 1-22

Klingner, Friedrich, *Römische Geisteswelt. Essays zur lateinischen Literatur*, ed. Karl Büchner, Stuttgart 1979 (= Munich [5]1965)

Knibbe, Dieter, 'Rhesos A', *PRE Suppl.* 12, Stuttgart 1970, 248-96

Koch, Carl, 'Pax', *PRE* XVIII 4, Stuttgart 1949, 2430-6

– , 'Roma aeterna', in *Prinzipat und Freiheit*, ed. Richard Klein, WdF 135, Darmstadt 1969, 23-67

Kraft, Heinrich, *Die Offenbarung des Johannes*, HNT 16a, Tübingen 1974

Kromayer, Johannes and Georg Veith, *Heerwesen und Kriegführung der Griechen und Römer*, Munich 1928

Kuhn, Heinz-Wolfgang, 'Die Kreuzesstrafe während der frühen Kaiserzeit. Ihre Wirklichkeit und Wertung in der Umwelt des Urchristentums', *ANRW* II 25.1, Berlin and New York 1982, 648-793

Kunkel, Wolfgang, 'Zum Freiheitsbegriff der späten Republik und des Prinzipats', in *Prinzipat und Freiheit*, ed. Richard Klein, WdF 135, Darmstadt 1969, 68-93

Lange, Karl Ernst, *Der Friedensgedanke in der augusteischen Dichtung*, Diss. Kiel 1956

Lampe, G.W.H., 'The Two Swords (Luke 22,35-38)', in *Jesus and the Politics of his Day*, ed. E.Bammel and C.F.D.Moule, Cambridge 1984, 335-51

Lampe, Peter, 'Die Apokalyptiker – ihre Situation und ihr Handeln', in *Eschatologie und Friedenshandeln. Exegetische Beiträge zur Frage christlicher Friedensverantwortung*, SBS 101, Stuttgart 1981, 59-114

Lapide, Pinchas, *Wie liebt man seine Feinde?*, Mainz [2]1984

– , *Er predigte in ihren Synagogen. Jüdische Evangelienauslegung*, Gütersloh [3]1982

Laruccia, Stephen D, 'The Wasteland of Peace: A Tacitean Evaluation of Pax Romana', in *Studies in Latin Literature and Roman History* II, ed. Carl Derouxer, Collection Latomus 168, Brussels 1980, 407-11

Liebenam, 'Exercitus', *PRE* VI 2, Stuttgart 1909, 1589-1679

Lietzmann, Hans, *An die Korinther I-II*, ed. Werner Georg Kümmel, HNT 9, Tübingen [4]1949

Linskens, John, 'A Pacifist Interpretation of Peace in the Sermon on the Mount?', *Concilium* 164, 1983, 16-25

Loader, William R.G., *Sohn und Hoherpriester. Eine traditionsgeschichtliche Untersuchung zur Christologie des Hebräerbriefes*, WMANT 53, Neukirchen-Vluyn 1981

Lohmeyer, Ernst, *Die Offenbarung des Johannes*, HNT 16, Tübingen [2]1953

Lührmann, Dieter, 'Liebet eure Feinde (Lk 6,27-36/Matt.5, 39-48)', *ZTK* 69, 1972, 412-38

MacMullen, Ramsay, *Enemies of the Roman Order. Treason, Unrest and Alienation in the Empire*, Cambridge, Mass. 1966

Maehler, see Sources (b)

Magie, David, *Roman Rule in Asia Minor to the End of the Third Century after Christ* I, II, Freiburg, etc. 1972

Matthiae, Jochen, *Die Genese des Amtspriestertums in der frühen Kirche, Der priesterliche Dienst III*, QD 48, Freiburg etc. 1972

Matthiae, Karl, and Edith Schörnet-Geiss, *Münzen aus der urchristlichen Umwelt*, Berlin 1981

Mehl, Andreas, '*Ubi solitudinem faciunt, pacem appellant.* Ein antikes Zitat über römischen, englischen und deutschen Imperialismus', *Gym.* 83, 1976, 281-8

Merkelbach, Reinhold, 'Der Rangstreit der Städte Asiens und die Rede des Aelius Aristides über die Eintracht', *ZPE* 32, 1978, 287-96

Metz, Johann Baptist, *Unterbrechungen. Theologisch-politische Perspektiven und Profile*, Gütersloh 1981

Meyer, Hans D., 'Die Aussenpolitik des Augustus und die augusteische Dichtung. Properz', in *Properz*, ed. Werner Eisenhut, WdF 237, Darmstadt 1975, 287-301

Michel, Otto, *Der Brief an die Hebräer*, KEK 13, Göttingen 1966

– , *Der Brief an die Römer*, KEK 12, Göttingen [12]1963

Mikat, Paul,'Der "Auswanderungsrat" (I Clem.54.2) als Schlüssel zum Gemeindeverständnis im 1.Clemensbrief', in *Bonner Festgabe Johannes Straub*, Bonn 1977, 213-23

– , 'Lukanische Christusverkündigung und Kaiserkult. Zum Problem der christlichen Loyalität gegenüber dem Staat', in id., *Religionsrechtliche Schriften. Abhandlungen zum Staatskirchenrecht und Eherecht* II, ed. Joseph Listl, Berlin 1974, 809-44

– , 'Die Bedeutung der Begriffe Stasis und Aponoia für das Verständnis des 1.Clemensbriefes', ibid., 719-51

Molthagen, Joachim, 'Der römische Staat und die Christen im zweiten und dritten Jahrhundert', *Hyp.* 28, Göttingen [2]1975

Mommsen, Theodor, 'Die Rechstverhältnisse des Apostels Paulus', *ZNW* 2, 1901, 81-6

Morgenthaler, R., 'Roma Sedes Satanae, Röm.13.1ff. im Lichte von Luk.4.5-8', *ThZ* 12, 1956, 289-304

Müller, Ulrich B., *Messias und Menschensohn in jüdischen Apokalypsen und in der Offenbarung des Johannes*, StNT 6, Gütersloh 1972

– , *Die Offenbarung des Johannes*, ÖTK 19, Gütersloh and Würzburg 1984

– , *Zur frühchristlichen Theologiegeschichte. Judenchristentum und Paulinismus in Kleinasien an der Wende vom ersten zum zweiten Jahrhundert n.Chr*, Gütersloh 1976

Mussner, Franz, *Der Brief an die Epheser*, ÖTK 10, Gütersloh and Würzburg 1982

Nebe, Gottfried, *Hoffnung bei Paulus. Elpis und ihre Synonyme im Zusammenhang der Eschatologie*, SUNT 16, Göttingen 1983

Nestle, Wilhelm, *Der Friedensgedanke in der antiken Welt*, PhS 31.1, Leipzig 1938

Opelt, Ilona, 'Augustustheologie und Augustustypologie', *JAC* 4, 1961, 44-57

– , *Die lateinischen Schimpfwörter und verwandte sprachliche Erscheinungen. Eine Typologie*, Heidelberg 1965

Perrin, Norman, *Rediscovering the Teaching of Jesus*, London and Philadelphia 1967

Pesch, Rudolf, *Das Markusevangelium*, HTK II, 1,2, Freiburg, etc. 1976, 1977

Peterson, Erik, 'Christianus', in id., *Frühkirche, Judentum und Gnosis, Studien und Untersuchungen*, Rome, etc. 1959, 64-87

Petzke, Gerd, 'Der historische Jesus in der sozialethischen Diskussion. Mk 12.13-17 par', in *Jesus Christus in Historie und Theologie, FS Hans Conzelmann*, ed.Georg Strecker, Tübingen 1975, 223-35

Pflaum, Hans-Georg, 'Das Römische Kaiserreich', *PWG* IV, Berlin, etc. 1963, 317-428

Plümacher, Eckhard, 'Apostelgeschichte', *TRE* 3, Berlin and New York 1978, 283-528

Preuschen, Erwin, *Die Apostelgeschichte*, HNT 4/1, Tübingen 1912

Raith, Werner, *Das verlassene Imperium. Über das Aussteigen des römischen Volkes aus der Geschichte*, Berlin 1982

Richter, Will, 'Römische Zeitgeschichte und innere Emigration', *Gym.* 68, 1961, 286-315

Riekkinen, Vilho, *Römer 13, Aufzeichnung und Weitererführung der exegetischen Diskussion*, AASF 23, Helsinki 1980

Roloff, Jürgen, *Die Offenbarung des Johannes*, ZBK NT 18, Zurich 1983

Rostovtzeff, Michael, *Gesellschaft und Wirtschaft im römischen Kaiserreich* I, II, Heidelberg nd.

Rubin, Zeev, 'Pax als politisches Schlagwort im alten Rom', in *Frieden und Friedenssicherung in Vergangenheit und Gegenwart. Symposium der Universitäten Tel Aviv und Mannheim 12-21. Januar 1978*, ed. Manfred Schunke and Klaus-Jürgen Martin, Munich 1984, 21-34

Schäfke, Werner, 'Frühchristlicher Widerstand', *ANRW* II 23/1, Berlin and New York 1979, 460-723

Scheibler, Ingeborg, 'Götter des Friedens in Hellas und Rom', *Antike Welt* 15/1, 1984, 39-57

Schille, Gottfried, *Die Apostelgeschichte des Lukas*, THK V, Berlin 1983

Schlatter, Adolf, *Paulus, der Bote Jesu. Eine Deutung seiner Briefe an die Korinther*, Stuttgart [2]1956

Schlier, Heinrich, *Der Apostel und seine Gemeinde. Auslegung der ersten Briefes an die Thessalonicher*, Freiburg etc. [2]1973

– , *Der Römerbrief*, HTK VI, Freiburg, etc. 1977

Schmithals, Walter, 'Zum Friedensauftrag der Kirche und der Christen', in *Christliche Ethik und Sicherheitspolitik. Beiträge zur Friedensdiskussion*, ed. Erwin Wilkens, Frankfurt 1982, 11-34

– , *Das Evangelium nach Markus*, ÖTK 2/1,2, Gütersloh and Würzburg 1979

Schnackenburg, Rudolf, *Der Brief an die Epheser*, EKK X, Zurich, etc. and Neukirchen-Vluyn 1982

Schneemelcher, Wilhelm, 'Kirche und Staat im Neuen Testament', in *Kirche und Staat, FS Hermann Kunst*, ed. Kurt Aland and id., Berlin 1967, 1-18

Schneider, Gerhard, *Die Apostelgeschichte*, HTK V, 1,2, Freiburg etc. 1980, 1982

– , 'The Political Charge against Jesus (Luke 23.2)', in *Jesus and the Politics of his Day*, ed. Ernst Bammel and C.F.D.Moule, Cambridge 1984, 403-14

– , *Das Evangelium nach Lukas*, ÖTK 3/1,2, Gütersloh and Würzburg 1977

– , *Verleugnung, Verspottung und Verhör Jesu nach Lukas 22.34-71. Studien zur lukanischen Darstellung der Passion*, SANT 22, 1969

Schottroff, Luise, 'Die Friedenspraxis Jesu und seiner Boten', in id., *Der Sieg des Lebens. Biblische Traditionen einer Friedenspraxis*, Kaiser Traktate 68, Munich 1982, 23-47

– , 'Gewaltverzicht und Feindesliebe in der urchristlichen Jesustradition. Mt 5,37-48; Lk 6,27-36', in *Jesus Christus in Historie und Theologie. FS Hans Conzelmann*, ed. Georg Strecker, Tübingen 1975, 197-221

– , ' "Gebt dem Kaiser was dem Kaiser gehört, und Gott, was Gott gehört." Die theologische Antwort der urchristlichen Gemeinden auf ihre gesellschaftliche und politische Situation', in *Annahme und Widerstand*, ed. Jürgen Moltmann, Kaiser Traktate 79, Munich 1984, 15-58

– , 'Die Schreckensherrschaft der Sünde und die Befreiung durch Christus nach dem Römerbrief des Paulus', *EvTh* 39, 1979, 497-510

– and Wolfgang Stegemann, *Jesus von Nazareth – Hoffnung der Armen*, Stuttgart, etc. 1978

Schrage, Wolfgang, *Die Christen und der Staat nach dem Neuen Testament*, Gütersloh 1971

– , *Ethik des Neuen Testaments*, NTD Ergänzungsreihe 4, Göttingen 1982 (ET in preparation, Philadelphia 1987)

– , 'Leid, Kreuz und Eschaton. Die Peristasenkataloge als Merkmale paulinischer *theologia crucis* und Eschatologie', *EvTh* 34, 1974, 141-75

Schulz, Otto Theodor, *Die Rechtstitel und Regierungsprogramme auf römischen Kaisermünzen (Von Caesar bis Severus)*, SGKA 13/4, Paderborn 1925

Schulz, Siegfried, *Q. Die Spruchquelle der Evangelisten*, Zurich 1972

Schwarz, Franz Ferdinand, 'Sehnsucht und Wirklichkeit, Reflexionen zu *pax* und *bellum* bei Tibull (I 10)', *Altsprachlicher Unterricht* 23, 1980, 40-58.

Schweizer, Eduard, *Der Brief an die Kolosser*, EKK XII, Zurich, etc. and Neukirchen-Vluyn 1976

– , *Good News according to Matthew*, Atlanta 1975 and London 1976

Sellin, Gerhard, 'Das Geheimnis der Weisheit und das Rätsel der Christuspartei (zu 1 Kor 1-4)', *ZNW* 73, 1982, 69-96

Sherwin-White, A.N., *Roman Society and Roman Law in the New Testament*, Oxford 1963

Simon, Erika, *Ara pacis Augustae, Monumenta artis antiquae*, Tübingen, nd (1967)

Speigl, Jakob, *Der römische Staat und die Christen. Staat und Kirche von Domitian bis Commodus*, Amsterdam 1970

Stemberger, Günther, 'Die Beurteilung Roms in der rabbinischen Literatur', *ANRW* II, 19/2, Berlin and New York 1979, 338-96

– , *Die römische Herrschaft im Urteil der Juden*, EdF 195, Darmstadt 1983

Stier, Hans Erich, 'Augustusfriede und römische Klassik', *ANRW* II,2, Berlin and New York 1975, 3-54

Stolle, Volker, *Der Zeuge als Angeklagter. Untersuchungen zum Paulusbild des Lukas*, Stuttgart, etc. 1973

Strecker, Georg, *Die Bergpredigt. Ein exegetischer Kommentar*, Göttingen 1984

– , 'Die Makarismen der Bergpredigt', in id., *Eschaton und Historie. Aufsätze*, Göttingen 1979, 108-31

Strobel, August, 'Apokalypse des Johannes', *TRE* 3, Berlin and New York 1978, 174-89

– , 'Furcht, wem Furcht gebührt. Zum profangriechischen Hintergrund von Rom 13,7', *ZNW* 55, 1964, 58-62

– , 'Zum Verständnis vom Rm 13', *ZNW* 47, 1956, 67-93

Stuhlmacher, Peter, 'Der Begriff des Friedens im Neuen Testament und seine Konsequenzen', in *Historische Beiträge für Friedensforschung*, ed. Wolfgang Huber, Studien zur Friedensforschung 4, Stuttgart and Munich 1970, 21-69

Stuhlmann, Rainer, *Das eschatologische Mass im Neuen Testament*, FRLANT 132, Göttingen 1983

Sutherland, C.H.V., *Roman Imperial Coinage*, London nd; German concise ed., *Münzen der Römer*, Munich and Fribourg 1974, to which references are made

Taeger, Jens-W., 'Einige neuere Veröffentlichungen zur Apokalypse des Johannes', *VuF* 29, 1984, 50-75

Theissen, Gerd, 'Gewaltverzicht und Feindesliebe (Matt.5.38-48/Luke 6.27-38) und deren sozialgeschichtliche Hintergrund', in id., *Studien zur Soziologie des Urchristentums*, WUNT 19, Tübingen 1979, 160-97

– , 'Die starken und Schwachen in Korinth. Soziologische Analyse eines theologischen Streites', ibid., 272-89

– , 'Die Tempelweissagung Jesu. Prophetie im Spannungsfeld von Stadt und Land', ibid., 142-59

– , *Untersuchungen zum Hebräerbrief*, StNT 2, Gütersloh 1969

– , *Miracle Stories of the Early Christian Tradition*, Edinburgh 1983

Trummer, Peter, 'Warum Gewaltlose selig sind. Exegetische Hinweise zum Verständnis von Mt 5,5', in *Gedanken des Friedens*, ed. id., Grazer Theologische Studien, Graz 1982, 203-36

– , 'Gewaltloser Widerstand in neutestamentlicher Zeit. Und was daraus zu lernen ist', ibid., 165-201

Ullmann, Walter, 'The Cosmic Theme of the *Prima Clementis* and its Significance for the Concept of Roman Rulership', *StPatr* 11, TU 108, Berlin 1972, 85-91

Unnik, Willem Cornelis van, ' "Tiefer Friede" (I Klemens 2,2)', *VigChr* 24, 1970, 261-79

– , 'Noch einmal "tiefer Friede". Nachschrift zu dem Aufsatz von Herrn Dr K.Beyschlag', *VigChr* 26, 1972, 24-8

– , 'Lob und Strafe durch die Obrigkeit. Hellenistisches zu Röm 13,3-4', in *Jesus und Paulus, FS Werner Georg Kümmel*, ed. E.Earle Ellis and E.Grässer, Göttingen 1975, 334-43

Vielhauer, Philipp, *Geschichte der urchristlichen Literatur. Einleitung in das Neuen Testament, die Apokryphen und die Apostolischen Väter*, Berlin and New York 1975

Vögtle, Anton, *Was ist Frieden? Orientierungshilfen aus dem Neuen Testament*, Freiburg, etc. 1983

Vogt, Joseph, *Kulturwelt und Barbaren. Zum Menschheitsbild der spätantiken Gesellschaft*, AAWLM.G.1967/1, Mainz 1967

– , 'Tacitus und die Unparteilichkeit des Historikers', in *Prinzipat und Freiheit*, ed. Richard Klein, WdF 135, Darmstadt 1964, 9-20

Walaskay, Paul W., *'And So We Came to Rome.' The Political Perspective of St Luke*, Cambridge 1983

Weber, Wilhelm, '... *nec nostri saeculi est*. Bemerkungen zum Briefwechsel des Plinius und Trajan über die Christen', in *Das frühe Christentum im romischen Staat*, ed. Richard Klein, WdF 267, Darmstadt 1971, 1-32

Weber-Schäfer, Peter, *Einführung in die antike politische Theorie II. Von Platon bis Augustinus*, Darmstadt 1976

Weinstock, S, 'Pax and the Ara Pacis', *JRS* 50, 1960, 44-58

Weiser, Alfons, *Die Apostelgeschichte*, ÖTK 5/12, Gütersloh and Würzburg 1981, 1985

Weiss, Johannes, *Der erste Korintherbrief*, KEK 5, Göttingen 1910

Wenger, Otto Paul, *Römische Kaisermünzen*, Orbis Pictus 63, Berne and Stuttgart 1975

Wickert, Lothar, 'Der Prinzipat und die Freiheit', in *Prinzipat und Freiheit*, ed. Richard Klein, WdF 135, Darmstadt 1969, 94-135

Wifstrand-Schiebe, Marianne, *Das ideale Dasein bei Tibull und die Goldzeitkonzeption Vergils*, Acta Universitatis Upsaliensis, Studia Latina Upsaliensia 13, Uppsala 1981

Wilckens, Ulrich, *Der Brief an die Römer*, EKK VI 1,2,3, Zurich, etc and Neukirchen-Vluyn 1978, 1980, 1982

Wimmel, Walter, 'Tibull II 5 und das elegische Rombild', in *Gedenkschrift Georg Rohde*, ed. Gerhard Radke, Aparchai 4, Tübingen 1962, 227-66

Windisch, Hans, *Imperium und Evangelium im Neuen Testament. Rede zur Verfassungsfeier, gehalten an der Christian- Albrechts-Universität am 28.Juli 1931*, Kieler Universitätsreden 14, Kiel 1931

Wissowa, G., 'Pax', *AGLM* III 2, Leipzig 1902-1909, 1719-22

Wlosok, Antonie, 'Die Rechtsgrundlagen der Christenverfolgungen der ersten zwei Jahrhunderte', in *Das frühe Christentum im römischen Staat*, ed. Richard Klein, WdF 257, Darmstadt 1971, 275-301

Abbreviations

AASF	Annales academiae scientiarum Fennicae
AAWLM.G	Abhandlungen der Akademie der Wissenschaften und Literatur in Mainz. Geistes- und sozialwissenschaftliche Klasse
ÄGU.G	Grieschische Urkunden aus den staatlichen Museen zu Berlin
AGJU	Arbeiten zur Geschichte des antiken Judentums und des Urchristentums
ALGM	*Ausführliches Lexicon der griechischen und römischen Mythologie*, ed. W. H. Roscher
ANRW	*Aufstieg und Niedergang der Römischen Welt*, ed. H. Temporini and W. Hesse, Berlin 1972ff.
BETL	Bibliotheca Ephemeridum Theologicarum Lovaniensium
BHT	Beiträge zur historischen Theologie
BMCRomEmp	*Coins of the Roman Empire in the British Museum*, ed. H. Mattingly, London 1923ff.
BR	*Biblical Research*
CSEL	Corpus scriptorum ecclesiasticorum Latinorum
CTM	*Concordia Theological Monthly*
Dig.	*Digesta*, see Sources (b) under *Corpus iuris*
EdF	Erträge der Forschung
EKK	Evangelisch-katholischer Kommentar zum Neuen Testament
ET	English Translation
EvTh	*Evangelische Theologie*
EWNT	*Exegetisches Wörterbuch zum Neuen Testament*
FRLANT	Forschungen zur Literatur des Alten und Neuen Testaments
FS	*Festschrift*
FTS	Frankfurter theologische Studien
GWU	*Geschichte in Wissenschaft und Unterricht*
Gym.	*Gymnasium*
HIRK	*Historische Inschriften zur römischen Kaiserzeit* (see Bibliography under Freis)
HNT	Handbuch zum Neuen Testament
HTK	Herders Theologischer Kommentar
Hyp.	*Hypomnemata*
JAC	*Jahrbuch für Antike und Christentum*
JBL	*Journal of Biblical Literature*
JdI	*Jahrbuch des deutschen archäologischen Instituts*
JRS	*Journal of Roman Studies*

KEK	Kritisch-exegetischer Kommentar
KP	*Der Kleine Pauly. Lexikon der Antike* (5 vols.)
LCL	Loeb Classical Library
MSSNTS	Monograph Series of the Society for New Testament Studies
NTA	Neutestamentliche Abhandlungen
NTD	Das Neue Testament Deutsch
NTS	*New Testament Studies*
OGIS	*Orientis Graeci Inscriptiones Selectae*, see Bibliography under Dittenberger
ÖTK	Ökumenischer Taschenbuch-Kommentar
PhS	*Philosophic Studies*
PRE	*Paulys Real-Encyclopädie der classischen Alterthumswissenschaft*, new ed. begun G. Wissowa, 1894ff.
PWG	Propyläen Weltgeschichte
QD	Quaestiones Disputatae
RAC	*Reallexikon für Antike und Christentum*
RGG	*Die Religion in Geschichte und Gegenwart*
SANT	Studien zum Alten und Neuen Testament
SBS	Stuttgarter Bibelstudien
SGKA	Studien zur Geschichte und Kultur des Altertums
SHAW	Sitzungsberichte der Heidelberger Akademie der Wissenschaften
StNT	Studien zum Neuen Testament
StPatr	*Studia Patristica*
SUNT	Studien zur Umwelt des Neuen Testaments
*Sylloge*³	*Sylloge Inscriptionum Graecarum*, see Bibliography under Dittenberger
ThA	Theologische Arbeiten
ThB	Theologisches Bücherei
TDNT	*Theological Dictionary of the New Testament*, ed. G. Kittel
THK	Theologischer Handkommentar zum Neuen Testament
ThZ	*Theologische Zeitschrift*
TRE	*Theologische Realenzyklopädie*
TU	Texte und Untersuchungen
UTB	Uni-Taschenbücher
VigChr	*Vigiliae Christianae*
VuF	*Verkündigung und Forschung*
WdF	Wege der Forschung
WMANT	Wissenschaftliche Monographien zum Alten und Neuen Testament
WUNT	Wissenschaftliche Untersuchungen zum Neuen Testament
ZBK	Zürcher Bibelkommentar
ZdZ	*Zwischen die Zeiten*
ZKG	*Zeitschrift für Kirchengeschichte*
ZNW	*Zeitschrift für die Neutestamentliche Wissenschaft*
ZPE	*Zeitschrift für Papyrologie und Epigraphik*
ZTK	*Zeitschrift für Theologie und Kirche*

Notes

Introduction (I)

1. The word 'peace' and its derivatives occur in exactly 100 passages in the New Testament, but very often in stereotyped phrases like 'go in peace', 'peace be with you', 'grace be with you and peace from God our Father and the Lord Jesus Christ', 'the God of peace'.

2. The unity of the death and resurrection of Jesus is the focal point for the formation of primitive Christian statements of faith, cf. Wengst, 'Glaubensbekenntnisse IV.Neues Testament', *TRE* XIII, Berlin and New York 1985, 392-9.

3. For crucifixion in antiquity cf. Kuhn, passim, and above all Hengel, *Crucifixion*, passim, esp. 33-63.

4. Cf. Mark 11.15-19 par.; 14.58 par.; 15.29 par. and in addition Theissen, 'Tempelweissagung', passim.

5. Kuhn, 733, cf. 678; also Hengel, *Crucifixion*, 47: 'Josephus gives us numerous instances from Judaea that it was used excessively to "pacify" rebellious provincials.'

6. Cf. Kuhn, 726; Hengel, *Zeloten*, 30, 265-8, 347.

7. The historicity of this information is disputed; against it cf. Bultmann, *Tradition*, 284; Schmithals, *Markus*, 683; for it, with what I find to be convincing arguments, e.g. Pesch, *Markus* II, 484.

8. Mark 15.33.

9. Mark 15.38.

10. The words 'by the blood of the cross' are usually taken to be an addition to the hymn by the author, cf. e.g. Schweizer, *Kolosser*, 53f., 55; Gnilka, *Kolosser*, 58, 71, 76.

11. He makes that quite clear by the definition of the 'body' (which in the hymn means the universe) as 'community' in v.18. That this is an addition by the writer of the letter is almost universally recognized; cf. Schweizer, *Kolosser*, 52f., 69f.; Gnilka, *Kolosser*, 58, 69f., 77. It is also shown by the prayer of thanksgiving with reference to baptism which is put before the hymn in vv.12-14, and finally through his demands in vv.21-23 which are addressed directly to the community.

12. We can leave aside the question whether the basis of this is a traditional hymn; both the most recent commentaries argue against this (Schnackenburg, *Epheser*, 106f.; Mussner, *Epheser*, 19).

13. Cf. Mussner, *Epheser*, 81.

14. II Cor.5.17; Gal.6.15.

15. Gal.3.28; I Cor.12.13; Col.3.11.

16. Cf. Metz's dictum about Ernst Bloch; Metz has spoken of the 'interruption of the rebellion against the graceless continuity which has made our souls so apathetic and so hopeless' (*Unterbrechungen*, 69).
17. Luke 24.39; John 20.20; cf. above all John 20.25,27.
18. Benjamin, 704.

Part One (II)

1. Aristides, *Eulogy of Rome*, 106.
2. Virgil, *Aeneid* VI, 791-5, cf. *Eclogue* IV.4-10: 'Now is come the last age of the song of Cumae; the great line of the centuries begins anew. Now the Virgin returns, the reign of Saturn returns; now a new generation descends from heaven on high. But do you, pure Lucina, smile on the birth of the child under whom the iron brood shall first cease and a golden race spring up throughout the world. Your own Apollo is king.' Cf. the whole of this famous eclogue and on it Ebach, *Konversion*, passim. In the course of the Roman empire the golden age has to be continually proclaimed afresh. It was already heralded by Augustus, and again awaited in the early days of Nero (see Seneca, *Apocol.*, 4.1; Lucan, *Bellum Civile* I, 33f.), but then hoped for only on the presupposition of its demise (cf. Seneca, *Octavia* 391ff.) (ML).
3. Here I need mention only the two earliest witnesses of this view handed down to us. In 175 Bishop Melito of Sardes wrote in his *Apologia* to the emperor: 'Our way of thought first sprang up in a foreign land, but it flowered among your own peoples in the glorious reign of your ancestor Augustus, and became to your empire especially a portent of good, for from then on, the power of Rome grew great and splendid... this way of thought began with Augustus and has grown to full stature along with the Empire... The greatest proof that the establishment of our religion at the very time when the Empire began so auspiciously was an unmixed blessing lies in this fact – from the reign of Augustus the Empire has suffered no damage, on the contrary everything has gone splendidly and gloriously, and every prayer has been answered' (cited in Eusebius, *HE* IV, 26,7f.). Origen (who died in 254) refers the quotation of Ps.72.7 ('In his days may righteousness flourish, and peace abound till the moon be no more') to the birth of Jesus under Augustus; through the Roman empire the fulfilment of the task of universal mission had been made easier: 'It is quite clear that Jesus was born during the reign of Augustus, the one who reduced to uniformity, so to speak, the many kingdoms on earth so that he had a single empire. Accordingly, how could this teaching, which preaches peace and does not even allow men to take vengeance on their enemies, have had any success unless the international situation everywhere had been changed and a milder spirit prevailed at the advent of Jesus?' (*Contra Celsum* II, 30). For the view of the principate by the church fathers as a 'time of coincidence', cf. Opelt, 'Augustustheologie', passim (further literature is mentioned there).
4. Pflaum, 384.
5. Aristides, 103.
6. Henze, 8.
7. Aristides, 99.

8. Augustus, *Res Gestae*, 13; cf. Virgil, *Aeneid* I, 291-6, where Jupiter prophesies to Venus: 'Then shall wars cease and the rough ages soften; hoary Faith and Vesta, Quirinus with his brother Remus, shall give laws. The gates of war, grim with iron and close-fitting bars, shall be closed; within, impious Rage, sitting on savage arms, his hands fast bound behind with a hundred brazen knots, shall roar in the ghastliness of bloodstained lips.' Nero had celebrated on coins the closing of the temple of Janus which he had ordered, cf. Sutherland, 163, no.309.

9. Augustus, *Res Gestae* 12.

10. OGIS 458.

11. *The Collection of Ancient Greek Inscriptions in the British Museum* IV, ed. G.Hirschfeld, London 1893, no.894.

12. Aristides, 6.

13. Ibid.

14. Cf the famous sequence in Tacitus, *Annals* I.4.1: '...as long as Augustus... upheld himself, his house and peace.'

15. Seneca, *De Clementia* I,4,1f. For the concept of the Pax Romana cf. also Seneca, *Ad Polybium* XV, 1; *De Providentia* IV,14. Somewhat later Pliny the Elder speaks of: 'The boundless grandeur of the Roman peace, which displays in turn not men only with their different lands and tribes but also mountains, and peaks soaring into the clouds, their offspring and also their plants. May this gift of the gods last, I pray, for ever! So truly do they seem to have given to the human race the Romans as it were a second sun' (Pliny, *Natural History* XXVIII, 3).

16. Of course modern admirers of Rome do not take this question into account. It is already almost comic that Stier should cite as 'the most brilliant example' of the statement 'In the long run the (!) ancient world did not regret the fact that it became Roman' Aelius Aristides' *Eulogy of Rome* (35) and refer the question 'what echo the first Princeps found among the (!) population of the *Orbis Romanus* with his new orientation for Roman policy' to the two inscriptions from Halicarnassus that I have already mentioned from Halicarnassus and Priene and to Suetonius, *Augustus*, 98 (50f.). The Suetonius passage, according to which as the aged Augustus was sailing past Puteoli 'the passengers and sailors on a ship from Alexandria that had just arrived, decked with garlands and burning incense, called out their good wishes to him and lavished the utmost praise; it was only thanks to him that they were alive, thanks to him that they voyaged and thanks to him that they enjoyed freedom and prosperity' is not, as Stier wants it to be, an expression of spontaneous enthusiasm by ordinary people but an incident staged by the well-to-do, as is clear from the uniform clothing, the garlands and the incense. So it is not surprising that Stier finds the praise of Augustus as 'Redeemer' or 'Saviour' in the inscription from Halicarnassus; after sketching out the development of this title he writes: 'More than two and a half centuries of vain and often bitterly disappointed hopes could not drive out this earthly expectation from the hearts of people tried by suffering, until finally they found fulfilment in the person of Augustus' (52).

17. Stier gives an account which, following the slogan that the end justifies the means, generously overlooks the victims. That becomes clear when he

supposes 'that not a little in the conduct and decrees of Augustus to which modern critics have taken exception is simply determined by his policy of peace' (15) and when he asserts: 'If there were wars which resulted in such a state (viz., the Roman empire as an empire of peace), it is unjustified simply to condemn them as aggression' (35). What counts is evidently the strong personality which has imposed itself by whatever means and is then supposed to bring blessings: 'It is difficult to get an appropriate picture of significant individuals from their behaviour in turbulent times, since such ties continually compel these particular individuals to adopt special measures, in which the general situation is reflected rather than the individual concerned. The situation of the historian only becomes more favourable for his judgment when he studies a "great man" at the height of the position of power that he has achieved, where he can shape things through his own power without being constrained by opposing forces' (13f.) A legitimation of the actual course of events on the basis of the alleged 'realization of the dream of world peace' also appears in Nestle, 61, 75; cf. further 11 below and notes 22, 23. In contrast to a merely affirmative historiography which legitimates what actually happened as being necessary, in a stimulating study Alexander Demandt advances methodological considerations which are meant to show that 'our picture of history remains incomplete unless it is brought within the framework of unrealized possibilities' (*Ungeschehene Geschichte. Ein Traktat über die Frage: Was wäre geschehen, wenn...?*, Göttingen 1984 (quotation on p.10).(ML)

18. Tacitus, *Annals* I, 9,5.

19. Tacitus, *Annals* I, 10,4. Here Tacitus is thinking of the blood of the Roman nobility; other blood will have to be recalled. Tacitus had already mentioned earlier one main aspect of the domestic political price which the Roman upper classes paid for the 'peace of Augustus'. After the mention of the sacrifice among the nobility in the battles before Augustus he continued, 'While the rest of the nobility found a cheerful acceptance of slavery the smoothest road to wealth and office, and, as they had thriven on revolution, stood now for the new order and safety in preference to the old order and adventure' (*Annals* I, 2,1).

20. See above 9f. and note 15.

21. Augustus, *Res Gestae*, 12.

22. Budde 6. Stier interprets the location on the Field of Mars in a similar way: '...certainly to indicate that now a new saeculum, the age of world peace, had fulfilled and transcended the old ordinances' (35, cf.20). Simon, passim, gives a description of the *ara pacis* with numerous illustrations. For this altar as an example of Augustan art which does not primarily depict circumstances but interprets them in terms of their ideological justification and is the occasion for a perspective which identifies a programme (golden age) with reality, cf. Borbein, passim. Weinstock, passim, questions whether the monument identified as the *ara pacis Augustae* really was this monument.

23. Klingner offers further examples of such an interpretation when he speaks of an 'initiation' which 'maintained the bloody course of Roman history' through the subjection of the 'nuisances' (653), as does Schulz when in reference to the relief of arms on the statue of Augustus by Primaporta he thinks: 'It is quite

evident that all success in war is there only for the purpose of the blessings of peace' (54 n.143).

24. Augustus, *Res Gestae*, 13. Koch describes 'the association of Pax with Victoria and the group of ideas around it' as typically Roman ('Pax', 2435).

25. Thus on a sestertius of Vitellius, Wenger, 33 no.13; cf. Sutherland, 181 no.333; Kent, 58 no.223. For a further description of Mars cf. ibid., pl.89 no.353R.

26. Franke, no.58. Cf. the similar motifs, ibid., no.504; Sutherland, 179 no.325.

27. Franke, no.39. Victoria standing on the globe: Wenger, 27 no.1; Sutherland, 120 n.213. Victoria is fixing a shield with a victory inscription to the palm tree; Wenger, 43 no.32; similarly Sutherland, 209 no.386. Victoria on the obverse and Octavian as Neptune (?) on the reverse with his right foot on the globe: Sutherland, 120 nos.214-15.

28. Kent, 34 no.133 V; similarly Sutherland, 132 no.237. Marcus Aurelius on the *sella curulis*, the seat of office, holds the globe in his hand and is crowned by Victoria: Franke, no.16.

29. Sutherland, 120 nos.210,211; further illustrations of Pax with the olive branch and cornucopia cf. ibid.119 no.209, 181 no.335.

30. Ibid., 122, no.227.

31. Stier justifies at length the conditions of the Pax Romana as an armed peace: 'At its basis is the universal human experience that weapons are the only means of effectively protecting those who are physically weaker against the attacks of the stronger' (21). Even Stier seems to feel that this statement is not enough in view of the then unique military power of Rome, and so he moves over to a contrast between barbarism and high culture and to a manifest natural superiority of the latter. 'The Roman empire was surrounded by plundering nations; the highly civilized lands which were united within it had a claim to armed protection against attacks from the realms of the "marginal nations"' (21). Thus for Augustus 'the idea of world peace served to secure the whole existence of high culture' (22 n.46) and 'Rome had inevitably to take upon itself the military burden... of protecting itself and civilized humanity against the "barbarian" peoples of the North' (32). A preparation for war is therefore an expression of a desire for peace; since Stier takes for granted a solution which is as unimaginative as it is heedless of experiences to the contrary: 'unfortunately violence can only be countered with violence', and he adds: 'precisely when the protection of world peace is at stake, which cannot be achieved only (?) by more or less pious forms of speech' (25). Now Stier can also simply overlook the fact that Rome was not content with mere defensive wars. But here too he resorts to the contrast between barbarism and high culture, the latter evidently supported by the course and goal of history, associated with a simple opposition between good and evil, and thus imperialism finds its legitimation as an instrument of the good. Stier quotes Cicero ('It is the nature of the barbarians to live day by day; our purpose must be to take note of the continuation of time') and then continues: 'The question of the destiny of history asked then, as it does now (!), whether the "barbarians", too, will get used to this attitude. In the last resort it is the task of high culture to realize the insights and discoveries that have been granted to it in the reality of human life as a duty to the good

and a protection against the bad, instead of casting words – however attractive they may sound – to the wind' (25). Therefore Stier asks what for him is a rhetorical question about Roman expansion with reference to the Roman sense of mission: 'Should they of all people be denied the right also to extend their cultural achievements to the barbarians?' (33). So in the end it is not surprising that he describes the attempt made under Augustus to extend the northern frontier to the Danube-Elbe line as 'an act of offensive defence' (33). Over against the 'harshness... of sending troops against hitherto free peoples to subject them' (34) he refers to similar occurrences during the formation of 'other great empires' and produces a mythology by dwelling on the concepts of destiny and tragedy: 'In all these cases the question is not a moral one; this is a tragedy which is bound up through destiny with the formation of great cultural empires' (35). It is quite painful to see such an ideological account continually presented with deep conviction as being unprejudiced scholarship *sine ira et studio*. It is worth putting the sober summary by Fuchs alongside Stier's apologetics: 'The *pax Romana* was a hostile confrontation brought about by blood and iron and the use of every fighting weapon of the state imaginable against the whole earth, based on a politics of compulsion; and in each individual instance there lay behind it an unbounded desire to preserve its own advantage' (*Friedensgedanke*, 201). In connection with the contrast between high culture and barbarism made by Stier we should recall first, that for the Greeks 'even the Romans, who came into close contact with Hellas, were first regarded simply as barbarians' (Vogt, *Kulturwelt*, 8; cf. Stemberger, 40f. and the Hellenistic-Jewish passages cited there); and secondly, it has to be stressed that here we have the expression of an 'egocentric view of the world' (Vogt, *Kulturwelt*, 9), according to which 'civilized people in the *orbis Romanus* represented the *genus Romanum* itself' (ibid., 12). 'There was a good deal of delusion, indeed falsehood, in this propaganda' (ibid., 18).

32. Cf.*BMCRomEmp* III, p.61 nos.212-15; 170 nos.800-3; 189 no.891; 197 nos.931f.; 205 (descriptions) pl. 13 no.4; pl. 29 nos. 3f.; pl.36 no.5 (illustration).

33. Cf. the dedicatory inscription '*Marti, Victoriae, Paci*' depicted in Wissowa, 1722.

34. Kent, pl.52 no.206R.

35. Franke, no.42; cf. also ibid., 46: the emperor Trajan in front of a victory sign holding his right hand above it with a fettered prisoner sitting below it.

36. Kent, pl.VIII no.266R (Trajan); ibid., pl.84. no.338R (Lucius Verus); Franke, no.34 (Commodus). The sovereign might of victorious subjection is also shown by an aureus of Augustus on which there is a depiction of how Victoria forces a bull, which symbolizes Armenia, to its knees by the horns (Kent, pl.34 no.138).

37. Wenger, 34 no.16; Kent, pl. VII no.240; similarly Sutherland, 188 no.351; for the same motive related to Germany under Domitian, Kent, pl.65 no.246R. Cf. also Sutherland, 174 no.319: a Jewish woman sitting mourning under a palm tree while on the other side Titus is standing in a victorious pose.

38. Kent, pl.VII no.249; Sutherland, 182 no.343. Cf. also ibid., 193 no.355; a fettered Dacrian sitting on weapons, on a denarius of Trajan.

39. That the so-called 'Constantinian shift' made no difference to the Pax

Romana as the victor's history in terms of the connection between war, victory and subjection is again shown impressively by the coins. On a solidus from the time of Constantine the emperor, moving to the right, is shielded with a victory sign on the left; with his right hand he is dragging a fettered prisoner behind him by the hair and is trampling on one sitting in front of him with the left foot (Sutherland, 70 no.542; cf. 278 no.569; further Wenger, 67 nos.79,81f.). The mere exchange of a symbol while conditions remain the same is documented very clearly by a solidus of Iovian: the emperor in the uniform of a general, with a globe in his left hand, is now holding the labarum, the imperial standard adorned with the Christogram, in his right hand instead of the victory sign, under which a fettered prisoner is crouching at the emperor's feet (Beck/Bol, 480 no.82; cf. nos.81,83).

40. Plutarch, *Caesar*, 12.

41. Tacitus, *Agricola*, 29.2.

42. Ibid., 20.2f.; cf. also the description of the different means which the Roman general Domitius Corbulo used in Armenia: 'In the case of the suppliants he employed pardon, in that of the fugitives, pursuit; to those lurking in covert he was merciless, firing the entrances and exits of their dens, after filling them with lopped branches and bushes' (Tacitus, *Annals* XIV, 23,2).

43. One might consider whether in our day the production of terror does not follow from fostering an image of the enemy, while 'the attractions of peace' are produced by the advertising industry.

44. Tacitus, *Annals* XII, 33.

45. Plutarch, *Numa*, 26; cf. Plutarch, *Moralia*, 323f.: 'Trophy upon trophy arises, triumph meets triumph, and the first blood, while still warm on their arms, is overtaken and washed away by a second flood. They count their victories, not by the multitude of corpses and spoils, but by captive kingdoms, by nations enslaved, by islands and continents added to their mighty realm.'

46. Tacitus, *Annals* I, 51.1.

47. Plutarch, *Numa*, 26, cf.5.

48. Plutarch, *Antony*, 6.

49. Virgil, *Aeneid* VI, 851-3.

50. '*Fatum* is the language of the gods; it is an expression of the *imperium Iovis* which manifests itself as *imperium Romanum*' (Weber-Schäfer, 145). And so Roman rule and the peace it achieves is indeed fatal. For fate as a Leitmotiv in Virgil's *Aeneid*, cf. Heinze, 54-6.

51. Virgil, *Georgics* IV, 561f.; Horace similarly wishes: 'let warlike Rome dictate terms to the conquered Medes' (Horace, *Odes* III 3,43f.); cf. also *Epistles* I,12,27f.: 'Phraates on humbled knees has accepted Caesar's imperial sway'.

52. Aristides, 91.

53. Cf. also Livy I, 16, which gives a report of the descent of Romulus from heaven shortly after his death: 'The will of heaven is that my Rome shall be the capital of the world; so let them cherish the art of war, and let them know and teach their children that no human strength can resist Roman arms.'

54. Plutarch, *Cato*, 14.

55. Virgil, *Aeneid* I, 278f.: for this passage cf. Koch, 'Roma', 25-8; see also VII, 98-101, where Latinus receives the oracle not to give his daughter to a native husband but to wait for strangers soon to come, 'who with blood will

bear our name to the stars and from whose tribe the descendants will tread under foot all the territory where the sun in its circling course looks upon the ocean in the east and in the west'. Cf. further VII, 257; VIII, 678-81, 714-23.

56. Virgil, *Aeneid* I, 282.

57. Suetonius, *Claudius*, 17,1.

58. Josephus, *BJ* III, 472f.; cf. VI,38, according to which Titus says before the storming of the third and last wall of Jerusalem: 'It is unfitting for you, who are Romans and my soldiers, who have in peace been taught how to make wars, and who have also been used to conquer in those wars, to be inferior to Jews.' So it is certainly no chance that a coin (AD 68) depicts the genius of the Roman people on the obverse and Mars on the reverse (Sutherland, 179 nos.322,323). For Roman self-awareness cf. further Plutarch, *Sertorius*, 6; *Cato*, 10. In this second passage Plutarch describes how Cato called in the help of the Celtiberi during his expedition to Spain: 'On their demanding 200 talents pay for such assistance all his officers thought it intolerable that Romans should agree to pay barbarians for assistance. But Cato said there was nothing terrible in it; should they be victorious they could pay the prize with the spoils taken from the enemy and not out of their own purse, whereas, should they be vanquished, there would be nobody left either to pay or to ask the price.' The same event is also described in Plutarch, *Mor.*, 199c.

59. Josephus, *BJ* III, 210; literally the end reads 'to make a profit'.

60. Josephus, *BJ* III, 480.

61. Josephus, *BJ* I, 135; V, 364; Plutarch also speaks of 'the incorruptible weapons of Rome' (*Lucullus*, 26).

62. Josephus, *BJ* V, 366f.; cf. II, 362, where Josephus makes King Agrippa II, who wants to prevent the Jewish revolt, give this warning at the beginning: 'Will you not carefully reflect upon the Roman empire? Will you not estimate your own weakness? Has not your army been often enough beaten even by your neighbouring nations? While the power of the Romans is invincible in all parts of the habitable earth?' The Jewish rebels acted according to the words which Josephus attributed to Titus, and did 'as the wickedest wretches would have done, and encouraged yourselves to act against us' (Josephus, *BJ* VI, 341).

63. Ibid., 378. For the statement that God is with the Romans cf. IV, 370; V, 39,60; VI, 39,110,311.

64. Plutarch, *Mor.*, 824c-e. A good deal of what Plutarch says here is impressively depicted in an illustration on the verso of a coin which was minted under Marcus Aurelius in Hierapolis in Phrygia: a river god in the centre with ears of corn and poppy seeds symbolizes fertility; helmeted Athene, on the left with a spear in her right hand and Victoria on her left hand, represents the military victory that has been achieved so that trade and commerce can flourish in the peace which has thus been made possible, portrayed by Hermes on the right with a staff of peace in his left hand and a bag of gold in his right (Franke, 207). Even before the passage cited Plutarch had thought that the statesman could only remind himself of what Pericles once said when he put on the garb of a general: 'Take care, Pericles, you are ruling free men, you are ruling Greeks, Athenian citizens,' but he must tell himself, 'You who rule are a subject, ruling a state controlled by proconsuls, the agents of Caesar.' He must have no illusions, 'since you see the boots of the Roman soldiers just above your head.'

He must listen like an actor to the prompter and must not allow himself any slip: 'For to fail in one's part in public life brings not more hissings or catcalls or stamping of feet, but many have experienced "the dread chastiser, axe that cleaves the neck"' (Plutarch, *Mor.*, 813c-f). 'And not only should the statesman show himself and his native state blameless towards the rulers, but he should always have a friend among the men of high station who have the greatest power as a firm bulwark, so to speak, of his administration' (*Mor.*, 814c). The resigned sound which these statements of Plutarch still have has completely disappeared in Aristides, when he is discussing the same question, *Eulogy of Rome*, 69.

65. Pliny, *Panegyricus*, 12.

66. Josephus, *BJ* III, 71-108. For a description of Roman military power cf. also the list of the legions in the various areas of the empire for the year AD 23 in Tacitus, *Annals* IV,5: twenty-five legions, the garrison in the capital, fleets of ships and in addition numerous auxiliaries.

67. Josephus, *BJ* III, 108.

68. Josephus, *BJ* III, 304. Cf. the similar reference which Eleazar makes in his last speech to the rebels besieged in the fortress of Masada before they all commit suicide: 'And as for those who are already dead in the war, it is reasonable that we should esteem them blessed, for they are dead in defending, and not betraying their liberty; but as to the multitude of those that are now under the Romans, who would not pity their conditions? and who would not make haste to die, before he would suffer the same miseries with them? Some of them have been put upon the rack, and tortured with fire and whippings, and so died. Some have been half devoured by wild beasts, and yet have been kept alive to be devoured by them a second time, in order to afford laughter and sport to our enemies; and such of us who are alive still, are to be looked upon as the most miserable, who being so desirous of death, could not come at it' (Josephus, BJ VII, 372-4). Cf. ibid. II, 75,79.

69. Aristides, 9. For the assertion of the universality of Roman rule cf. ibid., 10: 'Your possessions coincide with the way of the sun, and it is only your land on which it shines in its course'; also Virgil, *Aeneid* VII, 258, where according to an oracle the coming race of Romans will 'occupy the whole earth with troops'.

70. Aristides, *Eulogy of Rome*, 70f.

71. Horace, *Odes* IV, 5,27f.

72. That does not prevent him for lamenting over his task in respect of the time of Tiberius as compared to that of the earlier historians – for the following reasons: 'For this was an age of peace unbroken or half-heartedly challenged... and the prince was not concerned to extend the empire' (*Annals* IV, 32,2). For Tacitus' captivity to the city of Rome within a particular senatorial tendency cf. Vogt, 'Tacitus', 380-2; for the fundamental conflict in which he is involved, Jens, passim, esp.419; for a more sophisticated assessment of Tacitus the historian see von Fritz, 458-63.

73. Tacitus, *Annals* XIII, 41,4.

74. Ibid. XIV, 26,1.

75. Ibid. II, 21,2.

76. Seneca, *Epistles*, 95,30. At another point Seneca could, however, speak

in glowing terms of the emperor Claudius, who shows how much better it is to safeguard the empire by benefits than by arms (*ad Polybium* XII,3).

77. *Res Gestae*, 3. Plutarch describes a similar specific instance from early Roman history. The general Aemilius gives the beaten Ligurians 'humane and conciliatory terms; for it was not the wish of the Romans to extirpate altogether the Ligurian nation, since it lay like a barrier or bulwark against the movements of the Gauls, who were always threatening to descend upon Italy' (*Aemilius*, 6). Thus considerations of military utility decide whether they are kept alive or annihilated.

78. Horace, *Odes* III, 3,53f. What lies beyond the Roman frontier marks evidently does not deserve to be called the 'world'. Cf. also Propertius II, 10,17f.; 'and if there be any land withdrawn upon earth's furthest rim, captured hereafter let it feel your mighty hand'.

79. Aristides, *Eulogy of Rome*, 80.

80. Horace, *Odes* I, 21,13-16. The constant war on the frontiers also serves to ensure domestic pacification. It has a disciplinary effect. The victorious acts of subjection were made known to the inhabitants of the empire not least through coins.

81. *Res Gestae*, 26. Cf. also Seneca, *De Brevitate Vitae* IV,5, where he says of Augustus that 'he pacified (*pacat*) the Alps and tamed foes who had invaded peace and the empire (*paci et imperio*)', that 'he moved the frontiers beyond the Rhine, the Danube and the Euphrates'.

82. Tacitus, *Annals* XIII, 55,1-56,1.

83. Not to take the war on the periphery seriously – at any rate only presented in passing as on a newsreel – is probably a centre mentality.

84. OGIS 613; cf. *Sylloge*[3] 730, 8,11f.

85. Aristides, *Eulogy of Rome*, 104. In a comparison with Plato's view of the origin of the world Plutarch writes: 'In this way then did time lay the foundation for the Roman state and, with the help of God, so combine and join together fortune and virtue that, by taking the particular coalitions of each, he might construct for all nations a hearth, in truth both holy and beneficent, a steadfast cable, a principle abiding for ever, an anchorage for the swell and drift as Democritus says, amid the shifting conditions of human affairs' (*Mor.*, 316f.-317a). Shortly after that he notes, in a comparison with Democritus' theory of atoms: 'While the mightiest powers and dominions among men were being driven about as fortune willed, and were continuing to collide one with another because no one held the supreme power. but all wished to hold it, the continuous movement, drift and change of all peoples remained without remedy, until such time as Rome acquired strength and growth, and had attached to herself not only the nations and peoples within her own borders, but also royal dominions of foreign people beyond the seas, and thus the affairs of the vast empire gained stability and security, since the supreme government, which now knew reverse, was brought within an orderly and single cycle of peace' (317 b-c). Cf. further Velleius Paterculus II, 103.5: 'On that day there sprang up once more in parents the assurance of safety for their children, in husbands for the sanctity of marriage, in owners for the safety of their property, and in all men the assurance of safety, order, peace and tranquillity; indeed, it would have been hard to entertain larger hopes, or to have them more happily fulilled.'

86. Seneca, *Epistles*, 91.2.
87. Josephus, *BJ* IV, 94.
88. Josephus, *Antt.* XIV, 156f.
89. Josephus, *BJ* I, 199f.
90. Ibid., 155-7; cf. also Suetonius on Galba, who as proconsul in Africa had 'to restore order in this province disturbed by inner disputes and barbarian revolts' (*Galba* 7,1); similarly in *Caligula* 1,2 on Germanicus who is sent off 'to restore tranquillity and order in the East'.
91. Aristides, *Eulogy of Rome*, 69; cf. also Horace, *Odes* IV, 15,17-20, who celebrates Augustus: 'While Caesar guards the state, not civil rage, nor violence nor wrath that forges swords, embroiling hapless towns, shall banish peace.'
92. Horace, *Odes* III, 14,14-16; cf. Josephus, *Antt.* XIV, 247, who there cites a resolution of the Pergamenes according to which the Romans 'work to secure prosperity and peace for their friends and allies'.
93. Tacitus, *Histories* II, 21,2.
94. Ibid. II, 12,1; however, people are thoroughly disillusioned in this respect by Otho's troops.
95. Cf. Josephus, *Antt.* XIV, 158-60; XV, 344-8; also Velleius Paterculus II, 126,3: 'The Pax Augusta, which has spread to the regions of the east and of the west, and to the bounds of the north and of the south, preserves every corner of the world safe from the fear of brigandage.'
96. Aristides, *Eulogy of Rome*, 100. But cf. also Juvenal, *Satires* X, 19-22: 'Though you carry but few silver vessels with you in a night journey, you will be afraid of the sword and cudgel of a freebooter, you will tremble at the shadow of a reed shaking in the moonlight; but the empty-handed traveller will whistle in the robber's face.'
97. Seneca, *Epistles*, 73.5.
98. Pliny, *Epistles* X, 2.2f. cf. Tacitus, *Agricola*, 3.1.
99. Martial, *Epigrams* IX, 70. 7f.
100. Tacitus, *Histories* IV, 73f. Dio Chrysostom also legitimizes Roman rule with a reference to the prevention of internal strife, when he says to the Alexandrians in respect of the Roman occupation forces: 'For how otherwise could you keep your hands off one another?' (32.51).
101. *Sylloge*[3], 685.14f.
102. *Sylloge*[3], 742.I,1ff., 10ff.; cf. also Josephus, *BJ* II, 340f., according to which after the unrest caused by the bad governorship of Florus a Roman legate in Jerusalem convinced himself of the readiness of the population for peace and then on the one hand praised them for their loyalty to the Romans and on the other admonished them to go on keeping the peace. Plutarch makes similar remarks about Aemilius, who restored a province to peace and loyalty (*Aemilius*, 4).
103. See above 16 and n.64.
104. This concord means first that of citizens among themselves, above all members of the upper classes. In the context of advice to statesmen, after an admonition to reject unlawful and unseemly demands of friends Plutarch writes (*Mor.*, 808d): 'Then a man ought to ascribe to his friends a share in his own good and kindly acts of favour... Hand over to one friend a case at law... to another introduce a rich man who needs legal oversight and protection, and

help another to get some profitable building contract or lease' (*Mor.*, 809a). But cf. also Plutarch's criticism of the indigenous upper class, through whose conduct the in any case restricted autonomy is further undermined: 'And the cause of this is chiefly the greed and contentiousness of the foremost citizens; for either in cases in which they are judging their inferiors, they force them into exile from the state, or in matters concerning which they differ among themselves, since they are willing to accept an inferior position among their fellow citizens, they call in those who are mightier; and as a result senate, popular assembly, courts, and the entire local government lose their authority. But the statesman should soothe the ordinary citizens by granting them equality and the powerful by concessions in return, thus keeping them within the bonds of the local government' (*Mor.*, 815a).

Secondly, concord also embraces that between the different states. On this see Merkelbach, passim. This concord is a favourite theme on coins. Most frequently there are two figures, each representing a city, holding out hands. The earliest examples are in Franke, cf. nos. 234 (Nero), 238 (Domitian) and 230 (Commodus): 'All in all there are more than 78 cities which coined homonoia coins in about 110 combinations' (ibid., 24). That happened each time on the occasion of a treaty. According to Franke 'the considerable distances between two such homonoia places lead one to doubt the practical value of such treaties. Without doubt controversies over the first rank among cities were ended by a homonoia treaty, probably quite often on orders from Rome' (ibid). Dio Chrysostom attempts to show that on the other hand cities also must have had their own interest in doing away with such controversies and restoring concord in order to limit the scope for the misuse of power by the governor (38.34-37): he calls 'peace, concord and friendship among each other the first commandment' (39.2).

105. Tacitus, *Germania*, 33.2.

106. For the combination *pax et concordia* in Cicero and Sallust cf. Chantraine, 38f.

107. Plutarch, *Otho*, 15, cf. also Tacitus, *Histories* II, 20,2 on negotiations between Vitelliani and Othonians: 'Finally, when in vain and empty phrases they had handed back and forth the words "peace and concord".'

108. Tacitus, *Annals* XIII, 48.

109. Franke, no.20.

110. Aristides, *Eulogy of Rome*, 36.

111. Above, 21 and n.102.

112. Above, 16 n.64.

113. Plutarch, *Aemilius*, 29.

114. Pliny, *Epistles* VIII, 24,4f.

115. Tacitus, *Agricola*, 24,3. It is also very clear from Plutarch, *Philopoimen*, 17, that the price of Roman peace is freedom.

116. Tacitus, *Histories* IV, 17,2.

117. Tacitus, *Agricola*, 31,2.

118. Tacitus, *Histories* IV, 73,3. Would Tacitus really not have noticed in this formula that he had previously attributed such 'fine words' to Cerialis? Even if that were the case and, as Stier thinks, Cerialis's speech is to be regarded 'as the statement of a successful Roman soldier, much admired by the author (viz.

Tacitus)' (21 n.45), we cannot read the text other than as an unmasking of Roman imperialism (and any other kind of imperialism).

119. Josephus, *BJ* II, 346.

120. Ibid., 348f.

121. Ibid., 355.

122. Ibid., 379.

123. Ibid., 351, 354.

124. Tacitus, *Histories* IV, 74,2. In view of its relationship with the governor Dio Chrysostom advises the city of Tarsus to calculate the possibilities carefully (34.38-42). He stresses as a basic motto: 'Men who find themselves in such a situation as yours, which of course is the common situation everywhere today, should be so minded as not, on the one hand, to submit to any and every things and allow those in authority to treat them simply as they please, no matter to what lengths of insolence and greed they may proceed; nor, on the other hand, to be disposed to put up with nothing disagreeable whatever' (38). Unlike Agrippa and Cerialis he takes it amiss 'if no remnant of hesitancy or distrust is to be left in the minds of those who deal unfairly' (39). But if proceedings against an oppressive governor seem unlikely to succeed or are inopportune for other reasons, one must be submissive (40). Significantly Dio ends by comparing the relationships with the governor and thus with the power of Rome to bearing a burden.

125. See above, 12 and n.30.

126. Franke, no.473.

127. Seneca, *Epistles*, 73,8,10.

128. Tacitus, *Annals* I,81,2; cf. also I,4,1; 7.1; 8.6 etc; also Seneca, *De Constantia* II, 2: 'For Cato did not survive freedom nor freedom Cato.' Plutarch makes a similar comment on Lucullus (*Lucullus*, 44).

129. Plutarch, *Aemilius*, 11.

130. Tacitus, *Agricola*, 14.1.

131. Josephus, *BJ* I, 281f.

132. Ibid., 386.

133. Ibid., 393: he had evidently had practice in this, Josephus, *Antt.* XIV, 303, 327, 381f., 490; XV, 75.

134. Josephus, *BJ* III, 443; but cf. the judgment of Philip V of Macedon: 'that to reign by favour of the Romans was more the part of a captive satisfied with meat and drink than of a man possessed of courage and spirit' (Plutarch, *Aemilius*, 8). With an eye to the balance of power he nevertheless took this kingdom. Cf. also the 'arguments' of the German Flavus to his brother Arminius who was insisting on freedom: according to Tacitus, *Annals* II, 10: 'Roman greatness, the power of the Caesar: the heavy penalties for the vanquished: the mercy always waiting for him who submitted himself'.

135. Josephus, *Antt.* XIV, 385.

136. Pliny, *Epistles* IX, 5. Cf. also Aristides, *Eulogy of Rome*, 64, where as a consequence of the granting of Roman citizenship to citizens holding high positions in towns it is said: 'There is no need of any garrisons based on fortresses; for the most prominent and powerful men everywhere guard their own ancestral city in your interest, and so you have possession of the cities in two ways, first from here (viz. Rome) and in each places through these citizens.'

137. See above 14 and n.49.

138. Josephus, *BJ* V, 372f.

139. Josephus, *BJ* II, 336, 338.

140. Ibid., IV, 414.

141. Cf. Liebenam, 1657-9; Bechert, 14f.

142. Josephus, *BJ* III, 95.

143. A description of the use of such handcuffs can be found in Acts 21.33; cf. 12.6.

144. Pliny, *Epistles* VIII, 4,2; cf. the depiction of a bridge on a sestertius of Trajan in Sutherland, 201 no.375.

145. *Eulogy of Rome*, 101.

146. The building of roads and bridges could also primarily or simultaneously serve military purposes. That is clear in Tacitus, *Annals* I, 56,1f.; 61.1; II, 7,3.

147. Tacitus, *Agricola* 31,1.

148. As another example cf. the dam corvée in Egypt, as it emerges from a document relating to service in the annual five-day dam corvée from the time of Trajan: Hengstl, no.4, 38; also the explanation on p.39.

149. bShabb 33b; cf. Stemberger, *Herrschaft*, 112f. Imperial building works in the provinces could also serve to encourage loyalty. Thus Dio Chrysostom concludes from Trajan's 'concern' for Alexandria: 'You must make your country better... by means of good behaviour, by decorum, by showing yourselves to be sure and steady' (32.95).

150. According to Samuel Krauss, *Monumenta Talmudica* V, I, Darmstadt 1972 (= Vienna and Leipzig 1914), no.396; cf. also bAZ, 2b.

151. Pliny, *Epistles* VIII, 4.3.

152. Ehrhardt, I, 256.

153. Tacitus, *Agricola*, 12.6; cf. the list of booty in the state treasury in Lucan, *Bellum Civile* III, 154-68.

154. Josephus, *BJ* VI, 317.

155. Josephus, *BJ* VII, 132-52;

156. Josephus, *BJ* VII, 158-60. Ancient examples of the introduction of specific works of art into Vespasian's temple of peace can be found in Koch, 'Pax', 2435f. Vespasian was not an innovator in this respect, nor was Augustus, of whom Pausanias explicitly observes: 'Augustus evidently did not begin the carrying off of statues and images of the gods from the conquered, but was only following a long established custom' (VIII, 46, 2; cf. IX, 33,6: X, 7,1).

157. Plutarch, *Pompey*, 70.

158. For billeting cf. Liebenam, 1667f.

159. Plutarch, *Lucullus*, 29; cf. also Livy XXXIV, 9,12, according to which in the war in Spain Cato is said to have forbidden the suppliers to buy up grain in view of the grain that the Spaniards already had on the threshing floor, with the observation, 'The war will feed itself'.

160. Tacitus, *Histories* I,51,1.

161. Apuleius, *Metamorphoses* IX, 39,2-5. Apuleius then goes on to describe how the gardener offers physical resistance and to begin with is successful; however, after a time he is seized and faces the death penalty (39,6-42,4). Cf. also Horsley, A9 (pp.36-8), a Latin-Greek inscription from Pisidia from AD 18/

19, an edict of the governor of Galatia for the city of Sagalossa relating to its obligations towards the regional transport system; also Epictetus, IV, 1,79.

162. See above, 21 and n.100.

163. OGIS 669 (there is a German translation in HIRK no.39, 68-73). For an indisputable identification those liable to pay tax were evidently also registered with an indelible mark; cf. Horsley A28, Text II lines 10f., where it says of one 'without special mark' and of another 'a scar on the right side of the head' (p.80).

164. Josephus, *Antt.* XVIII, 1-3.

165. Plutarch, *Galba*, 4.

166. Hengstl, no.1, pp.30f.

167. Ibid., 32.

168. On this cf. also Mähler, 18-21; for a 'dam tax' raised in Egypt cf. ibid., 29f.

166. Suetonius, *Augustus*, 18.2.

170. Tacitus, *Annals* XIII, 50,1f.

171. Ibid., 51, 1.

172. Tacitus, *Germania*, 29.1.

173. Josephus, *BJ* II, 372.

174. Pliny, *Epistles* IX, 33, 2-10. An edict by a governor of Galatia from the period AD 13-15 runs: 'Hospitality must be provided free of charge for all members of our staff, individuals on imperial business from all the provinces, the freemen and slaves of the Princeps Optimus and their beasts of burden' (HIRK no.30, p.53). As is shown by the passage from Pliny quoted in the text, the peace evidently also offered the Roman officials the possibility of having time at their disposal and travelling. Despite the possibility of free travel throughout the enormous area of the Roman empire, as much praised then as it is today, for most people this was not much use. Mention need only be made of conditions in Egypt: 'For fiscal considerations – in order to keep the economy going and to keep a grip on the population – there was never general freedom of movement in Graeco-Roman Egypt, but particularly at this time (namely from the death of Augustus to the accession of Vespasian) ties to a locality were strict and the consequences of flight far-reaching' (Hengstl, 100).

175. Aristides, *Eulogy of Rome*, 11.

176. Ibid., 13. Aristides makes a similar comment about the lands: 'There is nothing which would escape you (viz., the Romans): no city, no people, no harbour, no stretch of land, even if you have declared an area to be worthless.' Cf. the similar statement by Josephus, above, 15 and n.62.

177. Pliny, *Panegyricus*, 29. For the significance of Alexandria and Egypt for providing grain for Rome see also Josephus, *BJ* II, 386; IV, 605.

178. For Aristides, *Eulogy of Rome*, 11, the city of Rome is 'like a common market for the whole world'. Cf. the splendid picture of the port of Ostia on a sestertius of Nero (Sutherland, 163 no.310).

179. Pliny, *Panegyricus*, 29. Of course Pliny deceives himself: 'abundance here and lack nowhere' applied at any time only to the upper classes.

180. Aristides, *Eulogy of Rome*, 60, 65, stresses that there is no hatred among those who are inferior.

181. Tacitus, *Annals* XII, 43.

182. Ibid., III, 54,4.

183. Seneca, *Octavia*, 434f. This work is attributed to Seneca, but was not written by him (*KP* 4,230). But Seneca himself continually refers in particular to the 'bottomless and insatiable maw which explores on the one hand the seas, on the other the earth, with enormous toil hunting down your prey' (*Epistles* 89,22; cf. further *Ad Helviam* X, 2-7; *De vita beata* XI,4; *Epistles* 60,2). Alongside the quest for pleasure he also censures the avarice which extends without limit beyond the frontiers of the different lands, and the extravagance which put up buildings everywhere and exploits every speck of nature (*Epistles*, 89,20f.). Virgil also mentions goods from all over the world: 'Do you not see how Tinolus sends us saffron fragrance, India her ivory, the soft Sabaeans their frankincense; but the naked Chalybes give us iron, Pontus the strong smelling beaver's oil, and Epirus the Olympian victories of her mares' (Virgil, *Georgics* I, 56-59; cf. also Aristides, *Eulogy of Rome*, 12, and on the luxury of the upper classes generally, Tacitus, *Annals* III, 52,1-54,1). In another passage Seneca suspects that Rome has got its riches from the conquered and that 'whatever one people has snatched away from all the rest may still more easily be snatch by all away from you' (*Epistles* 87.41).

184. Josephus, *BJ* IV, 587.

185. Lucius in Apuleius's *Metamorphoses* has the experience that 'my charges in the city of Rome were by far greater than in the provinces' (XI, 28,1).

186. Tacitus, *Annals* II, 33,2f.; cf. also Lucan, *Bellum Civile* I, 162-82.

187. *Res Gestae*, 19-21.

188. Suetonius, *Augustus*, 28,3; cf. 29.

189. Tacitus, *Annals* XV, 45,1. According to Pliny Trajan was restrained over private building, 'but when it comes to public building you do it on the grand scale!'. He then goes on to enumerate it (Pliny, *Panegyricus*, 51).

190. *Res gestae*, 15; cf. also Tacitus, *Annals* XIII, 31.2 on a distribution of gifts by Nero in 57 and the depiction of this on a sestertius (Kent, pl.V no.194R); there are similar portrayals on sesterces of Nerva (ibid., pl.66, no.255) and Commodus (ibid., pl.89, no.356). Cf. also on a further sestertius of Nero the portrayal of Annona and Ceres with the stern of a ship (!) in the background (Sutherland, 164 no.312) and the list of Domitian's distribution of gifts in Suetonius, *Domitian*, 4,5.

191. Pliny, *Panegyricus*, 25.

192. Ibid., 26.

193. Ibid., 27.

194. Suetonius, *Augustus*, 43.

195. *Res Gestae*, 22f.

196. Tacitus, *Dialogus*, 29,3. For the gladiatorial fights cf. Seneca, *Epistles*, 7,3-5, who describes them as 'sheer murder'; cf. further 95.33: 'Man, an object of reverence in the eyes of man, is now slaughtered for jest and sport... and it is a satisfying spectacle to see a man made a corpse.' In a comparison Marcus Aurelius speaks of a man 'who is inordinately without feeling and clings to life and is like those half-flayed gladiators set against wild beasts who, full of blood and wounds, yet ask that they be kept for another day, so that in this state they may again be thrown to the claws and teeth of the wild animals' (X, 8). The emperor had probably watched such spectacles often enough and is here showing

his 'feelings'. The Collosseum and the Circus Maximus, whose 180,000 seats Trajan had embellished with marble, were depicted on coins, the former on a sestertius of Titus (Sutherland, 181 no.337), the latter on a sestertius of Trajan (ibid., 194 no.357; Wenger, 37 no.20; Kent, pl.69 no.259R).

197. Seneca, *Epistles*, 18,1.

198. Juvenal, *Satires* X, 78-81. The connection between 'bread and games' also appears in Seneca when he says of Rome, 'in which the seating space of three theatres is required at one time, in which is consumed all the produce of the plough from every land' (Seneca, *De Clementia* I, 6,1), and in Tacitus, when he reports that Nero's cancellation of a major journey which had been announced and his consequent stay in Rome pleased the people, 'with its passion for amusements and its dread of a shortage of corn (always the chief preoccupation) in the event of his absence' (Tacitus, *Annals* XV, 36,4). Cf. also Plutarch, *Mor.*, 821f.: 'And so he who first said that the people was ruined by the first man who thought its favour was well aware that the multitude loses its strength when it succumbs to bribe-taking.' But shortly after that Plutarch recommends his reader not to covet 'the customary public contributions' (822a).

199. Petronius, *Satyricon*, 119,1-18, 27-36; cf. also Plutarch, *Mor.*, 325d-e.

200. Juvenal, *Satires* VIII, 87-90. Plutarch speaks of 'the procuratorships and governorships of provinces from which many talents may be gained' (*Mor.*, 814d).

201. Ibid., 106-12. Plutarch says of Caesar that he had become 'a rich man' as a result of his stay in Spain (*Caesar*, 12).

202. Pliny, *Epistles* III, 9,13.

203. Ibid., 17. The Indian in Philostratus, *Vita Apollonii* III, 25, has heard that the Greeks already call Roman governors just and praise them 'if they do not sell justice'.

204. Juvenal, *Satires* III, 46f.

205. Tacitus, *Agricola*, 6,2.

206. Ibid., 19,4.

207. Ibid., 20,1.

208. See above, 23 n.124.

209. Tacitus, *Agricola* 35, 2; cf. also Seneca, *De Ira* I, 11,4: 'Yet these are they whom the Spaniards and the Gauls and men of Asia and Syria (= auxiliaries), inured to war, cut down before they could even glimpse a Roman legion.'

210. Tacitus, *Histories* IV, 14,1; cf. further Plutarch, *Sulla*, 25; *Lucullus*, 20.

211. Cf. also Plutarch's report on the governorship of Brutus in Gaul: 'For while the other provinces, owing to the insolence and frivolity of their governors, were plundered as though they had been conquered in war, to the people of his province Brutus meant relief and consolation even for their former misfortunes' (*Brutus*, 6; further *Sertorius*, 6).

212. According to Tacitus, *Annals* IV, 46,1, a levy was the reason for the Thracian rebellion of 26. They refused 'to tolerate the military levies and devote the whole of their able-bodied manhood to the Roman service'. When this rebellion was defeated, the Thracian auxiliaries who had remained loyal to Rome were also motivated as a result 'to ravage, burn and plunder' (ibid., 48,1).

213. Tacitus, *Histories* IV, 14,2f. Caesar speaks in similar terms of taxation

measures by his opponent Scipio: 'Any mode of exaction, provided a name could be found for it, was deemed a sufficient excuse for compelling contributions' (*Bellum civile* III, 32,2). Tacitus can report further similar cases: those who wanted to revolt in Gaul in 21 'in assemblies and conventicles made their seditious statements about the continuous tributes, the grinding rates of interest, the cruelty and pride of the governors' (*Annals* III, 40,3). The revolt of the Friesians in 28 broke out 'more from our cupidity than from their own impotence of subjection' (IV, 72,1). Similarly the revolt of the Iceni in Britain in 61 broke out after bad attacks (XIV, 31).

214. Plutarch, *Marius*, 6.

215. Tacitus, *Histories*, IV, 74,1.

216. Virgil, *Aeneid* IV, 231; cf. also the passage VI, 852, mentioned above. Ovid, *Metamorphoses* XV, 829-32, is also evidence of the connection between subjection, peace and law. Cf. further Propertius III, 4,3f.

217. Tacitus, *Annals* XV, 6,4. According to Aelius Aristides it is a failing of Alexander the Great that the question put concerning him can only be regarded as rhetorical: 'What laws, then, did he give to individual peoples?' (*Eulogy of Rome*, 26). Cf. also Dinkler, *Friede*, 442.

218. Hengstl, no.17, 63f.

219. Epictetus, *Dissertations* III, 22,55. According to Epictetus himself, however, the Cynic should not go to the courts: immediately before that he had said: 'He must be beaten like an ass, and having been beaten he must love those who beat him like the Father of all, like a brother' (54). Epictetus is here concerned with the autarcic personality who can also live happily under the most difficult conditions (45ff.; cf. Theissen, 'Gewaltverzicht', 172f., 188). In another passage he shows that his trust in Roman 'state justice' is not very great when he asks: 'Should kinship with the emperor or simply contact with a person in a high position in Rome already be able to enable one to live without danger, without contempt and without fear of anything?' (*Dissertations* I, 9,7).

220. Apuleius, *Metamorphoses* III, 29,1f.; cf. also the little story told in X, 28,3-5, which is set in Corinth: a woman who feels that she has been poisoned runs to the governor's house, shrieks until she gains entrance, and makes a denunciation before she dies. The governor convicts her murderess by torturing her slaves and condemns her to death by wild beasts.

221. Seneca, *De Clementia* I, 1,7f.

222. Ibid. I, 8,2.

223. Pliny, *Epistles* X, 2,2f.

224. Tacitus, *Histories* I, 1,4; cf. *Agricola* 3,1.

225. Tacitus, *Annals* XV, 60,2-63,2.

226. How despotic even Augustus, the famous bringer of peace, was, is illuminated by the following incident narrated by Suetonius: 'When Quintus Gallius, a praetor, held some folded tablets under his robe as he was paying his respects, Augustus, suspecting that he had a sword concealed there, did not dare to make a search on the spot for fear that it should turn out to be something else, but a little later he had Gallus hustled from the tribunal by some centurions and soldiers who tortured him as if he were a slave, and though he made no confession, ordered his execution, first tearing out the man's eyes with his own hand' (Suetonius, *Augustus*, 27.4).

227. Tacitus, *Annals* II, 51. The atmosphere of anxiety in the later days of Tiberius is impressively described by Tacitus in IV, 69,3: 'In Rome, the anxiety and panic, the reticences of men towards their nearest and dearest had never been greater: meetings and conversations, the ears of friend and stanger were alike avoided; even things mute and inanimate – the very walls and roofs – were eyed with circumspection.'

228. Tacitus, *Histories* II, 84. Cf. also Josephus, *BJ* II, 308, who reports of the 'hitherto unknown cruelty of the Romans' by the governor Florus in Judaea, who had 'men of the equestrian order whipped and nailed to the cross before his tribunal, who although they were by birth Jews, yet were they of Roman dignity notwithstanding'.

229. Plutarch, *Pompey*, 10.

230. Apuleius, *Metamorphoses* IX, 35,2-38,7; cf. also Seneca, *Epistles*, 90.39: 'Although she adds one estate to another, evicting a neighbour either by turning him out or wronging him'. Plutarch writes that 'Some persons, through their foolishness, are so silly and conceited, either because of abundance of money, or importance of office, or petty political preferments, or because of position and repute, that they threaten and insult those in lower stations' (*Mor*. 103e-f).

231. Cf. Pliny, *Epistles* II,11; III,4; IV, 9.

232. Pliny, *Epistles* III, 4,7.

233. Pliny, *Epistles* III, 9,25.

234. Pliny, *Epistles* V,13,8. Tacitus reports that at the beginning of the reign of Galba 'the senate resolved to deal more thoroughly with the matter of informers'. 'This vote of the senate had had various fortunes and had been weak or effective according to the power or poverty of the defendant; yet it still retained some of its terror' (*Histories* II, 10,1).

235. Apuleius, *Metamorphoses* X, 12,4. Cf. also Aristides, *Eulogy of Rome*, 32: had the governors even the slightest doubt about legal decisions or investigations, they would refer them to the emperor 'if they (viz. the subjects concerned) are worthy'.

236. Petronius, *Satyricon*, 14,2.

237. Apuleius, *Metamorphoses* X, 33,1. Juvenal also takes for granted the venality of judges (Juvenal, *Satires* XIII, 3f.); cf. also Tacitus, *Annals* II, 34,1.

238. Juvenal, *Satires* XVI, 6-14.

239. Aristides, *Eulogy of Rome*, 39.

240. Tacitus, *Agricola*, 21. For the significance of *humanitas* cf. Gellius, *Noctes Atticae* XIII, 17,1, who points out that it does not correspond to the Greek word *philanthropia*, as was most often assumed in his day, but to *paideia* (= education). According to Plutarch's account, as governor in Spain Sertorius already made himself popular among the 'barbarians' by showing them Roman military practices and embellishing their equipment: he then continues: 'But most of all were they captivated by what he did with their boys. Those of the highest birth, namely, he collected together from the various peoples, at Osca, a large city, and set over them teachers of Greek and Roman learning. Thus in reality he made hostages of them while ostensibly he was educating them, with the assurance that when they became men he would give them a share in administration and authority. So the fathers were wonderfully pleased to see their sons, in purple bordered togas, very decorously going to their schools and

Sertorius paying their fees for them, holding frequent examinations, distributing prizes to the deserving, and presenting them with the golden necklaces which the Roman call *bullae*' (*Sertorius*, 14). When later there was a revolt, Sertorius disposed of these hostages, 'killing some and selling others into slavery' (25).

241. Aristides, *Eulogy of Rome*, 93; cf. 94.

242. Pliny, *Epistles* X, 37-42, 70f., 98f.

243. Aristides, 97.

244. Ibid., 98.

245. Josephus, *Antt.* XV, 328-30; cf. also 331-41, which depicts the building of Caesarea by the sea, and 268, according to which Herod instituted fighting games in Caesarea which were held every five years, and had a theatre built in Jerusalem and an amphitheatre in the plain.

246. Seneca, *Epistles*, 90,25. He goes on to mention 'a glass-blower who by his breath moulds the glass into manifold shapes which could scaaely be fashioned by the most skilful hand' (31). But he gives the impression of not being enthusiastic, but rather being satiated by civilization; instead of this he is enthusiastic about the early period and among other things says about it: 'The air, the breezes blowing free through the open spaces, the flitting shade of crag or tree, springs crystal-clear and not spoiled by man's work whether by water pipe or by any confinement of the channel but running at will, and meadows beautiful without the use of art' (43).

247. Plutarch, *Lucullus*, 23. For games in Asia Minor during the time of the Empire cf. Franke, 24-7, and the depictions on coins relating to it.

248. Apuleius, *Metamorphoses* X, 18,1f. In X, 29,4-32,4; 34,1-3 Apuleius describes the opening part of a programme in the amphitheatre of Corinth: Greek ballet, a representation of the judgment of Paris, executions by wild animals.

249. Apuleius, *Metamorphoses* IV, 13,2,4,6.

250. Ibid., 14, 2f.

251. Tacitus, *Histories* IV, 64,3.

252. Ibid., 65,2.

253. *Friedensgedanke*, 198f.; *Widerstand*, 18,47-9. The reference is to Pliny, *Natural History* XIV, 1,2-6.

254. Petronius, *Satyricon*, 88, 7f., 10.

255. Horace, *Ars Poetica*, 325-32. However, Seneca does not praise the technical progress which this spirit doubtless produced and which led to all the attractive things which he mentions in the quotation reproduced on p.42 above and clearly would not want to be without. He does not count these inventions as wisdom: 'All this sort of thing has been devised by the lowest grade of slaves' (Seneca, *Epistles*, 90.25).

256. Virgil, *Aeneid* VI, 847-50.

257. Cf. above 14 and n.49.

258. Cf. simply Propertius II, 10,10-20.

259. Propertius IV, 4,67f. This line is stressed one-sidedly by Meyer. He finds 'in Propertius the same notions, wishes and expectations with respect to the foreign policy of Augustus... as with Virgil and Horace, but put more naively and expressed with less disguise' (301). However, in this interpretation he does not take into account the passages I shall be going on to mention. Propertius's

comments are not free from contradiction, because his existence is contradictory; he lives by the prevailing system and at the same time at least partially dissociates himself from it.

260. Propertius III, 5,10-12.

261. Ibid., 3,6.

262. Ibid., 13-15.

263. Propertius II, 15,40-43.

264. Propertius III, 5,1f.

265. Ibid., 23-46.

266. Ibid., 46f. The reference is to the standards lost to the Parthians in 53 BC at the battle of Carrhae.

267. Tibullus II, 5,115-18.

268. Ibid., 39-64.

269. Tibullus I, 1,5-10.

270. The estate inherited from his ancestors had been reduced by confiscation, but 'a spot of earth is enough' (Tibullus I, 1,43).

271. Tibullus I, 10,7f. On the elegy I,10, cf. Schwarz, passim.

272. Ibid., 33, 39f.

273. Tibullus I, 1, 73f. Tibullus prefers the 'battles of Venus' (I, 10,53). Cf. also his wish in II, 5, 105f.: 'Through your peace, Phoebus, may bow and arrow disappear; Love should go through the lands without weapons.'

274. Tibullus I, 1, 75-78. Earlier, in 53-55, he had said: 'It is your due, Messala, to fight on land and water, so that your house can boast the adornment of booty from the enemy. But a lovely maiden holds me in her thrall.' Cf. also I, 10, 25-32.

275. Cf. also the description of the abundant blessings of peace in Tibullus I, 10,45-68. The Pax called on at the end, in 67f., is not to be associated with Augustus' programme of peace (thus Wifstrand-Schiebe, 92f.), since in the context the marks of soldiers appear twice as a contrast to peace, not as its presupposition (49f., 65f.). For the 'lack of specific references to the "Roman world"' in Tibullus I, 10, cf. also Laage, 120-5 (the quotation is on p.125).

276. Raith, 12.

277. The two Virgil passages mentioned in n.2 above and Seneca, *Apocol.*, 4,1 associate the golden age with a ruler figure.

278. Aristides, *Eulogy of Rome*, 89.

279. Ibid., 88.

280. Ibid., 31.

281. Pliny, *Panegyricus*, 72.

282. Ibid., 94.

283. Ibid.

284. Pliny says of Trajan that the emperor wants to be preserved by the gods only 'if he has ruled the state well and in the interests of all'. He then turns this statement into an ideology by drawing the opposite conclusion: 'you can be confident that you are ruling well, as long as they are preserving you' (Pliny, *Panegyricus*, 68; for this structure of argument in Dion cf. Eggenberger, 157f.). Pausanias speaks similiarly of the 'Emperor Hadrian who supremely revered the gods and created the greatest happiness for all (!) his subjects' (I, 5,5). Seneca describes the emperor wearing himself out for the well-being of the

world when he says of Claudius: 'His watchfulness guards all men's sleep, his toil all men's ease, his industry all men's dissipations, his work all men's vocation. On the day that Caesar dedicated himself to the whole world he robbed himself of himself; and even as the planets which, unresting, pursue their courses, he may never halt or do anything for himself' (Seneca, *Ad Polybium* VII, 2). It does not need to be stressed that this description does not of course correspond to reality.

285. Seneca, *De clementia* I, 1,2.

286. Ibid., I,1,5.

287. Aristides, *Eulogy of Rome*, 107.

288. Tacitus, *Annals* XV, 74,3.

289. Virgil, *Eclogues* I,6-8; cf. also *Georgics* I, 24-35, which says of Augustus, among others: 'And so the mighty world may receive you as the giver of increase and lord of the seasons, whether you come as god of the boundless sea and sailors worship your deity alone.'

290. Horace, *Odes* I, 12,49.

291. Horace, *Odes* III, 5,1-3; cf. IV, 5,32. The parallel between Jupiter and Augustus also appears in Ovid, *Metamorphoses* XV, 858-60: 'Jupiter controls the heights of heaven and the kingdoms of the triformed universe: but the earth is under Augustus's sway. Each is both Father and ruler.' Earlier he has said: 'So then that his son might not be born of mortal seed, Caesar must needs be made a god' (760f.).

292. Seneca, *Ad Polybium* XIII, 1.

293. Thus in *Epigrams* V, 8, he speaks of 'our gracious emperor' as 'our god', prays in VII,5 when he is absent from Rome: 'bring back our god to our urgent prayers'; and in IX, 64, he describes the worship of Domitian as Hercules in which the emperor is regarded as the 'greater god', as is already evident from the significant introduction: 'Caesar deigning to descend to the features of great Hercules.' Later, however, under Trajan, Martial writes: 'In vain, O flatterers, you come to me: I think not to address any man as master and god' (X, 72).

294. Aristides, *Eulogy of Rome*, 32; this description is meant seriously by Aristides and is not understood as a caricature.

295. Pliny, *Epistles* X,1,2.

296. *Res Gestae*, 9. For the oath of loyalty to the emperor see the survey in Freudenberger, 135-7 (with references to specialist literature).

297. Pliny, *Epistles* X, 35.

298. Pliny, *Epistles* X, 52; cf. 102, the report about the same ceremony in the following year, and Tacitus, *Annals* XVI, 22,1. Cf. the examples of the oath of loyalty to the emperor in the inscriptions nos.7-9 in HIRK 10-13.

299. Pliny, *Epistles* X, 36, 53, 103.

300. Seneca, *Ad Polybium*, VII, 4.

301. Apuleius, *Metamorphoses* XI, 17,3.

302. OGIS, no.458,40f. The Greek translation of the letter with which the proconsul gave the occasion for this decision speaks twice of 'the most divine emperor' (4,22).

303. Mähler, 60.

304. Kent, pl.38 no.149R; cf. pl.49, no.187R, where there is a parallel from Asia Minor for the time of Claudius. The front of a temple is depicted on a coin,

also with the inscription '*Romae et Augusto*'; in the temple on the right there is a female figure with a cornucopia, probably the personification of Asia, crowning the emperor Claudius who stands on the left beside her.

305. Tacitus, *Annals* IV, 15,3.

306. Ibid., 55f.

307. Franke, 11. According to Christensen, 'the most decisive thing about this cult was its character as a religion of political loyalty' (23; cf.25).

308. Franke, no.422.

309. Aristides, *Eulogy of Rome*, 66.

310. One of the reasons for Nero's accusations against the consul Thrasea was that he had not taken part in such ceremonies (Tacitus, *Annals* XVI, 22.1).

311. Pliny, *Epistles* X, 96,5.

312. Pliny, *Epistles* X, 96,3. This procedure was applied at the very time in which according to a rescript of Trajan the liberal principle held that 'it is better for the crime of a guilty person to go unpunished than to condemn an innocent person' (*Digest* 48,19,5). However, in connection with the passage from Pliny which has been cited it should be noted that 'obstinacy' and 'stubbornness' were regarded as dangerous political characteristics; cf. the similar combination, *contumacia cum pernicia*, in the speech by Cerialis which has already been mentioned several times (Tacitus, *Histories* IV, 74,4) and the sentence in the speech of Calgacus: 'Courage and high spirit in their subjects displease our masters' (*Agricola* 31.3). This is not, of course, a reference to any penal condition. Freudenberger rightly disputes that, with a reference to the Pliny passage (99-110). However it is wrong to see the description of those executed as obstinate and stubborn as an excuse for the swift action of the governor (though that is what Freudenberger, 107f., thinks). 'Pliny has no doubt about the correctness of his action' (Christensen, 49). These executions also served to fulfil the political task which he had of restoring order to the province (cf. the conclusion of the letter of Pliny and on it Freudenberger, 179). Josephus gives an analogy: after the Jewish war Sicarii had fled to Alexandria but they were caught and tortured there: 'For when all sorts of torments and vexations of their bodies that could be devised were made use of to them to get them merely to confess that Caesar was their lord, not one of them yielded or thought of saying the words' (*BJ* VII, 418). Not even any of the children could be persuaded 'to name Caesar as their Lord' (ibid., 419).

313. For Roman historiography from Sallust to Tacitus as 'a literary platform of political opposition and political resignation', cf. Richter, 289-309 (the quotation is on 307). The book by MacMullen covers a longer period and takes in the first four centuries. However, he takes a very broad view of enmity and in the first two chapters confines 'Roman order' to the principate.

314. Seneca, *Apocol.*. 1,1; 4,1.

315. In the drama Octavia, which is wrongly attributed to Seneca, vv.391-406 lament over the present in an almost apocalyptic way and see the last day coming on the world on which the present generation will be buried under the fall of heaven, so that the world brings forth a new one as once in the golden age. In the same work, however, there is a celebration of the time of Augustus (472-8) in which what here is above all regarded as 'beautiful' is fulfilled: 'To abstain

from cruel bloodshed, to be slow to wrath, give quiet to the world, peace to one's time.'

316. Seneca, *Epistles*, 19,7.

317. Seneca, *Epistles*, 9,18f.; *De constantia* V,6.

318. Seneca, *Epistles*, 9,19; according to 41.8 that should be praised in man 'which cannot be given or snatched away'. In *De Constantia* V.7 Seneca gives as the reason for Stilpo's answer that 'he had with him his true possessions'.

319. For a number of reasons Seneca had dismissed the other possibility, the solidarity of those affected by the snatching away in separation and thus the description of part of an alternative society. That would not least contradict his advice that 'the wise man will never provoke the anger of those in power' (Seneca, *Epistles*, 14,7).

320. Juvenal, *Satires* XIII, 28-30.

321. *Widerstand*, passim.

322. *Widerstand*, 19.

323. Plutarch, *Phocion*, 23.

324. *Widerstand*, 17.

325. This situation is of course depicted with wonderment by Aelius Aristides. 'You have so thoroughly investigated the ocean... that not even the island that lies by itself (viz. Britain) has escaped you' (*Eulogy of Rome*, 28). There is a collection of taunts of the Romans, like the accusation that they are 'robbers of the world', in Opelt, *Schimpfwörter*, 186f.

326. For this statement cf. Laruccia, passim, and for part of its influence Mehl, passim.

327. Tacitus, *Agricola*, 30,3-31,2. The speech by Calgacus should be compared with that of Critognatus of Gaul, in which he says: 'The Cimbri devastated Gaul, they brought great disaster upon us, yet they departed at length from our borders and sought other countries, leaving us our rights, laws, lands, liberty. But the Romans – what else do they seek or desire than to follow where envy leads, to settle in the lands and states of men whose noble report and martial strength they have learnt, and to bind upon them a perpetual slavery? This is the way in which they have waged wars. And if you do not know what happens in distant nations, look now on Gaul close at hand, which has been reduced to a province, with the changes of rights and laws, and crushed between the axes in everlasting slavery' (Caesar, *Bellum Gallicum* VII, 77,14-16). From the Roman point of view the change of Gaul 'to our laws' was of course praised (thus the Cerialis speech quoted on 21 above). Cf. further, from the speech of King Mithridates in the extract by M.Iunianus Iustinus from the history of Pompeius Trogus on the Romans: 'And as they themselves report, their founders were fed at the breast of a she-wolf, so now that whole people has the disposition of a wolf, insatiably bloodthirsty, hungry and lusting for mastery and riches' (XXXVIII 6,7f.).

328. For the very different Jewish views on Rome see Stemberger, *Herrschaft* (for the quotation from IV Ezra which follows cf. 26-30); cf. id., 'Beurteilung'.

329. 11.37-46, in Charlesworth, *Old Testament Pseudepigrapha*, 1, 549. 'This is not the account of a fight by the lion; it is, rather, a judgment' (Müller, *Messias*, 102f.). Cf. also Sib. III, 175-95. For the widespread hope in the East 'that a king from the East would seize rule', which is evidently not grounded

'on specific ethnic expectations of a redeemer but represents a standpoint common to the whole of the Near East' and its probable sociological setting in a peasantry uprooted by tribute and thus alienated from traditional loyalties, cf. Kippenberg, passim (the quotations are from 43 and 47).

330. Cf. *Eulogy of Rome*, 105: 'The all-seeing Helios discovered under your rule neither a crime nor an injustice nor any such other things as used to happen in former times. Therefore he rightly looks down on your kingdom with the greatest pleasure.'

Part Two (III)

III/1

1. See above, 8f. and nn. 10,11.

2. According to Schottroff this saying of Jesus clearly says what the Pax Romana is: 'The powerful exert force on the peoples. The aim of this force is to preserve the existing order, in which it is clear who profits by it' ('Friedenspraxis', 25).

3. Cf. above 52f. and n.327.

4. Josephus, *Antt.* XVIII, 116-18. This account, which gives political motives for the intervention of Herod Antipas, clashes with the narrative in Mark 6.17-29, according to which John was arrested because of his criticism of an illegitimate marriage of the tetrarch and finally executed by the intrigues of the infuriated Herodias.

5. Cf. the examples in Billerbeck II, 200f.

6. Schneider, *Lukas*, 310.

7. Cf. Delling, τελειόω, *TDNT* 8, (80-4) 84.

8. Cf. the short sketches in Petzke, 225-7, and Gnilka, *Markus* 2, 154f.

9. Although it is often claimed that the saying of Jesus in v.17 is independent of the scene which precedes it, which is supposed to have been created from the saying (e.g. Schrage, *Staat*, 32 n.57, though he considers this only very cautiously), that does not seem very credible. Without the scene the saying of Jesus is completely in the air and can be used for just about anything, as the history of its interpretation clearly shows. It does not seem probable that Jesus uttered such a saying 'without a situation'. So we would have to postulate that the original saying has not come down to us and the one that we have now has been invented. But why assume this when the present connection between v.17 and v.16 is as smooth as one could imagine and the behaviour of Jesus depicted in it corresponds precisely with his situation, as I shall go on to show?

10. The instructions from the Sanhedrin, which must be discovered from the wider context, might go back to Marcan redaction (cf. Gnilka, *Markus* 2, 150f.).

11. Against Schrage, *Staat*, 31.

12. In 3.6, which is probably a redactional passage, Pharisees and Herodians similarly appear in a joint action.

13. Both in their actions and in the way in which they are treated by Jesus the questioners, though given different names, appear as a single group; there is nothing here to indicate that they differ from one another over the problem at issue.

14. There is no evidence for the designation 'Herodians' outside Mark 3.6;

12.13. Analogous formations make it clear that this kind of term denotes political supporters of a man (cf. above, 73), in this case therefore supporters of a Herod. It seems improbable that Mark would have invented such a group. This designation existed before him. It is referred either to Herod Antipas, tetrarch over Galilee and Peraea from 4 BC to AD 39, or to Herod Agrippa I, at first successor to Philip in AD 37 until he had extended his territory by expansion during 39 and 41 to about the size of the empire of Herod the Great; he died as early as 44. In both cases the reference is to a Herod as reigning king (cf. e.g. Hans-Friedrich Weiss, Φαρισαῖος B, 'The Pharisees in the New Testament', *TDNT* 9, (35-48) 39f. Against this is the fact that analogous designations of parties are not formed with names of persons who rule without competition. It is certainly no coincidence that the only passage in Josephus which mentions 'supporters of Herod' with other terms (*Antt.* XIV, 450) relates to a time when Herod was still fighting for his rule. Another possibility is therefore more probable. As I shall go on to demonstrate, the narrative in Mark 12.13-17 must be set in Judaea. At the time of Jesus 'Herodians' in Judaea can only denote a party the political aim of which was again to remove Judaea from direct Roman procuratorial rule and make it subject to the rule of a Herod. That can then be Herod Antipas or even (Herod) Agrippa (I), who at that time was living in Rome. Both had this aim and the latter finally achieved it, though of course with the help and favour of Rome. In connection with the question about taxation that means that the Herodians can in no way have been in favour of refusing to pay tax. Their political aim called for absolute loyalty to Rome. Generally speaking, loyalty towards Rome was also characteristic of Pharisaism, otherwise the reconstitution of Judaism under its leadership after the catastrophe of the Jewish war would have been impossible. But there were certainly also Pharisees who sympathized with the Zealots (cf. Hengel, *Zeloten*, 340f.). There is nothing to indicate that this is what was meant in Mark 12.13. The connection between Pharisees and Herodians in Mark 12.13, for which there could be a historical reason, was already made before the evangelist. That led him to write 3.6 as he did.

15. There is a detailed account in Hengel, *Zeloten*, 132-50.

16. Schrage, *Staat*, 33.

17. Schmithals, *Markus*, 528.

18. As far as I know, Eisler was the first person to interpret this saying in terms of Jesus' situation, namely that of someone completely without possessions (196-201; cf. 201: 'Anyone who no longer has money, no longer uses money, need no longer pay tax to Caesar').

19. Cf.Schrage, *Staat*, 34f.

20. Cf. e.g. the depiction in Matthiae, 99 no.51, with the description on p.98. The obverse shows the 'head of the emperor with a laurel wreath facing right'; the inscription runs 'Tiberius Caesar, son of the divine Augustus, Augustus'. The reverse bears the inscription 'high priest' and depicts 'Livia as goddess of peace..., sitting turned to the right; in her outstretched left hand she is holding an olive branch and with the right she is supporting herself on the sceptre'. Cf. above all Hart, passim.

21. It is possible to understand the text in an even more pointed way. Literally the question is 'Is it lawful to give tax to the emperor or not? Should we give or

not give?' The answer contains a composite verb for 'give' which can have the same significance as the simple verb and is also used 'of any payment in the context of a debt' (Dibelius, 'Rom', 177 n.2), but also has the meaning 'give back'. The change of the term in the answer could therefore emphatically produce, 'Give back to the emperor what is the emperor's'.

22. Petzke, 230.

23. As the final part of Jesus' answer is added unasked and as he thus transcends the question put to him, the connection is surely to be understood in an adversative sense.

24. Bornkamm, 123 and n.31 on 207.

25. This saying has a close but also characteristically different parallel in Luke 12.51-53. Both evangelists have taken it over from the Logia source (Q). On the whole Matthew has probably kept the original form here. I shall discuss only the most important points. In Luke there is a prophecy: the division in the family appears as a *consequence* of the coming of Jesus. According to the Matthaean formulation, however, the division is his *aim* and *goal*. From the first part of the saying one would expect an indication of aim and goal here. Moreover it seems more probable that such a saying (division in the family as the aim and goal of the activity of Jesus) would later be toned down to a prophecy (division as an inevitable consequence of confessing Jesus) than vice versa. In Matthew the division takes place exclusively from below upwards, but in Luke it is the other way round. The latter necessarily follows if the statement appears as a prophecy which describes the consequences of confessing Jesus. In that case it would be difficult to see how the division should come about only from one side. It is no argument against the assumption that here too the priority is with Matthew to say that at a secondary stage he assimilated the terminology more closely to Micah 7.6. It is indeed correct that the Matthaean version is close to the Old Testament text, but the substance is fundamentally different from Micah 7.6 and the tradition of exegesis based on this passage. I shall go into that later. – Luke 12.52 has no parallel in Matthew. It is an anticipatory generalization from v.53, which must be regarded as a redactional expansion because of the Lucan terminology. On the other hand Matt.10.36, the conclusion of the quotation of Micah 7.6, has no parallel in Luke. Here Matthew could have expanded the Micah text at a later stage. This general statement would have fitted very well indeed into the Lucan version. However, one cannot rule out with certainty an omission by Luke because of the generalization which has already been made in v.52. If one leaves aside the introduction and construction of this first sentence, which I shall not discuss here and which remain questionable – in terms of content that is irrelevant – it thus follows that Matt.10.34f. reproduces the traditional text, whereas there has been a transformation in Luke 12.51-53. For an analysis of the text cf. also Schulz, *Q*, 258f.

26. Matthew and Luke present it in very different contexts. Luke puts it at the end of a lengthy 'sermon' by Jesus to the disciples beginning in 12.22 and only interrupted in v.41 by a question from Peter which has been produced by the collection of various sayings. In Matthew it appears within the mission discourse. It follows from this that in the sayings source it was loosely connected, without any particular framework.

27. But Matthew, too, understands it in this way by the context he gives it; cf. especially the reciprocity of father and son and mother and daughter in v.37.

28. Micah 7.1-6 complains about the collapse of good order, a collapse which has progressed so far that in the most intimate sphere, the household, the family, people rise up against those to whom they owe respect and obedience. For the history of the exegesis of this passage in ancient Judaism see the details in Bill. I, 586; IV 2, 982. The respect of children for their parents is taken for granted not only in Judaism but also in the Hellenistic world; cf. the saying in this connection from an Isis aretalogy from the second and first century BC in Macedonia: 'You (viz. Isis) have made parents be respected by their children' (in Horsley 10 [Text A.2 lines 31f.]).

29. If we see this intention arising out of the wording of the saying, in my opinion it certainly cannot be explained as a community construction. The reformulation in Luke 12.51-53 certainly rests on the experiences of the community that confessing Jesus led to grievous divisions in the most intimate spheres. This is matched by the formulation in the style of a prophecy and also the reciprocity. A parallel saying, an expression of the same experiences and formulated on the basis of them, can be found in Mark 13.12f. parr. Mention should also be made of passages like Matt.5.10 par.; 10.18; Mark 13.9, where there are prophecies of the sufferings of disciples which arise as a consequence of confessing Jesus. As in Luke 12.52f. here we constantly have a reflection of the experience of the community. Matthew 10.34f. is characteristically different from this. How could this formulation, which did not correspond to the experience of the community, be formulated in it? So it must go back to Jesus himself.

30. For them cf. the passages in Hengel, *Zeloten*, in the index s.v. 'Friedens-partei', esp. 210f., 218.

31. Dibelius regarded Mark 3.20f. 'by the evangelist as an introduction preparatory to the story in 3.31ff.' (*From Tradition to Gospel*, reissued London 1971, 47). But it is extremely improbable that such a report in which the family of Jesus accuse him of being mad should be redactional or that it should have been invented before Mark in the community, in view of the prominent position of the members of the family of Jesus in the Jerusalem community (cf. just Gal.1.19; 2.9). And so Mark 3.20f. was left out by Matthew and Luke, and in some textual evidence the statement that Jesus was out of his mind has been changed and indeed put on the lips of opponents (cf. the text-critical details on Mark 3.21 in the synopsis by Aland). For the designation of kin as οἱ παρ' αὐτοῦ cf. Hengstl, 129 (no.46, lines 13f.): τινὲς τῶν παρ' ἐμοῦ.

32. The very general statement added in v.35, 'Whoever does the will of God is my brother, my sister and my mother' is not specifically rooted in the preceding scene. On the contrary, the scene is completely rounded off with the reference in v.34 and does not need v.35. According to Bultmann the closing saying in v.35 is primary and the preceding scene has been built on it (*Tradition*, 29). That is utterly improbable. As is shown by the adoption of Mark 3.34f. in Matt.12.49f. and Luke 8.21, later writers had difficulties with v.34 and not with v.35. According to v.34, for Jesus mothers and brothers are simply those who are around him, without any further specification or condition; according to v.35 they are those who do the will of God. This simultaneous generalization

and specification can be explained in terms of the situation after Easter: now beyond the possibility of being able to become a physical disciple of the earthly Jesus, people looked for a practicable, generally binding criterion for affinity to Jesus and found it in doing the will of God. By contrast the scene itself can only be understood in the pre-Easter situation and therefore is hardly conceivable as an invention of the community.

33. Cf. the parallel Matt.20.26f.; Luke 22.26f.; Mark 9.35.

34. Hoffmann, *Eschatologie*, 143.

35. It thus follows another principle, precisely the opposite to the one that Aelius Aristides describes for Roman soldiers, when he says of the soldiers: 'When you go against the enemy they are of one mind, but they fight among one another for preeminence as long as they live and the only thing therefore that they ask of all men is that they should meet a foe (*Eulogy*, 85)'

36. In the lists of disciples in Luke 6.15: Acts 1.13 a Simon is described as 'the Zealot'. At the corresponding point in Mark 3.18; Matt.10.3 he is called the Canaanite. That goes back to the Aramaic equivalent for Zealot. Cf. Hengel, *Zeloten*, 72f.

37. Cf. Hoffmann, *Moral*, 164f.

38. There is no need to analyse this text here as it may be taken as certain that Jesus had close and friendly dealings with 'publicans and sinners', and that is the only important point.

39. To the saying of Jesus in Mark 2.17b, 'I am not come to call the righteous but sinners', Luke in 5.32 adds the words 'to repentance'. Evidently he can understand the invitation of Jesus to sinners only as a call to repentance. In so doing he presupposes a common concept of the sinner and the correctness of distinguishing between righteous and sinners, whereas Jesus puts precisely this distinction in question: he does not make the sinner 'righteous', as those who attack him for his conduct would understand the term.

40. Luke has essentially preserved the original text of the Beatitudes. They are addressed to people who are marked out by their difficult social situation. That corresponds to the situation of Jesus and his followers. Therefore the form of an address seems to me to be primary, even if the third person plural is universally customary for beatitudes (Bultmann, *Tradition*, 109 and n.4). Matthew has altered and further expanded the beatitudes which he has in common with Luke. Here it is not people in a particular condition who are said to be blessed but those who behave in a particular way. So there are 'indirect demands' (Strecker, 'Makarismen', 123). The 'now' in the second and third beatitudes in Luke 6.21 is secondary, 'because an addition is more probable than a deletion; moreover *νῦν* is a favourite word of Luke's' (S.Schulz, 77; cf. also Strecker, *Bergpredigt*, 38).

41. That happens in Seneca, and significantly, therefore, with a rich man, when he says, 'Poverty is free, is without cares' (*Epistles*, 17,3).

42. Hoffmann, *Moral*, 35.

43. *Miracle Stories*, 250.

44. Ibid., 249.

45. According to Luke 11.14 the demon is dumb. As the continuation shows – the person from whom the demon has been driven out can speak – this means that he makes people dumb. It is similarly said in the Matthaean parallels (9.32;

12.22) that the possessed person is dumb. In the narrative of the healing of the boy who is possessed (Mark 9.14-29 par.) Jesus says to the 'unclean Spirit': 'You speechless and dumb spirit' (v.25). It follows from the crying out of the spirit mentioned in v.26 that it is therefore also addressed as one which makes dumb and is not dumb itself. In Mark 1.23-28 par. it is clear that the person possessed is not in control of himself; although introduced in v.23f. as someone who can speak he does not do so, but his words are those of the one by whom he is possessed. It is the same in the narrative indicated in Mark 5.1-15 par., as vv.6-10 show. In addition vv.3-5 describe the possessed person as crazy, making wild and self-destructive gestures, and as having been rejected from the community.

46. *Miracle Stories*, 255.

47. Ibid. In this connection it is worth noting that the Roman empire is occsionally compared with swine by rabbis: BerR LXV on Gen 26.34.

48. For the complex Mark 3.22-27/Matt.12.22-30 (9.32-34)/Luke 11.14-23 Matthew and Luke offer further similar material in addition to that in Mark and also both together characteristically differ from Mark in the material they have in common with Mark. Therefore we must conclude a double tradition: the same piece of tradition was in the Logia source in a version different from that in Mark. The saying quoted above represents the original answer of Jesus to the charge that he is in league with Beelzebul; for here there is a direct reference in terminology and content (cf. Schweizer, *Matthew*, 287). The saying has been transmitted in the same form almost word for word in Matthew and Luke. The only difference worth mentioning is that Matthew writes 'spirit of God' instead of 'finger of God', which may be a secondary explanation of the vivid image.

49. Theissen, *Miracle Stories*, 278, 279.

50. Cf. Hengel, *Zealots*, 127-32.

51. They are in Luke 6.27-36/Matt.5.38-48. I must dispense with an analysis here and just mention the following points. There are two different complexes in Matthew (5.38-42, 43-48) and only one in Luke. Matthew has inserted the similar but differing contents into the antithesis pattern as a secondary stage (cf. Bultmann, *Tradition*, 148f.). But Luke, too, worked redactionally. That is evident not only from the incorporation of the golden rule (vv.31f.) into this complex – it appears in Matthew in quite another context – but also above all from the fact that he twice introduces the commandment to love one's enemy. He puts it programmatically in front of the whole passage so that the individual instances of the renunciation of retribution which are listed afterwards appear as its exegesis, and then repeats it in v.35, evidently because it has a close connection with the theme of being children of God (Matt.5.44f.). That Luke 6.27-36 is a single complex is also a result of secondary composition (cf. Bultmann, *Tradition*, 96). In the Logia source used by Matthew and Luke the admonitions to refrain from retribution and to love one's enemy followed one another. As the second person singular is used throughout the one and the second person plural in the others, these are originally independent units.

52. That essentially corresponds to the text of Luke, for the originality of which see also Hoffmann, *Eschatologie*, 133; Schulz, *Q*, 121-3, differs. In Matthew, the second example presupposes the situation of a trial in which one party is 'taking the shirt off' another; it was impossible to sue for the cloak (cf. Bill. I, 343f.). In Luke, by contrast the situation in view is that of a robbery, in

which of course the upper garment is taken first. In Matthew the first example, too, is within the sphere of the law. Striking on the right cheek is striking with the back of the hand, which is regarded as an insult (cf. Bill.I, 342f.); by contrast Luke envisages a punch-up. The situations presupposed in Matthew are more appropriate to a settled community; those in Luke to the itinerant life of Jesus and his disciples. The further scene which is presented only in Matthew (5.41) has in view requisition by Roman occupying forces (cf. above, 29 and n.161). However, Galilee, the homeland of Jesus, was ruled by the tetrarch Herod Antipas, who maintained his own army. The other text common to Luke and Matthew (6.30/5.42) consists of generalizations and might be secondary in comparison with the two evocative scenes. Only it is to be assumed to be original (cf. also Linskens, 17f.). For an analysis of Matt.5.39b-42/Luke 6.29f. cf. most recently Hoffmann, 'Verbindlichkeit', 57-63.

53. To demonstrate the dimension of what is spoken of in this saying of Jesus a student once said in a seminar that it was not a matter of, 'If someone takes away your house, give him your daughter for his harem as well.'

54. Cf. Ex.22.25f. and the rabbinic exposition of this story given in Bill.I, 343f.

55. Vögtle, 96.

56. Hoffmann, *Moral*, 94.

57. 'Gewaltverzicht', 192f.; cf. also Trummer, 'Widerstand', 183-7, 194f.

58. Blank, *Dienst* 25. At this point reference should be made explicitly to the comments by Hoffmann, 'Verbindlichkeit', 111-17.

59. Two relevant differences in the text common to Luke and Matthew should be discussed: 1. In contrast to the indicative statement by Luke in the third line (6.35), the final version in Matthew (5.45) fits his ethicizing tendency (cf. Theissen, 'Gewaltverzicht', 161f.) and is therefore to be regarded as secondary. 2. In view of the final reason I find a decision difficult. The Matthaean version which describes God as the one who makes his sun rise on the evil and the good and the rain fall on the just and the unjust is usually taken to be original because of its vivid imagery (e.g. Schulz, *Q*, 18). On the other hand the one-sidedness of the Lucan formulation should be noted. It seems more unlikely that a statement that the goodness of God is shown to the ungrateful and evil should be transformed at a later stage into a statement about a goodness which is poured out over everyone without any distinction than vice versa. But whatever the original may have been, in both cases it is important that in his approach God acts contrary to human forms of behaviour. For the analysis of Matt.5.43-48/Luke 6.27f., 32-36, cf. most recently Hoffmann, 'Verbindlichkeit', 51-7.

60. Hoffmann, *Eschatologie*, 131.

61. For the 'interpretation of the love of one's enemy as a militant overcoming of the enemy through love' cf. Schottroff, 'Gewaltverzicht', 200-3 (the quotation is on 202). Love of one's enemy 'does not accept the enemy as he is; it wants everything from him; it wants to change his enmity' (202).

III/2

1. It is impossible here to enter into a thorough discussion of 'the legal foundations for the persecutions of Christians in the first two centuries' (thus

the title of an article by Wlosok), nor is there any need to; for that see this article and the further works in the volume of essays edited by R.Klein, *Das frühe Christentum im römischen Staat*, WdF 267, Darmstadt 1971; and above all the book by Molthagen which, in addition to the information given in its title, also deals with the first century; see further Freudenberger, *Verhalten*, 1-125; id., 'Christenverfolgungen', 23-5. In what follows I shall merely attempt to sketch out the situation of Christians in the Roman empire at the time of Paul.

2. *Annals* XV, 44.2-5.

3. In the statement in Tacitus that after the accusation by Nero 'those were first arrested who made a confession' we should understand the further words 'that they were Christians', not 'that they were responsible for the fire'.

4. Wlosok, 280; cf. 280f., 282; further Dibelius, 'Rom', 206-11.

5. Blank, 'Kirche', 17. It is significant that in the passage mentioned in n.2 Tacitus also points out that 'the man from whom this name (viz. Christians) is derived, Christus, had been executed in the rule of Tiberius on the orders of Pontius Pilate'.

6. Here I shall cite those letters of Paul which are universally reckoned to be authentic: Romans, I and II Corinthians, Galatians, Philippians, I Thessalonians, Philemon.

7. For punishment by flogging cf. Bill. III, 527-30.

8. For the situation presupposed in II Cor.11.32f. cf. Jewett, 30,31.

9. Phil.1.7,12-14, 16f.; 4.14; Philemon 1,9,13.

10. Phil.1.12-17. In the letter of Philemon the terms 'prisoner of Jesus Christ' (1.9) and 'my fetters of the gospel' (= my imprisonment caused by the gospel, 13) express that.

11. Cf. the Philippians passage mentioned in the previous note. Unfortunately we know neither the accusation nor the argumentation of the other Christians. As it cannot be supposed that the accusation fell under the category of a criminal charge relating to property, and as the claim of Paul that he is accused as a Christian must be taken seriously, the accusation can lie only in the political sphere. So Paul's proclamation must have been of such a kind or had such effects that it also touched on this area. Here he evidently regarded as essential the point which provoked this contact, whereas the other Christians it as an unnecessary provocation.

12. On this cf. Vielhauer, 155-70, 173f.

13. Cf. also 1.21-26, according to which, however, Paul expects an acquittal rather than the death penalty, though that, too, is within the bounds of possibility.

14. Cf. Mommsen, 89f.; according to him the verb used by Paul indicates 'a leading authority using lictors or the legal officers who act for them in non-Roman legal communities' (89 n.1).

15. Cf. Acts 16.22f.

16. Cf. Acts 21.39 and 16.37f.; 22.25-29; 23.27.

17. I Thess.2.9; I Cor.4.12; cf. Acts 20.34; according to Acts 18.3 he was a tentmaker.

18. I Cor.9.19; II Cor.11.7; cf. Hock, passim.

19. That is not to make a decision as to whether Paul's relationship with his

fellow workers was authoritarian or one of partnership. Wolf Henning Ollrog, *Paulus und seine Mitarbeiter. Untersuchungen zu Theorie und Praxis des paulinischen Mission*, WMANT 50, Neukirchen-Vluyn 1979, and Part II of the book by Walter Rebell, *Gehorsam und Unabhängigkeit. Eine sozialpsychologische Studie zu Paulus*, Munich 1986, provide a detailed account of Paul and his fellow workers.

20. Cf. Applebaum, 443, 444, 449, 451, 453f.; he thinks it difficult to estimate how far such Hellenization was 'synonymous with apostasy' (447). In this connection reference should also be made to Dio Chrysostom, 34,21-23, according to which 'linen weavers' did not have citizenship even in Dio's time. If Paul belonged to this trade, that also puts the information in Acts 21.39 in question.

21. Phil.3.5f.; cf. Gal.1.13f. In the first of these passages, after mentioning his 'inherited advantages', Paul stresses that 'for his part he did everything possible to prove himself worthy of this heritage' (Gnilka, *Philipper*, 190).

22. This is claimed in Acts 22.28 for Paul's Roman citizenship.

23. Cf. Josephus, *BJ* II, 306-8, according to which the procurator Gessius Florus himself had Roman *equites* flogged and crucified.

24. That would also have fitted admirably in the context: 'From the Jews five times I received the forty lashes save one; although a Roman citizen, I have been flogged three times...'

25. In complete contrast to the Paul of Luke.

26. Cf. Schlatter, 466.

27. There is, however, dispute as to how I Cor.15.32 is to be understood. Fighting with wild beasts is usually understood metaphorically. Lietzmann, for example, gives three reasons against a literal understanding: 1. In II Cor.11.23-29 Paul does not mention fighting with wild beasts. 2. Acts says nothing about it. 3. If Paul had been condemned *ad bestias* he would have lost his Roman citizenship, to which according to Acts 22f. he later refers. On 1: the list is not complete; the tribulation so strongly stressed by Paul in II Cor.1.8f. is not mentioned there. On 2: Acts omits a good deal: Paul's condemnation by a Roman governor would not fit its line (cf. above 94-7). On 3: No conclusions should be drawn from Paul's supposed Roman citizenship (see the previous excursus and above 101f.). – There is no way in which Paul can be referring to his apostolic sufferings with the expression 'fighting with beasts'; the location 'in Ephesus' calls for a specific event (as does the verb in the aorist). But in that case how could the reader see that the expression was meant metaphorically? Ignatius, Rom.5.1 is often cited as an answer, but there it must be noted that 'Ignatius himself draws attention to his metaphor' (Weiss, 365) and that he 'is imagining a real fight with wild beasts' (Conzelmann, *I Corinthians*, 278). So in the context Paul is concerned to demonstrate the presupposition 'If the dead do not rise' to be false. Therefore the statement about fighting with wild beasts 'must include a real and serious danger of death' (Weiss, 365f.). So with Weiss we can understand v.32 as follows: '...if things had gone in a human way; if at that time I had really been thrown to the wild beasts and died, what use would that have been?' (365) – if the presupposition is that the dead do not rise. But one could also understand v.32 as saying: 'If in Ephesus I had had to fight with wild animals (as in fact happened) in a human way (and thus, as is usually the

case, had perished – but I did not fight in a human way because the God who raises from the dead saved me) what use would that have been?'

28. Cf. Haenchen, 588; Jewett, 18f.

29. See above 94f.

30. Cf. I Clement 5.5-7.

31. What Paul goes on to list in v.35 is certainly not something he sees as rhetorical exaggeration but a description of reality: 'tribulation, anxiety, persecution, hunger, nakedness, peril, sword'.

32. Conzelmann, *I Corinthians*, 105.

33. When Conzelmann continues the quotation I have just given by writing that Paul is fighting more against 'the recognition of the world as an authority in matters concerning the community' (*I Corinthians*, 105), it should be noted that these are 'everyday legal matters', which usually fall within the sphere of competence of the courts.

34. For the relationship between the two proposals cf.Schrage, *Ethik*, 183.

35. According to Conzelmann v.8 is 'aggressive', but that does not mean that 'they have become criminals in the legal sense' (*I Corinthians*, 106).

36. Cf. I Cor.4.12.

37. Carr, *Angels*, 118.

38. I Cor.2.6-8. However there has been dispute over the interpretation of this passage since antiquity, and above all over the question whether the rulers 'are demons or political powers' (Conzelmann, *I Corinthians*, 61). Nowadays the first thesis is usually defended – against the customary usage of the Greek word and applying the idea of the unrecognized descent of the redeemer through the planetary spheres, for which there is evidence only in esentially later texts. Conzelmann himself puts the contradiction which this theory produces like this: 'If the *archontes* did not recognize Jesus, why then did they crucify him?' However, his reply, that this contradiction is the very means of bringing out the *theologia crucis*, is very unclear. Recently Carr, *Angels*, 118-20, has argued that the rulers are to be understood as political powers: id., *Rulers*, passim, which also takes up the arguments advanced in the opposite direction; Sellin, 84f., who refers to the synonymity of the 'wisdom of men' in 2.5 and the 'wisdom of this world and the rulers of this world' in 2.6 (85 n.55). If, then, we are to think of human and not demonic rulers, then given the way in which I Cor.2.8 is formulated ('the rulers of this world') it is probable that Paul has Romans and not Jews in mind, even if in I Thess.2.15 he writes of 'the Jews who killed the Lord Jesus and the prophets and persecuted us'. On I Thess. 2.14-26 and the later correction in Rom.11 cf. Stuhlmann, 103f., 164-88. What appears in just one passage in Paul, which moreover seems to have been written in great emotion, is then systematized in Luke (see above. 99f).

39. Cf. Phil.2.7f.

40. Despite what 'they' say, the Christians listed in v.2 and v.4 are clearly set apart; they are distinct from 'the rest'(v.6).

41. See above, 19–21, 37f.

42. Hardly any of the exegetical literature notes that there is a thesis about the Pax Romana in I Thess.5.3. The exceptions are Ehrhart (II, 21) and Goppelt, though the latter does not mention the passage in the part of his *Theology* devoted to Paul.

43. Schlier, *Apostel*, 87.
44. Cf. I Thess.1.10.
45. For the use of the quotation from Ps.110.1 in this and other New Testament passages cf. Carr, *Angels*, 89-92.
46. Blank, 'Kirche', 25.
47. But see how Aelius Aristides speaks of Roman citizenship (*Eulogy of Rome*, 59-64). Windisch comments on Phil.3.20f.: 'It is a genuine Christian eschatological doctrine of the state, anti-imperialist and anti-Roman' (28).
48. Cf. the inscription from Halicarnassus quoted at 9 above.
49. Cf. Phil.3.21a with vv.10f.
50. For this arrangement of the text see Riekkinen, 35f.
51. 'Verständnis'; 'Furcht'; for 13.3-4 cf. the expansion by Unnik, 'Lob'.
52. 'Verständnis', 79; cf. Käsemann, *Romans*, 354: 'As the apostle's terminology shows, he has in view very different local and regional authorities and he is not so much thinking of institutions as of organs and functions, ranging from the tax collector to the police, magistrates, and Roman officials. It deals with that circle of power with whom the common man may come in contact and behind which he sees the regional or central administration.' As this last remark is also the case, it should not be asserted here that Paul 'does not say anything about the state as such or about the Roman empire' (ibid.).
53. That is clearly shown by the construction of the passage; in this respect I would mention here only that the imperative of v.1a is taken up again in v.5, summarizing what has gone before, and is finally re-extended again in v.7. The various reasons given are connected with these statements which determine the structure.
54. Cf. I Thess.5.4-8 and 78 above.
55. *Romans*, 351.
56. Ibid., 359.
57. Friedrich, etc., 157-9.
58. 165; in italics in the original.
59. Cf. above 74 and n.11.
60. Cf.3.8,31; 6.1f.,15; 7.7.
61. Käsemann, 'Generation', 373.
62. Schrage, *Ethik*, 227; cf. id., *Staat*, 55.
63. The section I Cor.11.2-16 with its multiplicity of partially contradictory and largely separate reasons shows the degree to which such reasons have a functional significance in paraenetic contexts in Paul and how little suited they are to systematization, in which the balance is completely shifted.
64. Wilckens III, 33.
65. This view theoretically also opens up the possibility of criticism; but that is not hinted at in the least by Paul in this section.
66. Josephus, *BJ* II, 140; on this cf. Dibelius, 'Rom', 182 n.13, according to whom the reasons come from Josephus, who 'in this way reads into the oath the general duty of loyalty'. Cf. further Josephus, *BJ* II, 390, where in Agrippa's peace speech it is said of the Romans: 'For without God it is impossible that so great an empire could have come into being.' At this point, however, there is a clear danger of the theological legitimation of *de facto* power which is impressive as a result of its magnitude.

67. Campenhausen wants to understand Rom.12.17-13.14 and I Thess.5.1-15 in parallel ('Auslegung', 96-101). Significantly he leaves out I Thess.5.3. Only on this impossible presupposition can Wilckens then claim that 'the political aspect is lacking' in I Thess 5 (III,4 n.59).

68. Similarly, for the Christian it is a matter of service in the everyday life in which he finds himself; cf. Käsemann, 'Interpretation', 207, 212f. Here is the starting point for the further thinking on Rom.13.1-7, which Bindemann (passim) undertakes.

69. Thus the basic admonition in Rom.12.2 is already an admonition not to be adapted to this aeon.

70. See above, 75f.

71. Cf. Käsemann, *Romans*, 246.

72. One could even talk, in a literal translation, of a 'super-victory'.

73. Wilckens II, 175.

74. When Paul continues in II Cor.2.14, 'And reveals the fragrance of his knowledge through us all everywhere', he is retaining the image of the triumphal procession. For the mention of 'fragrance' might be made in this context against the background of the custom of carrying containers with incense alongside the triumphal chariot, from which clouds of incense ascended to heaven (cf. Carr, *Angels*, 62f.). This would give a single metaphorical background to v.14 and therefore makes this interpretation probable. Bultmann, *II Korinther*, 66-70, differs.

75. For the section Rom.5.1-5 cf. the thorough exegesis by Nebe, 123-36, 289-96.

76. Schlier, *Römer*, 136.

77. Cf. e.g. the commentaries by Käsemann, Schlier and Wilckens ad loc.

78. Verses 1 and 9 are parallels. In both verses the starting point is the justification which has alrady taken place. In v.1 faith as the mode of appropriation from the human side is attached to that, and in v.9 at this point the blood of Christ is mentioned as its objective basis; and the peace with God is matched by the deliverance from anger.

79. I Thess.1.10; cf.5.9.

80. Rom.1.18, 24-32.

81. In I Thess.5.3 at this point there is mention of the destruction which comes upon those who use the slogan 'peace and security'.

82. Here, too, Paul shows himself to be a Christian apocalyptist; cf. the similar Jewish apocalyptic evidence in Foerster, 408f.

83. 'Under the dominion of Christ strife with God ends and so does subjection to the power of wrath', Käsemann, *Romans*, 132.

84. On this cf. Schrage, 'Leid', passim.

85. What Käsemann writes on Rom.8.37 also applies here:'Standing under the cross characterizes the position of the victor' (247).

86. The final judgment is thought of here, cf. Nebe, 129f.

87. It is perhaps worth noting – though the fact should certainly not be played off against Eph.6.13-17 – that in mentioning breastplate and helmet Paul is only citing defensive weapons. Would not that too be a reflex againt the Pax Romana, based as it is on aggressive force? Breastplate and helmet express the certainty

of Christian existence in faith, love and hope; they do not denote isolation and insensitivity, as Paul himself shows.

88.The Greek word for 'faith', which also has the significance of 'trust' and 'loyalty', is quite often used by Josephus of the Romans: *Antt.* XIV, 186; XIX, 289; *BJ* II, 341; III, 31; IV, 93f.; *c.Ap.* II, 134; *Vita* 30, 34, 39,43,46, 61, 10, 346, 349. Cf. also Dio Chrysostom 31, 113.

89. It is already that on the basis of its composition, in so far as national religious, social and sexual-specific conflicts are done away with in it: Gal.3.28; I Cor.12.13. Cf. also the image of the body and its members, which in itself can also serve as a legitimation for rule, as is shown by the famous parable of Menenius Agrippa (cf. 116 and n.75 above); but in I Cor.12.14-26 Paul emphatically attacks such claims to superiority.

90. Given our sense of order, that is particularly striking in v.30, where Paul says in respect of prophets of whom two or three are to speak: 'If a revelation is made to another sitting by, let the first be silent.'

91. In Paul 'building up' refers to the community, not to isolated individual Christians (cf. Philipp Vielhauer, 'Oikodome. Das Bild vom Bau in der christlichen Literatur vom Neuen Testament bis Clemens Alexandrinus', in id., *Oikodome. Aufsätze zum Neuen Testament* 2, ed. Günther Klein, ThB 65, Munich 1979, [1-168] 71-115). The leading question for the individual participants in the assembly is not 'How am I edified?' Rather, it is 'What can I contribute to the edification of others?' If this question is answered positively, the first question looks after itself.

92. Wilckens, III, 25.

III/3

1. The church tradition names 'Luke' as the author of the Gospel and Acts. I am not presupposing that this man was the fellow-worker of Paul mentioned in Philemon 24, who is also mentioned in the Deutero-Pauline Epistle to the Colossians as 'Luke the physician' (4.14; cf. II Tim.4.11) or another person of the same name.

2. Conzelmann, *Theology*, 141. There he is even mentioned as the 'first convert', but this ignores Acts 8.26-40.

3. The word used in the parallel by Matthew in 8.5,8,13, and taken up by Luke in v.7, is ambiguous: it can mean 'child' or 'servant'. In Luke vv.2,3,10 Luke speaks of a slave; in the parallel John 4.46-54, there is 'son'.

4. As in the tradition, so too in Luke this story is set in Capernaum (7.1), a city which according to 4.31 is in Galilee; it was ruled over according to 3.1 by Herod (Antipas). Hence this non-Jewish centurion would not be a Roman even for Luke. But may we really draw this conclusion where he is concerned? At all events it is striking that in 4.4 Luke has Jesus preaching in the synagogues of *Judaea* (as opposed to Mark 1.39: Galilee), that in 6.17 he deletes the Galilean audience from Mark 3.7 and that according to 7.17 the news of Jesus' raising the dead in Nain is spread 'throughout Judaea'. More important, however, is the stylization of the centurion in analogy to Cornelius, who is clearly a Roman. According to Walaskay, Luke presents 'the centurion to his readers as a model of Roman citizenship, stationed in the provinces' (32f.).

5. For the redactional character of this passage cf. Schulz, *Q*, 237f.

6. Luke 7.5. Here, too, we need not be concerned to ask whether a centurion could have had the resources to found a synagogue. (For pay in the principate cf. Kromayer/Veith, 526.) What is more important is the picture drawn by Luke.

7. For a demonstration that there is tradition in v.11, but Lukan redaction in vv.12-14, cf. Schottroff and Stegemann, 138f.

8. A historicizing interpretation which concludes that the publicans and soldiers addressed by John the Baptist must have been those of Herod Antipas is wrong. Here it does not just need to be stressed that Luke had no exact knowledge of historical and geographical conditions in Palestine. Given the fundamental nature of the questions and answers in 3.12-14 he must have also been thinking of the publicans and soldiers whom he saw elsehere, i.e. of Roman officials. That would be even more true for his readers. Cf. Conzelmann, *Theology*, 138, according to whom Luke 'selects two examples of ethical instruction, those directed at the organs of the State, the military and the government'.

9. Walaskay, 29-32, shows that here Luke is formulating Augustan ideals. That too makes it probable that he has Roman bodies in mind.

10. Campenhausen, 'Kriegsdienst', 206.

11. Ibid., 207.

12. Mikat, 'Christusverkündigung', 811.

13. At this point Luke changes Mark 15.39. Whereas in Mark there is a confession of Jesus as Son of God on the basis of the circumstances of his death of Jeuss, here the centurion gives God the glory by saying that Jesus is 'innocent'.

14. On the basis of the situation in the tradition Luke here had an essentially freer hand than in his portrayal of the death of Jesus.

15. The fear of the tribune mentioned in v.29 is meant to 'show how greatly the tribune respects the law and Paul's status as a Roman citizen' (Haenchen, 634).

16. Haenchen here comments sarcastically: 'Fortunately the troops still appear in time to snatch Paul away from the *rabies theologorum* and bring him back to the peace of the barracks' (641).

17. Conzelmann, *Acts*, 127.

18. I shall later go into the point that that is not the only purpose Luke has for this scene; cf below, 98f.

19. 'But in that this transfer of the prisoner is coupled with the conspiracy, a dreary matter of routine is transformed into a narrative full of breathless suspense; at the same time Luke could thus present the intervention of the Roman authorities on Paul's behalf in the brightest light' (Haenchen, 650). 'The Romans not only protect the accused but above all give him the possibility to give an account of himself undisturbed' (Stolle, 52).

20. 'The expense is fantastic...; it is meant to illustrate the significance of this man (viz. Paul), the magnitude of the danger and the quality of Roman measures' (Conzelmann, *Acts*, 129).

21. Haenchen, 648.

22. Schille has shown in a particularly impressive way that these verses are

not to be interpreted in a historicizing way but that they are a literary contribution by Luke *ad maiorem Pauli gloriam* (466f.).

23. Cf. above, 37f.

24. We may conclude that Luke was informed about the fate of Paul from the indications which he makes the apostle give in his farewell speech to the presbyters of Ephesus in Miletus (Acts 20.23-25; cf. v.38) and from the prophetic and symbolic action of Agabus and Paul's reaction to it (21.10-14).

25. Cf. Walaskay, 43.

26. This is matched by the question put by the procurator Felix to Paul about his home province (23.34).

27. See above, 91. Luke had to pass over the similar report in Mark simply because he does not have Jesus condemned before Pilate (see below), and flogging and mockery followed the judgment; he could not and did not want to attribute to a Roman procurator cynical use of the power to have Jesus flogged and mocked before a judgment in the way depicted by John 19.1-3.

28. This is *fustigatio*, 'the lightest form of Roman flogging' (Walaskay, 44); cf. Sherwin-White, 27. 'In comparison with what happens before the Sanhedrin and Herod Jesus is in fact treated very well by the Romans' (Walaskay, 49).

29. Sherwin-White claims that the agreement between Mark 15.15 and Matt.27.26 that Pilate, 'after he had had him flogged, delivered him up to be crucified' is correct as over against the imprecise information in Luke, since such treatment ended with condemnation to a specific punishment (26). If Luke, who is elsewhere so knowledgeable about Roman legal proceedings, seems so unknowledgeable at this point, it is clear that he wants to conceal reality. He describes the event in Acts 3.13-15 in a similar way to Luke 23.24f.

30. 'Luke does not report any condemnation of Jesus by Pilate. Pilate merely "delivers" Jesus to the Jews, who themselves put him to death... We might accuse Luke of obscurity if we did not know his source, but as we do know it, we can prove that his account is a deliberate modification' (Conzelmann, *Theology*, 140).

31. He does that once again in the Gospel (Luke 24.20) and then continually in the speeches in Acts: Acts 2.23 (here he adds: 'through the hand of the lawless'); 2.36; 3.15; 4.10; 5.30; 7.52; 10.39; 13.27-29. That also rules out the conjecture that at the beginning of Luke 23.26 a change of subject is to be assumed from the Jews to Roman soldiers.

32. Acts 3.17; cf. Luke 23.34.

33. Walaskay stresses as an effect of the picture drawn by Luke the contrast between orderly Roman justice and the chaotic legal practice of the Jews.

34. See above, 91f.

35. That 'accords with the ordering of the trial'; cf. the commentaries ad loc., e.g. already Preuschen.

36. 'The short hearing by Felix... shows this governor as an impartial and correctly-acting official' (Haenchen, 650).

37. Schneider, *Apostelgeschichte* II, 350.

38. If we recognize that Luke's purpose is also to present Felix as demonstrating Paul's innocence of Paul, while at the same time being aware of the need to give an explanation for his ongoing arrest – for that cf. in detail

Haenchen, 656-9, 668-70 – , we cannot say with Schille that Luke's real estimation of the Romans is expressed in the critical comments in vv.25f.

39. Conzelmann. *Acts*, 134.
40. Thus Preuschen, 104.
41. Schille, 349.
42. Conzelmann, *Theology*, 142.
43. Schneider, *Apostelgeschichte* II, 263.
44. Cf. above, 37 and n.218.
45. Schrage, *Ethik*, 151.
46. Tacitus, *Histories*, V,9,3; cf. *Annals* XII, 54,1, according to which as procurator of Judaea Felix 'believed that he could commit all crimes undetected'. The assessment of Felix by Josephus agrees completely with this (*Antt.* XX, 162f., 182).
47. This information appears at the beginning of the accusation of Paul by the orator Tertullus before Felix and is therefore conventional. 'Tertullus naturally flatters Felix – that every reader knew. But Luke would not have given so much space to it if he had wanted like Tacitus or Suetonius to depict Rome's representative as a degenerate and unscrupulous rascal' (Haenchen, 657).
48. Thus, however, Schrage, *Staat*, 46; cf. Cassidy, 39.
49. Walaskay, 36, cf.12.
50. Walaskay, 37.
51. Conzelmann, *Acts*, 10.
52. Haenchen, 662.
53. For this last passage cf. Haenchen, 662; the quotation given above also relates to it.
54. Mikat, 'Christusverkündigung', 827, cf. 810.
55. Schneider, *Apostelgeschichte* I, 143; cf. id., *Lukas*, 478.
56. 'In Acts there is no instance of Roman intervention without previous Jewish agitation' (Conzelmann, *Theology*, 140).
57. Ibid., 144.
58. Cf. above, 72f.
59. For this group see Marcel Simon, 'Gottesfürchtiger', *RAC* II, Stuttgart 1981, (1060-1070) 1064-8.
60. Cf. Karl-Georg Kuhn/Hartmut Stegemann, 'Proselyt', *PRE Suppl.* IX, Stuttgart 1962, (1248-83) 1259f.
61. Suetonius, *Claudius*, 25,4; cf. Acts 18.2.
62. Cf. above, 73f.
63. Cf. above, 93.
64. Mikat, 'Christusverkündigung', 810, cf. 820.
65. Preuschen, 25.
66. Similarly in 4.19 Peter and John ask the same body 'whether it is right before God to listen to you rather than to God'.
67. Luke 1.1-4; Acts 1.1-3. There are examples from antiquity in Weiser, 47f.
68. The difference in the way in which the two books live up to this claim is considerable. Whereas in the first, the Gospel, 'an absolute break may be noted' (Vielhauer, 377) between the prologue and the following explanation, things are different in Acts (Dibelius, *Studies*, 88). For the influence of ancient historiography on them cf. Plümacher, 501-13.

69. Luke 1.3. The procurators Felix and Festus are addressed as 'Excellency' elsewhere in Acts: 23.26; 24.3; 26.25.

70. Cf. on this Haenchen, 136 n.4.

71. Vielhauer, 368.

72. Ibid., 45; that Luke 'is not thinking of people completely without knowledge' follows from the fact that 'his books would be incomprehensible without some prior knowledge of Judaism and Christianity' (ibid.).

73. Cf. Schottroff and Stegemann, 113-19; Frankemölle, 100-2; Theissen, 'Gewaltverzicht', 183. However, Theissen speaks of 'Lucan communities', and my question would be whether the Third Evangelist is not merely a representative of better-off Christians within communities in big cities.

74. Haenchen assumes that she is a well-to-do woman, because'purple materials were a markedly luxury item for rich people' (494).

75. For the areopagus cf. Gerhard Schneider, *EWNT* I, 361f.

76. Haenchen, 403.

77. Here he is even more ahead of his time than there; cf. above 90. Even Tertullian does not think it inconceivable that if a Christian takes over any honorary position or administrative office he can keep himself free of idolatry (*De idolatria*, 17). But that would mean that anyone holding office, let alone a proconsul, could not become a Christian and at the same time retain his office. It is remarkable that – as far as I can see – no commentator on Acts has marvelled at what Luke says here.

78. 'In an answer which deviates only at the last moment [Agrippa] accords Paul the highest assent possible for him' (Haenchen, 689).

79. Cf. Plümacher, 517.

80. According to Conzelmann 'the significance of this freely developed scene of splendour is to be seen purely in terms of its literary aim; Paul and thus Christianity are introducing themselves to a wider public' (*Acts*, 137).

81. Cf. *KP* 1, 637; Merklebach, 288.

82. The Asiarchs 'have the duty of advancing the cult of Caesar (and the goddess Roma). In spite of this, when they hear about the riot, their first thought is of Paul's safety' (Haenchen, 576).

83. Cf. above, 74f.

84. In addition, on the basis of his use of the Septuagint, the Greek translation of the Hebrew Bible, and the way in which it has a major influence on his language, it may be assumed that Luke comes from the group of 'godfearers' (above n.59; cf. Schneider, *Apostelgeschichte* I, 146; Weiser 40). In support of this is 'a striking knowledge of Hellenistic-Jewish tradition' (Gerhard Sellin, *Studien zu den grossen Gleichniserzählungen des Lukas Sonderguts*, Munich Protestant Faculty Dissertation 1973, 196f.). Given all that has been said it is obvious that he belongs in the world of the cities. Probably he did not live in Rome but in the provinces. The way in which he makes the town clerk of Ephesus speak in 19,40 agrees with the perspective of Plutarch at the end of the quotation given on 16f. above (*Mor.* 824e).

85. Luke 1.5; 2.1f.; 3.1f.; Acts 11.27f.; 18.2; cf. Plümacher 517.

86. For the way in which this awareness governs the whole account in Acts cf. Haenchen, 691f.

87. Ibid., 679.

88. Ibid.

89. 'Over everything there presides, like a blue sky darkened only by a few clouds, that harmony that goes with divine guidance. It is as if there were a premonition of the Constantinian epoch that was to come more than two centuries later' (Käsemann, *Freedom*, 122).

90. For the text of Mark cf. above, 63f.

91. 'In the transition in v.26a those addressed (not, as in Mark, those in the prevailing circumstances in the community, cf. Mark 10.43a) are contrasted with the kings and those who bear authority in the state' (Hoffmann, *Moral*, 189).

92. Hoffmann, *Moral*, 227.

93. 'Luke already knows great men and leaders in the community and requires of them a style of leadership which takes its bearings from that of Jesus' (Hoffmann, *Eschatologie*, 141; cf. id., *Moral*, 130).

94. Hoffmann, *Eschatologie*, 142.

95. Is it not a typically structural conservative attitude to treat structural demands as questions of style by means of personalization? At all events, that is not Jesus' answer.

96. 'Luke has carefully related the story of the entry of Jesus into Jerusalem to the birth narrative by means of redactional alterations' (Brandenburger, 33).

97. Cf. Edward Lohse, ὡσαννά, *TDNT* IX, (682-4) 682f.

98. That has a parallel in 2.14, where the peace is for those with whom God is well pleased.

99. Cf. Lohse, *TDNT*, 683.

100. Cf. Conzelmann, *Theology*, 139: 'The acclamation at the entry loses all political significance in Luke... Accordingly the Temple is the only goal of the Entry, and the only place of Jesus' activity.'

101. This is confirmed by another join in Luke's two volumes, namely the story of the ascension in Acts 1.4-11. According to v.6 the apostles ask Jesus whether he will establish the kingdom for Israel in the imminent future. They are given a negative answer: Jesus is going away into heaven and only his return will bring about the kingdom of God. For the intermediate period the disciples receive the gift of the Spirit, which enables them to fulfil their task of world mission. That is their concern. The kingdom of God is not on the agenda. Certainly, in view of the coming of the Lord they must always be prepared (Luke 12.35-40; 21.46), but he is not expected to come in the imminent future. Therefore the perspective is 'backward rather than forward' (Käsemann, *Freedom*, 117) and so Luke's description is characteristically different from that of Paul, who can speak of triumph only in a paradoxical way, against all appearances (cf. above, 85), 'the unceasing triumphant march, even amid blood and tears, where Christian faith overcomes the world' (ibid., 123). On the other hand abandoning an imminent expectation corresponds to a belief in the beyond of the kind that is expressed in Luke 23.42f. in the conversation of one of those who are crucified with him (on this see Gerhard Schneider, *Parusiegleichnisse im Lukas-Evangelium*, SBS 74, Stuttgart 1975, 83f.).

102. Schottroff/Stegemann, 100. Cf. also the replacement of the programmatic proclamation of the Gospel in Mark 1.15 that the kingdom of God is at

hand with the 'inaugural sermon' in Nazareth (Luke 4.16-30), which stresses the fulfilment of the saving message of scripture in the person of Jesus.

103. Thus Foerster, 411, on Luke 19.38.

104. Cf. Stuhlmacher, 59.

105. Cf. Schrage, *Ethik*, 147.

106. If we see that all of v.37 is regarded as the basis for the previous admonition, as the introduction shows, we cannot 'identify the time of enmity for the disciples of Jesus with the passion to Jesus' (against Schneider, *Lukas*, 456); the passion of Jesus, as the introduction of his heavenly enthronement, divides the times. Schneider's remark to this effect makes it sufficiently clear that it is extremely unsatisfying to understand v.38 as a preparation for the scene in 22.49-51. Above all according to G.W.H.Lampe, in v.38 Luke means to combine the scene of vv.35-37 with that of vv.49-51. Here the evangelist identifies the disciples as being the lawless in the quotation from Isa.53.12 in v.37 (342, 346). But that is to attribute too much to Luke: Jesus calls on his disciples to buy a sword – simply that they can be said to be lawless. The 'now' in v.36 which is contrasted to the 'then' of v.35 cannot be limited to the time leading up to the arrest. For according to Lucan chronology this is the Passover night. Quite apart from the fact that the possibilities of buying a sword must have been very limited, the other imperatives of v.36 cannot be thought of as being limited to this particular period.

107. In my understanding of this somewhat obscure passage I am thus following the remarks of Blank, 'Dienst', 29-34, which seem to me to offer the most convincing solution despite the objections of Vögtle, 84-6. I would refer to the exegesis by Eisler who regards the account as historical; in his view – 'of course' – each of the disciples had two swords (268). There is an echo of this in Lapide, *Feinde*, 59-61.

108. Käsemann, *Freedom*, 125. I find a similar differentiation between the period of the disciples of Jesus and the time of the church in connection with attitudes to property; cf. Helmut Merkel, 'Eigentum III. Neues Testament', *TRE* 9, Berlin and New York 1982, (410-13) 412.

109. Walaskay has in mind here the late period of Domitian. Luke would have had the same view of this as Pliny, see above 38 and n.223.

110. Mark 1.14/Matt.4.12 (cf. Matt.14.12f.); Mark 3.6f./Matt.12.14f.; Mark 7.24/Matt.15.21 in connection with Mark 7.1/Matt.15.1.

111. Luke 5.16; 6.12; 9.18, 29f.

112. *Acts*, 10.

113. IX; cf. the 'concluding comments' on 64-7. Here Luke is portrayed virtually in terms of Luther's doctrine of the two realms, above all on 66. That is certainly an exaggeration.

114. 65; cf. IX: 'That the Christian church survived the critical first century may largely rest on Luke's cautious wisdom in this respect.'

115. See above, 101.

116. Therefore Walaskay's positive evaluation of Luke's apologetic must be firmly challenged. In his work it is connected with a view of Roman reality under the Flavian emperors which is as naive as it is positive: 'Vespasian (69-79) restored peace, order and prosperity after the Civil War of 69. Titus continued the tolerant and liberal policy of his father. Even the first dozen years (81-92)

of the reign of Domitian went well for the people. His rule was sound and just; he continued the economic and social policy of his predecessors by which Rome (!) flourished' (64f.). The threat to the church evidently did not come from Rome but from those in Rome who were critical of her: 'With considerable skill he (Luke) succeeded in stemming the apocalyptic outcry of the antinomian wing of the church in which he wisely saw the primary internal threat to the Christian movement' (67). So the threat came from the critics who were still putting questions to those who were seeking a doubtful arrangement with the realities of power politics! From where does anyone who accepts the political apologetic of Luke today in an affirmative way take his bearings?

III/4

1. For the origin of this designation in the seventeenth century cf. Fischer, IX.

2. Vielhauer, 532.

3. In Eusebius, *HE* IV, 23,11.

4. In Eusebius, *HE* IV, 22,1. The next witness, Irenaeus of Lyons, in *Haer.* III,3,3, also quoted by Eusebius, V, 6,2f., mentions Clement as the third bishop of Rome after Peter and a disciple of Peter and Paul. Neither piece of information can be true. I Clement gives no indication whatsoever of a monarchical episcopate; even the Shepherd of Hermas, written some decades later in Rome, still presupposes that the community there functions in a collegiate way. As far as the supposed discipleship of Peter and Paul is concerned, the letter itself makes no claims in that direction, nor is there even an implicit reference.

5. Cf. also Vielhauer, 539f.

6. E.g.Fischer, 19.

7. See above, 111f.

8. Cf. Fischer, 19, who cites further indications that it is somewhat removed from the time of Nero.

9. Mention should be made here above all of Tacitus, Pliny and Juvenal (ML).

10. 59.2-61.3.

11. See above, 21f.

12. See above, 48f.

13. It always refers to God or Christ except in Titus 2.9 and Hermas, *Sim.* 2,2, where it is used of the good behaviour of slaves towards their masters. There is a close parallel in content, however, in Plutarch, *Demetrius*, 24, where the Athenians have made the decision that 'whatever King Demetrius commanded was pious before the gods and just in the eyes of men'.

14. According to Speigl, in Clement 'not only does constant and benevolent prayer for the Roman state have a fixed place, but even subordination to it is directly a gift of God and to this degree worship of God' (17). When he observes on Romans 13 that 'to set up a relation of analogy or a polarizing harmony between the heavenly and the earthly is just what our text does not do' ('Interpretation', 201), Käsemann demonstrates a significant difference between it and I Clem.60.

15. This condemnation of any kind of revolution whatever, so abundantly evidenced in church history, combined at the same time with a sanctioning of

existing conditions of rule, can thus be found at this early period. Eggenberger rightly says that here we are 'on the threshold of the negation of the *ius resistendi*' (23).

16. Eggenberger gives two possible ways of understanding this statement: 'Either in such a way that the will of God calls for subjection: the very bestowing of power and authority involves *de facto* recognition of them, as the divine indication of the God-given superiority of the ruling powers, so that in this way the hegemony of the *imperium Romanum* is and ought to be recognized as divinely willed in terms of the development of its power. Or in such a way that the divine will is itself immanent in the dispositions of the ruler and thus the emperor represents something like a branch of the divine rule of the world' (23).

17. Cf. Ullmann, 89.

18. See above, 106f.

19. *Eulogy of Rome*, 88; in 87 he had already stressed that every soldier keeps to his post, 'and the subordinate does not envy the one who holds a higher rank, but himself keeps strict control of those under his command'. Cf. also the following extract from Otho's speech to his soldiers according to Tacitus, *Histories* I, 84,1: 'If Vitellius and his comrades were given a free choice as to what spirit or what disposition they would most like for us, what else would they wish us than the spirit of revolt and division? For the soldier to refuse to obey the centurion, the centurion to refuse to obey the tribune, so that infantry and cavalry lost contact and thus brought us to ruin. In war, comrades, blind obedience is more important than cheeky questioning of the orders of the generals.'

20. Cf. II Kings 1.9-14; esp. Isa.3.3; I Macc.3.55, where there are similar sequences to I Clement 37.3. So this is not a 'careless mistake' (thus Speigl, 15). There were also leaders of fifties in Greek armies, so that the information in I Clem.37.3 could be a result of Clement's Greek education (thus Jaubert); however, it is more likely that he was influenced by the Bible.

21. He had already written of '*our* leaders' in 60.2.

22. According to Knopf it is 'a significant feature of the good disposition towards the ordering of this world that the Roman is proud of "our army"' (108).

23. Speigl, 14; cf. 15. Beyschlag sees in I Clement 'a firm will on the part of the church to remain in the parish of the world – over against any apocalyptic enthusiasm' (*Clemens*, 333). Moreover, the world is only alien to the degree that it does not accept Christians as Christians accept the world.

24. Beyschlag, *Clemens*, 191.

25. Clement is referring to Judith 8-13.

26. Knopf rightly observes on 1.3: 'The *presbyteroi* here are not to be seen as ministers standing over against the *neoi* mentioned immediately afterwards, but as the older leading group within the community.'

27. Harnack recognizes a Latin, Roman spirit in the letter: 'a sense of authority, order, law and obedience' (*Einführung*, 97f.). He then goes on to comment: 'In addition, throughout the letter there emerges a political significance of the kind that we usually judge to be the characteristic of more senior Roman officials.'

28. Cf. Ebach, *Leviathan*, 29-38.

29. Ibid., 30.

30. Job 19.26a is quoted loosely. Clement, of course, uses the Septuagint in all his biblical quotations.

31. The basis is Job 14.4f.

32. Job 38.11. For the speeches by God cf. Ebach, *Leviathan*, 67-77.

33. 30.4f. corresponds word for word to Job 11.2f; 19.3-9 similarly has the text of Job 4.16-5.5 along with an insertion from Job 15.15f.; Job 5.17-26 again appears word for word in 56.6-15. Job 5.11 is quoted, partly word for word and partly in paraphrase, in 59.3.

34. Ebach, *Leviathan*, 36 (n.4 on p.30).

35. Eggenberger, 175.

36. For the historical background to 20.1-10 cf. Knopf, 77-82; Fuchs, *Friedensgedanke*, 101-4; above all Eggenberger, 74-104, especially 87-91, whose comparison with Dio Chrysostom continues to retain its value even if the attempt to demonstrate a direct dependence on him does not work.

37. Knopf has suggested that 19.2f. and 20.11 are a redactional framework for the praise.

38. 19.2; 20.1, 9,10,11. This transfer is then carried out in 21.1ff. Interest in obedience is documented by 'the constant use of derivations of the root ταγ' (Knopf, 77). For the transfer of the fixed structures in the cosmos and nature to human society cf. Ullmann, 87-9; also the comments by Martin that the order of creation understood 'as essential superiority and subordination is transferred into the sphere of the church, and it is no coincidence that this happens in a letter written in Rome; in the capital of the empire the division of society into states and a hierarchy could be seen most clearly... It is decisive that the theory of the letter came about in a quite particular historical context and one has to remember this in referring to it' (75).

39. It is impossible to determine whether the leaders in 1.3 and 21.6 are to be understood as leaders in the Christian community (thus e.g. Knopf, 45, 83) or political leaders (detailed arguments in Eggenberger, 27-29; cf. also Speigl, 15). At all events Clement has 'the deep conviction that order must be preserved in the world as in the community, *homonoia* of the macrocosm (20.11), of the political cosmos (60.4; 61.1) and of the microcosmos of the community (34.7; 50.5; 63.2; 65.1)' (Dibelius, 'Rom', 198f.).

40. Eggenberger, 176.

41. Eggenberger stresses that 'the Neronian persecutions of Christians are depicted without any derogatory comment being made on Nero or on the official authorities' (171). According to Speigl the way in which Clement speaks of the martyrdoms of Peter and Paul is not determined by a political attitude but by the literary form of the agonistic discourse: 'Nowhere is the state blamed for the persecution. It is always only wicked individuals who persecute' (14). Clement's political attitude is, however, demonstrated in precisely such an unpolitical way of speaking. Cf. Dibelius, 'Rom', 202, according to which Clement 'does not seek to provide a narrative in the section on Paul but to put well-known things in what seems to him to be the right light – that of the philosophical *agon*. We can now say why he does this; he wants to avoid

characterizing counterparts in the state and speak only of the *ponoi* and *erga* of Paul.' Cf. the whole section and 216f.

42. Thus e.g. Knopf, 44.

43. Dibelius speaks of 'mild expressions' ('Rom', 193) and of 'an almost disguised mode of expression in which the letter speaks of the persecution which the community has just surivved' (ibid., 192).

44. 'They (viz., the Christians) are fought against by the Jews as Gentiles and persecuted by the Greeks: and those who hate them cannot say why they do so.'

45. It is conceivable that Clement attributed them to the unpredictability of the late Domitian and thus shares in the estimation of this ruler expressed by Pliny and Tacitus, who are delighted at the period after his death, cf. above 38.

46. Cf. Eggenberger, 171: 'The tendency here is clear; blame for the persecutions is not primarily to be attached to the authorities but to Christians.'

47. This must be said against Eggenberger, who regards the letter as a fiction (cf. above all, 189-93) and has to expend some imagination in defending this theory.

48. At no point does Clement indicate the content of this; his argument is exclusively formal. Thus Harnack conjectures 'simply a dispute between cliques which has got out of hand' (*Einführung*, 92; similarly Fischer, 3).

49. Cf. further 46.7,9; 47.6; 51.1; 54.2; 57.1; 63.1. The Greek στάσις corresponds to the Latin *seditio* (cf. Mikat, 'Stasis', 735), a term used to describe the worst political behaviour.

50. Cf.3.2; also 30.1, where the synonymous νεωτερισμός (revolution, agitation) is cited in a list of serious vices.

51. The natural way in which Clement looks through the 'political spectacles' of Rome also emerges from the way in which he inserts the term στασιάζειν (engage in rebellion) in his rendering of biblical texts (4.12; 43.2; 51.3) and in his praise of love in ch.49, which has echoes of I Cor.13, writes the line 'Love does not engage in revolts' (49.5). Beyschlag stresses that on the one hand Clement often uses 'concord' as a 'keyword' and on the other 'decisively rejects anything that goes by the name of "unrest", "quest for innovation", "overthrow" and "change", and sweepingly puts people who even seem to hint at being involved in this sort of thing on the same level as the fratricide Cain' ('Veränderung', 29).

52. In describing events in Corinth as 'rebellion', 'Clement is not to be understood as exaggerating in order to be able to speak of the abominable character of the revolt' (thus Eggenberger, 35). This is more a perception from a Roman perspective. It almost goes without saying that for Clement rebellion is something extraordinarily negative, with the result that he can depict what is going on in Corinth as particularly bad. Cf. also Mikat, 'Fürbitte', 844: 'Clement speaks of the rebels in Corinth in just the way that Jews friendly to Rome (e.g. Josephus) had been accustomed to speak about the Zealots and rebels in Jerusalem'. The characterization of the deposition of presbyters in Corinth as rebellion is reinforced by the addition twice of *aponoia* (folly, 1.1; 46.7); cf. Mikat, 'Stasis', 736f.

53. That the *status quo*, described in 14.2 as a good condition, is in fact in accord with the will of God follows from 14.1, where Clement contrasts

obedience to God with acceptance of the deposition of presbyters which has taken place.

54. Eggenberger comments on this passage: 'So here the awkward customer joins the fool and the fool the revolutionary as an enemy of God.'

55. For this term see above, 21f. we shall shortly be looking at its frequent use in I Clement.

56. Cf. Mikat, 'Auswanderungsrat', 216: 'The order that he wants consists in the restoration of the *status quo ante*.'

57. Tacitus, *Histories* IV, 74,4; cf. the further quotations from this speech on 21.

58. This follows very clearly from 3.4, according to which in Corinth now 'righteousness and peace are a long way off, because there is a revolt' (3.2f.). By contrast once, according to 2.2, a 'deep and blessed peace' prevailed. In an impressive collection of evidence van Unnik has demonstrated that 'where there is a clear context the expression "deep peace" is always associated with the situation of a state and indicates that this state is in a very fortunate position, bothered neither by enemies outside nor by revolutions within, and is therefore in perfect harmony (' "Friede" ', 277; the evidence is on 264-77). He notes that the term first appears in the time of Augustus (277); the Pax Romana is therefore characterized by it. The same context appears in I Clement with the terms στάσις (rebellion) and ὁμόνοια (concord), so that van Unnik concludes that Clement 'used this terminology for the church' (278). Therefore for Clement this peace is 'a periphrasis for the state of affairs in which it lives undisturbed by external and internal tensions and can engage in the activity to which it knows itself to be called by God' (261). Here, too, the parallel between Clement's idea of peace in the church and his Roman view of the Pax Romana is evident.

59. Against this understanding of 15.1 one could object that at this point Clement is not thinking of the situation in Corinth but is speaking in quite general terms. However, it is the particular merit of Brunner's work that he has demonstrated that at no point does Clement lose sight of his goal, but pursues it thoroughly and consistently.

60. According to Harnack this at the same time gives the title for the letter (*Einführung*, 54).

61. Cf. also 62.2.

62. According to Dinkler the idea of order is connected with the conception of 'peace and concord' in Clement 'without any tangible reference to Jesus Christ' (*Eirene*, 44).

63. A delegation from Rome was 'composed of senators and consisted of two to ten persons' (*KP* 3, 554): it 'had to bring the message sent by the Senate, to carry on negotiations and to report to the Senate' (ibid.). The community in Rome is not content with a postman but sends a delegation; cf. 65.1: 'Be quick to return our delegates in peace and joy, Claudius Ephebus and Valerius Bito, along with Fortunatus. In that way they will the sooner bring us news of that peace and concord we have prayed for and so much desire, and we in turn will the more speedily rejoice over your healthy state.' Clement had already mentioned the delegation in 63.3f.; there its status and task is indicated, namely to see to peace in Corinth.

64. Cf. Mikat, 'Stasis', 743, 747.

65. However, it should be noted that it comes into view in 41.3, though somewhat remotely.

66. In 54.3 Clement promises anyone who acts in this way that he will get praise in Christ and any place will accept him. As support for his advice in 55.1 he also cites famous examples of pagan kings and leaders.

67. Thus Knopf, 131, twice.

68. Cf. Mikat, 'Stasis', 740f.

69. Ulrich Wickert, 'Paulus, der erste Klemens und Stephan von Rom: drei Epochen der frühen Kirche aus ökumenischer Sicht', *ZKG* 79, 1968, (145-58) 155.

70. Cf. above 21 and n.100.

71. Cf. above 14 and n.49.

72. Cf. above, 107.

73. Cf. above, 108f.

74. Cf. also Rom.12.3-8.

75. Cf. Wilhelm Nestle, 'Die Fabel des Menenius Agrippa', in *Ideologie und Herrschaft in der Antike*, ed. Hans Kloft, WdF 528, Darmstadt 1979, 191-204. Nestle shows that 'the notion of the organic idea of the state' proved so 'elastic' that it could be used in a variety of ways (203). The image of the body and its members can be used to describe the nature of a brotherly and sisterly community or to disguise and legitimate power relationships.

76. For Pauline ecclesiology cf. above all Walter Klaiber, *Rechtfertigung und Gemeinde. Eine Untersuchung zum paulinischen Kirchenverständnis*, FRLANT 127, Göttingen 1982; for the conception of the body of Christ and the gifts of grace see esp. 41-8, 104-13, 214-28.

77. Granted, it comes at the end of remarks on the temple cult, after mention of the high priest, priests and levites; but for Clement the temple cult clearly represents the Christian community, as is indicated both by the introduction in 40.1 and the conclusion in 41.1. It should also be noted that the term 'lay person' does not appear in the Septuagint.

78. Unfortunately I Clement does not say what the λειτουργία, the service, of the laity is to be, but it is probably little more than to obey and to partake in the eucharist (Knopf, 114).

79. For these passages see Karlmann Beyschlag, '1.Clemens 40-44 und das Kirchenrecht', in *Reformatio und Confessio*, FS Wilhelm Maurer, ed. Friedrich Wilhelm Kantzenbach and Gerhard Müller, Berlin and Hamburg 1965, (9-22) 10-18. Martin aptly comments: 'The acuteness of Clement's conception lies in the fact that it ties services or functions to structures established once and for all and gives theological sanction to this tie' (72: cf. the whole section on I Clement, 67-78). How different things are in this respect not only in Paul's own work but also in Ephesians and I Peter and Acts is clear from the thorough investigation by Anton Vögtle, 'Exegetische Reflexionen zur Apostolizität des Amtes und zur Amtssukzession', in *Die Kirche des Anfanges*, FS Heinz Schürmann, ed. Rudolf Schnackenburg et al. (original ed., ETS 38, Leipzig 1978), Freiburg etc. 1978, 529-82. For the problems discussed in I Clem.42, 44 cf. also Joachim Rohde, *Urchristliche und frühkatholische Ämter. Eine Untersuchung zur frühchristlichen Amtsentwicklung im Neuen Testament und bei den apostolischen Vätern*, ThA, Berlin 1978, 109-13.

80. It is then no longer the case that even majority decisions can be wrong – given the lack of information about the deposition of the presbyters of Corinth it is not possible to pass any judgment – but rather that as a result democratic processes of decision in the community are made impossible and replaced by authoritarian dispositions.

81. Cf. Brunner, 89, who comments on Clement's use of scripture: 'The action of God documented in the work is not a challenge to existing conditions. Rather, the processes taking place in the present are simply related back to what alone is valid and unchangeable, to structure, with the help of scripture, seen ad a collection of arguments and illustrations.'

82. Mikat in particular has called attention to this, and rightly cited 14.2; 47.7; 59.1f. in this connection ('Stasis', 737-9; 'Fürbitte', 843; 'Auswanderungsrat', 215). As a summary, he says of intercession that with it Christians pray 'like the state cults for the emperor and empire. They give God his due, but also the emperor his. The community of Christians does not behave like a *superstitio* (viz. a superstitious sect hostile to the empire); rather, Christians are *religiosi* (viz., pious people); they pray for the Pax Romana, *pro salute populi Romani* (viz., for the well-being of the Roman people). But this prayer can only be credible if *everything* is avoided which *can* be regarded as στάσις (viz.rebellion) and ἀπόνοια (viz. folly)', 'Stasis', 751, my italics).

83. Here, too, a comparison with Paul is illuminating. For him the humility of Christ described in the hymn Phil.2.6-11 is the basis for the humility of members of the community, in that each is to think the other higher than himself and not seek his own good but that of the other (v.3f.) whereas Clement is concerned with subordination. It is generally striking how small a role Christ, who usually is mentioned only in stereotyped formulae, plays in I Clement. It simply cannot be claimed that there is much thought based on him.

84. *Einführung*, 87.

85. Cf. n.39 on Part II. In this connection the pillar of Trajan in Rome is very telling, no longer containing a statue of the emperor but one of Peter.

III/5

1. What Käsemann says in comparing Revelation with Luke's works applies even more to a comparison with I Clement: 'There are gulfs separating its message' (*Freedom*, 130).

2. 'A number of factors combine to point us to the end of the reign of Domitian' (AD 95/96)' (Strobel, *Apokalypse*, 187). For this indication of a period already suggested by Irenaeus (*Adversus Haereses* V, 30,3) cf. also Vielhauer, 503; Böcher, *Johannesapokalypse*, 41; Müller, *Apokalypsen*, 41f. There is a thorough discussion of the problem in Collins, 'Myth', passim; ead., *Crisis*, 54-83. She comes to the same result.

3. 'Although Rome and the Romans are nowhere mentioned by name in Revelation, the Roman world empire with its religious policy plays a significant role for the apocalyptist' (Böcher, *Kirche*, 51). According to Lohmeyer, however, 'no (!) historical experience or observation governs the eschatological drama' because the author 'is not concerned with time and history but only with the suprahistoircal and subterranean powers which stand in the way of the

consummation' (194; cf. sections 7 and 8 on 192-4 and also the exegesis of chs.13, 17). Only an interpretation that does violence to the text can challenge the fact that Revelation must *also* be interpreted in historical terms. What Lampe has said in connection with another apocalyptic book applies here: 'It is about as meaningful to see traditional and historical interpretations of the narratives in Daniel as alternatives as it is to force someone to make a choice between "green" and "round"' (72). In this section I shall consider the Book of Revelation against the background of the Pax Romana; in so doing I make no claim to be seeing the full dimensions of the apocalyptic imagery.

4. 'There is no doubt that the view of the apocalyptist is basically critical of the state' (Strobel, 'Apokalypse', 179). Bousset put it even more strongly: 'Hardly ever can such resounding, fulminating polemic have been written against a rule system as we have in this remarkable book' (137). Attempts at a comparison with Romans 13 (cf. e.g. Cullmann, 47f., 52f., 64f.) fail. For the problem cf. Ebach, *Leviathan*, 77 n.4; Roloff, 146f.

5. 1.1, 4,9; 22.8. It is now taken for granted that he is not identical with John the son of Zebedee or the author of the Fourth Gospel (cf. Vielhauer, 501f.; Böcher, *Johannesapokalypse*, 35; Collins, *Crisis*, 25-9). It is possible that this is John of Ephesus, well known from church tradition (Vielhauer, 502; cf.458). However, according to Collins all attempts at identification have failed (*Crisis*, 29-34); Müller, *Apokalypsen*, 45,46f., is also sceptical.

6. Cf.1,3; 10.10f.; 19.9f.; 22.6-10, 18f.

7. Cf. Müller, *Theologiegeschichte*, 35: Collins, 'Revelation', 11; ead., *Crisis*, 34-50 (with a survey of scholarship), 134-7; Lampe, 109-11, and especially Aune, 18f., 22 and 27: 'John was probably an itinerant prophet in the sense that he travelled round a particular area to a limited number of Christian communities, with some regularity.'

8. Cf. here above all Collins, 'Persecution', 732f., 742-4; id., *Crisis*, 102-4. Rather than being 'a kind of prison' (Lohmeyer, 15, 194), Patmos is described more aptly by Käsemann as 'the place for exiled rebels deprived of their eager activity, and with every idly spent hour burning into their marrow' (*Freedom*, 139). The interpretation of 1.9b as indicating that John stayed on Patmos for missionary purposes or to lead the community' (thus e.g. Vielhauer, 501) is questionable not so much because 'as a missionary field Parmos was too uninhabited and poor' (Kraft, 41) but because of the terminology of Revelation, in which διά with the accusative always gives reasons and not purposes (passages outside statements about suffering are 4.11; 13.14; 18.10, 15; statements about suffering are 2.3: 6.7: 12.11; 20.4). The three last-mentioned passages in particular come very close to the phrase in 1.9b or are identical with it. But that also removes the decisive objection to Kraft's theory that John withdrew to Patmos to receive a revelation (41f.).

9. 'The mode of expression also seems to assign this martyr death to the past' (Dibelius, 'Rom', 224).

10. The designation of Antipas as a faithful witness 'supports the assumption that he was interrogated by the governor of the province and executed' (Collins, 'Persecution', 742 n.71; cf. also Kraft, 65, who rightly refers to the proceedings described by Pliny).

11. Cf. the comments in Kraft, 64f.

12. The term 'souls' here is not to be understood in terms of Greek anthropology, for 'as they are visible to the seer, have a voice and above all are later clothed, they cannot be supposed to be incorporeal' (Stuhlmann, 127).

13. Cf. 12.11 and Schrage, *Staat*, 69; *Ethik*, 319. He stresses that such a formulation presupposes that executions have in fact taken place. Against Kraft's restriction to the Old Testament martyrs cf. Stuhlmann, 156 n.11; 157 n.17.

14. Cf. Collins, 'Myth', 394-7; ead., *Crisis*, 69-73.

15. It should be recalled that such a situation is in fact attested by I Clement, but the author assesses it in quite a different way from John.

16. Collins points out that apocalyptic comes into being 'in a situation of social crisis or alienation', but she stresses 'that the crisis is much more a matter of perspective than an objective reality, about which different observers would agree' ('Persecution', 729). 'The decisive point is not so much whether anyone is in fact oppressed as whether he feels oppressed' (ead., 'Revelation', 4; ead., *Crisis*, 84). Cf. also ead., 'Perspective', 252.

17. Here I am attacking the approach of the stimulating book on Revelation by Ellul, as evidenced in his comments on p.85: 'We should always return to the central notion that the seer of Patmos uses present history as a stage and a springboard, a sign and a means of expressing a universal truth.' John is not concerned to 'express a universal truth' about the state in itself but to bear witness to the reality of God in the situation of distress brought about by Roman rule. He feels that this situation is much too oppressive for him to use it either as a stage or as a springboard, so in any case the move is from the concrete to the abstract.

18. 1.9; 6.9; 20.4; cf. 12.17; 14.12.

19. Cf. 13.12,15.

20. Cf. above 50f. and nn.311–12.

21. 'After the first hearing only the confession of the *nomen Christianum* and nothing else was referred to; no further indications of its confession were sought' (Weber, 18).

22. Pliny, *Epistles* X, 96.1f.

23. Pliny, *Epistles* X, 97.

24. Stuhlmann interprets those who are said to have been 'slain' in this way: 'So the reference is to those who remained steadfast even in the face of the threat of execution which they could have escaped only by ceasing to bear witness'; he then points to the phrase 'faithful to death' in 1.20 (155). Cf. also 12.11, according to which the martyrs gave priority to their testimony over saving their lives, and 14.12, where keeping faith with Jesus is an element in the perseverance of Christians.

25. Kraft, 61.

26. Cf. in detail Theissen, 'Starke', 275-82.

27. Pliny, *Epistles* X, 96, 9f. Cf. Schäfke, 495; ibid., 556, for an enumeration of all the economic damage done by a boycott on food offered to idols.

28. If we take this context into account, there is no basis for the hypothesis put forward by Dibelius that the letters in which the question of sacrificial meat is discussed were only conceived of later ('Rom', 224).

29. The opponents attacked by John at this point should not be regarded as

Gnostic libertines engaging, say, in somewhat free sexual intercourse. The original Gnostic sources at no point support the charge, so popular among the later church fathers who wrote against heresy, that their ethics were libertinistic. Lohmeyer rightly notes that the word 'harlot' is not 'an indication of a basic moral libertinism', and he sees those under attack as 'a trend which sought to solve within the realm of the possible the difficult problem how the earliest Christian communities were to behave in pagan culture which they could not avoid in everyday life, by an assimilation to pagan circumstances' (31, cf. the following note). Müller, *Apokalypsen*, 113, and Roloff, 55, also argue that 'harlotry' implies sexual behaviour deviating from the community norm.

30. 'The question of assimilation is at issue here: what pagan customs Christians can appropriate for the sake of economic survival, business success or simple sociability' (Collins, 'Persecution', 740f.; cf. ead., *Crisis*, 87f.).

31. Cf. Gross, 94-101.

32. Ibid., 98; Knibbe, 282.

33. 16.13; 19,20; 20.10..

34. Cf. Knibbe, 281.

35. Schrage, *Staat*, 74.

36. Cf. Weber, 13: 'The imperial priests would be most strongly affected by a movement directed against the authoritarian symbols of the empire, the Roman gods and the ruler god; and they would inevitably have been joined by the rest of the priestly colleges in so far as this movement also affected the local deities, for these colleges were the strongest factors in economic and political life, along with the *koinon* and the municipal authorities.'

37. Käsemann, *Freedom*, 131.

38. It is evident in the portrayal of the emperor as an aping of Christ, cf. Schrage, *Staat*, 73; Böcher, *Kirche*, 55; Roloff, 135f.; above all Ebach, 'Apokalypse', 51-3.

39. Cf. 17.15.

40. It is an exact opposite to the hymn which begins 'I pray for the power of love'. From this point, too, one should consider the significance of singing this particular hymn at a military ceremony.

41. 17.2; 18.3,9.

42. 17.4; 18.7,16.

43. 18.3,15,19.

44. 18.12f. 'This very detailed list, including the slave market, gives those who are interested a glimpse of what the members of the rich upper classes, and the world of fashion, were accustomed to at the time' (Schrage, *Ethik*, 318). Cf. also 33 and n.183 and 35 and n.199.

45. The passage is, of course, in the context of the four apocalyptic horsemen (6.1-8) who symbolize what is expected to happen in the end-time. But this sequence of war, civil war, price increases and death from plague is not a mere fantasy. There is evidence of three specific examples of price increases for Asia Minor at the time of the composition of the book of Revelation: 1. In Pisidian Antioch in 92 or 93 after a severe winter the price for grain had gone very high because the producers held it back to make more profit. A decree from the governor called for the release of whatever grain had been stockpiled and set a maximum price, though this was twice the price of the year before (HIRK 65,

132f.). 2. Apollonius of Tyana calmed down a riot which had arisen in Aspendos in Pamphylia as the result of a famine: 'The people fed only on cheap vegetables and the bare necessities, as the well-to-do held on to the grain in order to be able to sell it at a higher price outside the country.' Apollonius persuaded the grain hoarders to sell on the domestic market (Philostratus, *Vita Apollonii* I,15). Dio of Prusa managed to calm down a crowd which had gathered to protest against exorbitant prices for grain and wanted to stone him and set fire to his house (Dio Chrysostom 46; cf. Collins, *Crisis*, 95-7). The edict of Domitian mentioned in Suetonius, *Domitian*, 7, may point in the same direction, though it does not specifixally relate to Asia Minor. In view of the lack of grain and surplus of wine it orders that no new vineyards are to be planted in Italy and that in the provinces half the vines are to be destroyed. However, this edict was immediately repealed. Attempts have been made to connect this directly with Rev.6.6, where after the mention of the increase in the price of grain it is said that no damage is done to wine and oil. John is 'disturbed that the measure which from his ascetic standpoint he thought to be good and healthy... has been repealed again. So now he prophesies a great increase in prices which will affect the necessities of life, whereas luxury articles will be spared as a mockery' (Bousset, 135). That cannot be substantiated; above all it should be noted that there were constant famines. The general economic background to the phenomenon described in Rev.6.6 – a lack of basic foods, a surplus of wine and oil – is a result of the extension of the *latifundia* which took place in the first century AD with the cultivation of wine and oil, which was more profitable than grain. For the edict of Domitian and the evidence mentioned under 1 and 3 above, and its possible connection with Rev. 6.6. cf. Magie I, 580-2; II, 1443f. It should also be noted that the cities of Asia Minor were dependent on imports of grain because of bad harvests (Magie I, 580); these came from areas on the north shore of the Black Sea. But the Roman armies in the East (above all in Pontus, Cappadocia and Armenia) and in the Danube area also had to draw grain from there (Rostovtzeff, II, 4f.). Reinforcement of these armies during hostile actions would increase the need for grain, so that the war may also have had negative effects on the provisioning of the cities of Asia Minor.

46. 17.3-5; Rome is also described as 'the harlot' in 17.15f. and as 'the great harlot' in 17.1; 19.2. The designation 'harlot' takes up the description of pagan idolatry as harlotry in Old Testament prophecy. In John the thought may above all be of the emperor cult, cf. further 14.8; 17.2; 18.3,9. Moreover the personification offered the possibility of depicting the luxury.

47. Cf. I Peter 5.13 and the commentaries ad loc., which give further examples.

48. For 17.5 that is confirmed by 17.1; cf. further 14.8; 18.2,10,21.

49. 11.7; 17.8. This beast can hardly be other than the one described in ch.13, i.e. Rome. The traditions taken up are different in each passage. Cf. Ebach, *Leviathan*, 19f. (n.9).

50. Aristides, *Eulogy of Rome*, 29-33, 103f.

51. Schrage, *Staat*, 72.

52. 12.9; 20.2.

53. 12.12. Therefore there might also be a connection between the approach of the dragon to the sea in 12.18 and the subsequent rise of the beast from the sea in 13.1. Further designations of Roman power as satanic can be found in

2.10,13. According to 2.10 the one responsible for the expected arrest of Christians in Smyrna is the devil. According to 2.13 'the throne of Satan' is in Pergamon, and Satan 'dwells' there. This passage has been interpreted in different ways: (*a*) 'the residence of the Roman governor or the place where judgment is given' (mentioned as a possibiilty in Collins, 'Persecution', 733); (*b*) the temple of Augustus and Roma, the earliest and most famous centre of emperor worship in Asia (Ehrhardt, II, 300; Collins, 'Persecution', 733f.; further possibilities are given in Fiorenza, *Priester*, 242f., 243 n.28); (*c*) the famous altar of Zeus (Dibelius, 'Rom', 223; Böcher, *Kirche*, 53; Lampe, 94). There would also be a reference to the emperor in the last instance as Domitian 'had himself celebrated as the new Jupiter (= Zeus) and often appears on coins with Jupiter's lightning flash' (Gross, 96). 'It is not clear whether "the throne of Satan" is a specific reference to one of these cult places; there is more evidence to suggest that this is a general reference to Pergamon as the stronghold of pagan religion' (Roloff, 54).

54. Thus Kraft comments: 'The authorization of the Antichrist by Satan demonstrates the difference between apocalyptic dualism and biblical creation faith clear. In the biblical view only God gives power and majesty to the children of men' (175). For the latter he then refers to Rom.13.1 and I Clem.16.1. For these references, see the discussion of the passages in III 2c and III 4a above. On the other hand the remarks by Ebach, 'Apokalypse', 48-54, show that it is too simplistic to talk of an apocalyptic dualism in contrast to biblical creation fatih; cf. also his exegesis of the speeches of God in Job, *Leviathan*, 67-77.

55. 13.5,7.

56. In terms of content that would correspond to the idea of eschatological measure in the form of a 'limited period of disaster', a point which has been worked out by Stuhlmann (46-52); cf. the summary on 52: 'Disaster is from the beginning subordinate to God's power. So it is not infinite, but limited. That is guaranteed by God's promise. The time of disaster to come is shorter than that which is past.'

57. Cf. the narrative of the 2000 swine which rush into the lake with the demon called Legion, and on it 66 above.

58. 19.17-21, the quotation from v.18, the following quotation and the allusion from v.17 and v.21. 'The apocalyptist quite deliberately puts the call to the banquet of God before the battle. Its outcome is so certain and sure that the call can already be given beforehand' (Bousset, 433). It is almost pointless to say of the talk of 'war' in 19.11-21: 'To seek to derive from this apocalyptic imagery a basic justification of war or simply a belligerent approach to the gaining of freedom of religion would be completely to misunderstand its meaning and function' (Vögtle, 26).

59. I demonstrated on p.122f. above how this passage bears witness to an acute perception of an exploitative reality, particularly in the part of the text which is not quoted here but was already cited above. For the parallels in content between Book 8 of the Sibylline Oracles and Rev.18 cf. Collins, *Crisis*, 92-4; for Rev.18 generally see ibid., 116-24; ead., 'Taunt Song', passim.

60. 'Here and in IV Ezra 33, 35 the questions "How long?", "Till when?", originally just an extension and parallel to the question "Why?" in the book of

Lamentations, has virtually been transformed into a cry of protest' (Stuhlmann, 126).

61. 'What is envisaged here is not its vengeance..., rather, this is a matter of the triumph of God's righteousness, the manifestation of his glory in vengeance' (Ellul, 151).

62. 6.11; for textual criticism and translation cf. Stuhlmann, 159-61.

63. Stuhlmann, 159.

64. The conception of a preordained number of martyrs can certainly be developed into the idea that the martyrs bring in the promise through their suffering, and that an accumulation of martyrdoms even hastens its coming, so that Stuhlmann can say: 'In this way suffering becomes not only tolerable but even desirable' (162). However, he then rightly affirms: 'But this intention is not yet that of the author of Revelation' (ibid). There is no indication in Revelation of a systematization of this conception with the aim of providing consolation. So it would not be appropriate to speak in this connection of 'a kind of synergism' (Collins, 'Perspective', 249; cf. 252).

65. Stuhlmann, 156; cf. 157 n.17.

66. It is not the case that 'the death of martyrs has a purificatory significance in itself' (Collins, 'Perspective', 255). This theory cannot be supported with a reference to 7.14, as both there and in the parallel 12.11 'the blood of the lamb' has the decisive significance, cf. Bousset, 286.

67. 'Like those still alive, the martyrs too are still in a state of waiting' (Stuhlmann, 158). Only in the context of this waiting for the final demonstration of the righteousness of God can one speak of reward (and punishment), and the heavenly investiture with white robes can be described as 'the reward for earthly martyrdom' (ibid.). But this 'reward' does not make the suffering meaningful and desirable.

68. 18.20; this cry of joy directly follows the lament of the kings, merchants and seafarers.

69. Cf. also 14.9-11.

70. 21.8 presents a traditional catalogue of vices which differs from others by the way in which 'cowardice and unbelief are mentioned at the beginning and lies at the end... the common factor between cowardice, unbelief and lies is that they represent the opposite of confession' (Kraft, 266).

71. Ebach, 'Konversion', 39; for what follows cf. also id., 'Apokalypse', 47.

72. 'The triumphant wrath of the seer is evident in the abundance of names for the dragon' (Lohmeyer, 101).

73. 12.9; cf. the whole section 12.1-12.

74. Cf. 12.12.

75. 14.8; cf. 18.2f. In 14.8 'by way of chronological anticipation the Roman harlot is spoken of as though she has already fallen, although in 14.9 there is still talk of the existence of the cult of the emperor throughout the empire. The fall of the harlot is sealed in the victory of Christ, without already having taken place' (Lampe, 98f.).

76. 11.17; cf. 19.6.

77. Cf.7.12; 15.3f.; 19.1.

78. 11.15; cf. 5.13; 12.10.

79. See above, 53.

80. 'In the OT the horn is always a symbol of power (see e.g. Num.23.22; Deut.33.17; Ps.74.4; 88.17ff.) and royal status (e.g. Ps.111.9: 147.14; Zech.1,18; Dan.7.7,20; 8.3)', Lohmeyer, 55.

81. 17.14; cf. 19.16.

82. Cf. also Schrage, *Ethik*, 311, on the 'legitimate element' in the hope of the thousand-year kingdom described in Rev.20: 'This element is the visible realization of the Lordship of Jesus Christ within this world, which cannot simply be abandoned to the demons and imperial minions of the dragon as being demonic. For the seer, the Lordship of Jesus Christ also needs to be manifested in this aeon.'

83. Here and in the following paragraphs I am taking up ideas and phrases from a short paper, given in my main seminar in the summer semester of 1984 by Heike Nadolph, on 'Continuity or Interruption?'.

84. 'So the new creation is no longer depicted as the island of order which has just been snatched out of the ocean of chaos and has to be constantly protected against its raging attack' (Georgi, 353f.).

85. One might recall 18.11-13; cf. also Sib.V, 447f.; 'In the last time, one day the sea will be dry, and ships will no longer sail to Italy.' Aelius Aristides, *Eulogy of Rome*, 10f., 13, gives a positive picture of the sea as the centre of the Roman empire, over which cargo ships bring the produce of the world to Rome (see above, 32 and n.175). Cf. also Roloff, 133, 136.

86. On this cf. Burr, 119-31, esp.127, where he makes it clear that the term was not understood in terms of local geography but also expressed a relationship of possession: 'If the ecumene was constantly thought of as being under Roman rule, so too of course was the sea within it' (127).

87. Bousset, 443.

88. For this collage extending as far as v.7, cf. Ebach, 'Apokalypse', 17-20.

89. 13.7; 17.13.

90. So the change from the singular 'people', which appears in the Old Testament passages alluded to here, to the plural 'peoples', may be motivated by this opposition to Rome and not be occasioned by an explicit antithesis to a particularism of Judaism; cf. Fiorenza, *Priester*, 355; Ebach, 'Apokalypse', 19f. In John, particularist and universalist statements stand side by side. With Georgi it is important to stress that 'Precisely in view of the outcome of Rev.20 it is surprising that there is no reference to the selection among human beings made there but that without qualification men and nations are said to be God's partners' (357; cf.357f. on 'promises to the nations in 21.1ff. and 21.9ff.' generally). However, between them comes 21.8f., a passage which can hardly be eliminated as 'a later orthodox correction to the all too universalist statements in the context' (which Georgi, 361 n.45, raises as a possibility). There is a function for both statements, so here, too, we should not be too systematic.

91. Georgi, 362; in the article to which I am specifically referring here Georgi also interprets the remarks about the new Jerusalem against the background of the planning and building of Hellenistic cities. It follows that 'John can claim for the eschatological city that it will realize ideals for which the pluralistically orientated Hellenistic city strove: the reconciliation and integration of all nations and the equalization of the classes' (369). 'The heavenly Jerusalem also fulfils a further ideal for which the Hellenistic cities strove but which they never

realized; the reconciliation of city and surrounding countryside. In the city in John's utopia there is no longer any differentiation between those inside and those outside: all are citizens. The new city is itself also paradise. It integrates nature. It gives the water of life and contains the tree of life. not only once, but in infinite variety, in the form of avenues which extend along the river and the (main) street' (369f.).

92. Thus the title of a book by Ebach mentioned in the Bibliography.

93. 21.11, 18-21.

94. According to Tacitus, *Annals* XV, 42.1, precious stones and gold had 'long since been customary' in Nero's Rome and 'as a result of a desire for extravagance had become a commonplace'.

95. Of course there is a basis for the mention of such valuable building material in the history of the tradition and it has symbolic significance, as is indicated in the commentaries on the passage. For the precious stones cf. especially Böcher, *Kirche*, 144-56; Bergmeier, 96-8; in 104-6 the latter firmly rejects the connection which is often made between the twelve precious stones and the signs of the zodiac.

96. Böcher, *Kirche*, 167.

97. The statement in 1.6 and 5.10 that Christians have been made a kingdom is also interpreted in the second passage in terms of the future exercise of rule. For 'as long as the world is dominated by anti-Christian powers, the active exercise of rule is possible only for those who are on the side of the ruling power, namely Rome' (Fiorenza, 'Religion', 265).

98. It is different with the statement of the lordship of Christ which is already made in connection with the present, and thus challenges the rule exercised by Rome.

99. According to Lohmeyer 'this is probably connected with legal and religious conceptions in antiquity and with the experiences of Jews as a nation...; the wall constitutes the city' (173).

100. Lampe writes about 'the early apocalyptic literature of Judaism' as follows; 'Underground literature, leaflets which were eagerly circulated among those who were persecuted, perhaps hidden in camps somewhere in the hills or in caves in the wilderness' (65). However, with Revelation we find ourselves in the sphere of Hellenistic Roman cities; but there it was certainly not read in public libraries.

101. According to Collins, 'the projection of the conflict (viz. with Rome) has a redemptive power on an almost cosmic canvas, in that it clarifies and objectifies the conflict' ('Revelation', 9; cf. ead., *Crisis*, 152-4).

102. 13.10; cf. 14.12; further 1.9: 2.2, 3,19; 3.10. Revelation is a text which enables its hearers or readers to stand fast in extreme circumstances. In a situation in which direct political action is not practicable, it is a text which keeps alive the hope for a better world.

103. Cf. above, 120f. and Müller, *Apokalypsen*, 96-9. According to Fiorenza the view rejected by John represented 'an important theological solution for Christians in Asia Minor, as the eating of food sacrificed to idols at banquets and taking part in the religious ceremonies of trade associations and the state cult was unavoidable for any Christian who wanted to take an active part in the social, economic and political life of his time'('Religion', 267; cf. further 267f.).

104. Lampe, 106 n.114, with reference to I Cor.8.4 as a parallel. It makes no difference whether John is quoting those whom he is attacking correctly or whether he is distorting their thesis by substituting Satan for God, in a situation where they spoke of 'knowledge of the divine origin' (thus Kraft, 70), as the effect of the knowledge claimed is the same in either event: eating food offered to idols without hesitation.

105. That applies even to the state cult: 'As loyalty to Roman state state religion... simply meant participation in cultic acts and ceremonies, it was possible for a Christian theology to put forward the view that one could adapt to pagan society and religion without violating one's Christian faith and Christian convictions' (Fiorenza, *Religion*, 268).

106. Cf. Aune, 28f.: 'John with his apocalyptic tradition of non-conformity and opposition to the dominant alien culture represents a conservative answer to the question of adaptation to paganism... "Jezebel" and the Nicolaitans represent liberal movements in the same community... However, the majority of Christians seems to belong to a middle trend or party which had not yet moved over into the camp of the Nicolaitans but which - from John's point of view – has departed from its first works (2.5) or whose works are insufficient in God's eyes (3.2) or which is neither cold nor warm (3.15f.).'

107. Cf. above, 126.

108. Cf. Lampe, 108: 'The uncompromising preservation of Christian identity has priority over any diminution of external unpleasantness and harassment. Those who are ready to adapt put the priority elsewhere by doing away with the constraints and lack of freedom which are bound up with separation from the customs of the pagans.'

109. Collins, 'Persecution', 741: 'Revelation', 11f. 'It is not improbable that Christian faith and life-style as John understood it was irreconcilable with normal participation in the social and economic life of the cities of Asia Minor' ('Persecution', 745). See also her comments on 13.17, 'that the connection of buying and selling with the sign of the beast relates to the fact that as a rule Roman coins bore the image and name of the ruling emperor. So the impossibility of buying or selling would be the result of a refusal to use Roman coins' ('Perspectives, 253; cf. *Crisis*, 124-7).

110. According to Käsemann the communities to which John writes 'are spent and either do not see it or try to come to terms with it. They praise Christ as the Lord of heaven, and do not hear him saying to them: "The world and all that is in it is mine." They know the first commandment, and they think it is enough if they keep themselves unspotted from the world, although the Antichrist has to be faced squarely if one is to keep alive. They take comfort from the resurrection and do not know that it begins here and now with the sovereignty of Jesus in the midst of his enemies and with the glorious freedom of God's children who, being ostracized, despise the mark of the beast under the Pax Romana. They suffer as though that were not exactly what they are called to do. They ought to make common cause with all those who are oppressed, insulted and appealing in vain to the tyrants, they await him who tramples underfoot the unrighteous' (*Freedom*, 139).

111. Cf. Ellul, 19: 'The Apocalypse is... a key to the deciphering of events of the present, and anyone who understands it will not only be encouraged to hold

fast, but even more will himself become a witness to this truth, a specific sign of the presence of God in the world.'

112. According to Collins the social withdrawal of Christians would 'amount to a political act which would be an invitation to intensified hostility and persecution. The author seems to be fully aware of this consequence' ('Revelation', 12).

113. 13.10; for the text of v.10b cf. Lohmeyer, 113.

114. John and those whom he attacks are also involved in a struggle over 'reality'. What one regards as 'real', how 'real' one holds the lordship of Christ to be, is evidently not completely independent of the social status that one has. The greater the social integration, the stronger seems to be the tendency to take account of the 'realities'. Cf. the observation by Collins that 'the Christians in Smyrna are portrayed as being economically poor and threatened by persecution (2.8-11), while those of Laodicea are said to be well-to-do and evidently avoid persecution (3.14-22)' ('Persecution', 745; cf. ead., 'Taunt Song', 202; *Crisis*, 132f.).

115. Cf. the sayings in the letters about the 'one who overcomes' (2.7,11,17,26-28; 3.5,12,21) and 15.2; 21.7.

116. Against Collins, *Crisis*, 172, who sees the imagery of Revelation as suggesting only 'a reversal of roles'.

117. 'A basically optimistic tenor is predominant in the book; it does not know of any resignation, let alone allowing it' (Strobel, 'Apokalypse', 175).

118. On this cf. the book by Jörns, esp.166-74.

119. On the function of the hymns in chs. 4 and 5 Jörns writes: 'Even before... one of the seven seals is opened, the aim of the final event, the consummation, is already celebrated in the songs. Before the terrors of judgment come upon the earth, joy rings out in the salvation which is achieved in them. Before the old creation passes away, God is celebrated as the new creator. The hymns are full of the certainty of salvation; the good tidings shine out over the tribulation of judgment' (76).

120. Cf. Jörns, 178f.

121. Cf. Jörns, 161-4.

122. According to Strobel 'the question remains whether elements of the liturgy of the Johannine community are echoed here and how far what is said has a basis in a particular Jewish-Christian tradition' ('Apokalypse', 182).

123. Pliny learns from apostate Christians that they are accustomed in their assembly 'to sing hymns to Christ as to a god' (*Epistles* X, 96,7). Hymns are mentioned in Col.3.16; Eph.5.19 and in Phil.2.6-11; I Tim.3.16; Col.1.15-20; Heb.1.3; Eph.2.14-16. They are characterized by praising the power and the glory of Christ. The thesis which is put forward in many variant forms that a liturgical structure can be detected in Revelation has been refuted by Jörns (180-4).

124. This is the only way in which John can envisage the circulation of his work; cf. 1.3: 'Blessed is he who reads aloud the words of the prophecy, and blessed are those who hear, and who keep what is written therein.'

125. Cf. also Lampe, 99f., and Roloff, 25, who on the basis of observations on the division in the second half writes of the community living 'in the end event with its catastrophes and tribulations': 'Although it is branded and

threatened by this event, even now it has a part in the new reality which is appointed in heaven by the Lordship of Christ and lives in hope that the power of its Lord which has still to be shown will be made manifest.'

126. In this connection I could take up the comments that Stuhlmacher makes at the end of his work: 'The living reality of reconciliation is disclosed in the living expression of faith. To this degree the practice of active praise of God is one of the testimonies to peace which are required of the church today, and we must hope that the practice of liturgy, confession and paraclesis, which is all to easy to despise but which nevertheless needs to be kept in high esteem, will result in the present day in further spheres of Christian activities of reconciliation which have yet to be discovered' (69).

Conclusion (IV)

1. Cf. Benjamin's eighth thesis on the concept of history, the first sentence of which runs: 'The tradition of the oppressed teaches us that the state of emergency in which we live is the rule' (697)

2. Thus Gerhard Gloege, 'Schriftprinzip', *RGG*[3] 5, Tübingen 1961 (1540-3), 1543.

3. Cf. Hengel, *Crucifixion*, 88: 'The earliest Christian message of the crucified messiah demonstrated the solidarity of the love of God with the unspeakable suffering of those who were tortured and put to death by human cruelty, as this can be seen from the ancient sources. This suffering has continued down to the present century in a passion story which we cannot even begin to assess.'

4. Lucan, *Bellum civile* V, 339-43.

5. Cf. Käsemann, *Freedom*, 136: 'It is true that the 8,000 crosses that the Romans set up on the Via Appia after the slaves' insurrection are not to be compared to Jesus' cross if one asks about the reason for them. But can the Christian pass them by without recollecting that his Lord, too, suffered precisely that torture? Is there not a community of those who are oppressed and insulted, which goes beyond all guilt, and which Christians cannot evade?'

6. In connection with an individual text, the tradition of Matt.5.38-48 par., Linckens notes that it 'cannot be doubted that these sentences had their function in quite particular historical situations and that those who proclaimed and heard them considered the world from the standpoint of the oppressed and the marginalized' (17). Cf. also the summary of the political protest of the New Testament writings given by Ehrhardt: 'The new message of "peace through Jesus Christ: he is the Lord of all things" (Acts X.36) applied to these, the poor, the weak, those who had been deprived of their rights, about whom neither the world empire nor its opponents cared, and it was in their language that it was written' (II, 444).

7. The cautious remarks by Collins about the Revelation of John should therefore be put much more decisively and basically: 'The portrayal of the Roman empire in Revelation is one-sided and therefore a caricature. Nevertheless it reminds us that creation and human life are not unmixed joy and clarity. The splendour of Rome was achieved by the unwilling sacrifice of many. The Book of Revelation can serve to remind those with privileges that the system which benefited them can in fact cause distress to others' ('Persecution', 747).

She writes in similar vein in other passages: 'Revelation reminds those with privileges what it means to live on the periphery' ('Revelation', 12).

8. 'The composition of this letter by an unknown author falls in the eighties or nineties' (cf. Vielhauer, 250f.; the quotation is on 25f.).

9. Given the context there, the statement that the readers and hearers have been illuminated, which also appears in 6.4, clearly refers to their baptism.

10. The Greek word used in 10.33 'here denotes someone who participated in word and deed in the fate of those who suffer' (Michel, *Hebräer*, 356).

11. The author does not hesitate to call such confiscation 'robbery', even if it follows the letter of the law.

12. Braun stresses that in 10.32-34 there is 'a *specific* reference to earlier time' (325).

13. Loader suggests that it is likely 'that there is as it were a constant threat of persecution not only in the past but also in the present or in the imminent future' (256).

14. In this context *parrhesia* must denote not being afraid of others. The need to stand fast stressed in v.36 also suggests this.

15. That the author is concerned with the theme of fearlessness and must therefore have a topical interest in it emerges especially from v.27, according to which Moses left Egypt without fearing Pharaoh, while according to Ex.2.14 he fled for fear.

16. '*diatagma* is a technical term for an official decree' (Braun, 377; cf. Michel, *Hebräer*, 408).

17. The explosive nature of the situation immediately becomes clear when in connection with Braun's remark about 'concealing' (376) – they 'show faith in running the personal risk involved in concealment' – one thinks of the proven faith of those who hid Jews under the Nazi régime, which often enough people failed to do.

18. Michel is too vague when he says: 'This sin would have consisted in becoming detached from the people of God' (*Hebräer*, 409).

19. Cf. Braun, 380: 'When Moses takes the side of the suffering people of God he has chosen the shame of Christ'. This 'is not for the sake of Christ..., but it is analogous to the shame of Christ' (381).

20. Cf. on 12.2 Hengel, *Crucifixion*, 7 n.10; Kuhn, 771.

21. Braun, 467: cf. ibid.: 'That Jesus went his way does not save the Christian from folowing him; on the contrary, it is a summons to do that.' Theissen also stresses that 11.26 belongs with 10.34; 13.13 (*Untersuchungen*, 98).

22. Theissen mentions this contrast to *Roma aeterna* at the end of a note: 'The emperor cult, the temple of Augustus and Roma (Asia Minor), belief in Rome and its power, find an opponent in 13.14' (*Hebräer*, 517 n.1). This reference is much more probable than the one to Jerusalem which he mentions earlier, since at the time the author was writing this city lay in ruins and the hope of Judaism was not for an abiding Jerusalem but for an eschatological Judaism that would be made new.

23. 'What human beings can never do, Christians must never even wish to do, namely build impregnable citadels on earth, take their stand on what is conventional so as to abandon the future for the sake of the past' (Käsemann, *Freedom*, 115).

24. For the future understanding of the city to come in Heb.13.14 cf. Theissen, *Untersuchungen*, 102-5.
25. Cf. Matt.25.31-46.
26. Metz, 92 in no. 29 of the 'Unfashionable Theses on Apocalyptic'.

Index of References

(a) Old Testament and Judaism

(b) Greek and Latin Writers

(c) Earliest Christianity

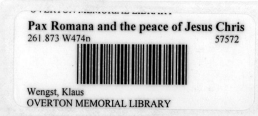